Postcard History Series

Jamestown

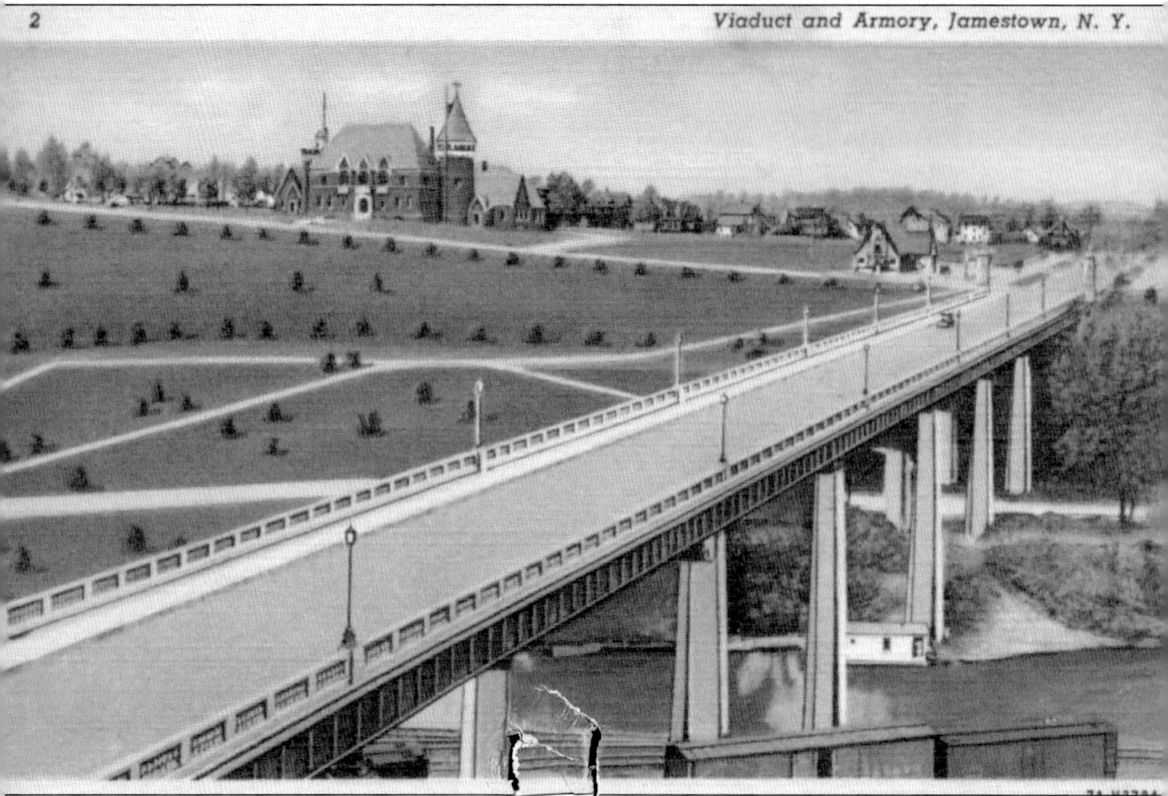

Although this view is after the armory's construction in 1933, it illustrates the valley carved by the Chadakoin River, which had to be spanned to get people easily from the west side of Jamestown to the business district. Before the Third Street Bridge was built in 1924–1925, residents had to find their way down the steep banks to one of the few bridges that spanned the river at water level. (Courtesy of the author's collection.)

On the Front Cover: The corner of Third and Main Streets is a center of the activity in the business district of Jamestown, New York. Anchoring Brooklyn Square's south side, the Gifford Building is in the center, down Main Street. Brooklyn Square was the early business district and was built on the banks of the Chadakoin River. At the writing of this book, some of these Main Street buildings still remain. (Courtesy of the author's collection.)

On the Back Cover: City hall, built in 1895 at the southeast corner of Third and Spring Streets, was across Third Street from the Lyric Theater, which featured vaudeville acts. Ellicott Hook and Ladder and Prendergast Hose Company shared the city hall station south of city hall. Shown are the 1909 American LaFrance chemical-hose unit; the first horse-drawn ladder wagon, which arrived in 1909; and Jamestown Police Department's "Black Mariah." (Courtesy of the author's collection.)

POSTCARD HISTORY SERIES

Jamestown

Karen E. Livsey and Dorothy E. Levin

ARCADIA
PUBLISHING

ISBN 978-0-7385-7566-7

Published by Arcadia Publishing
Charleston, South Carolina

Printed in the United States of America

Library of Congress Control Number: 2011937153

For all general information contact Arcadia Publishing at:
Telephone 843-853-2070
Fax 843-853-0044
E-mail sales@arcadiapublishing.com
For customer service and orders:
Toll-Free 1-888-313-2665

Visit us on the Internet at www.arcadiapublishing.com

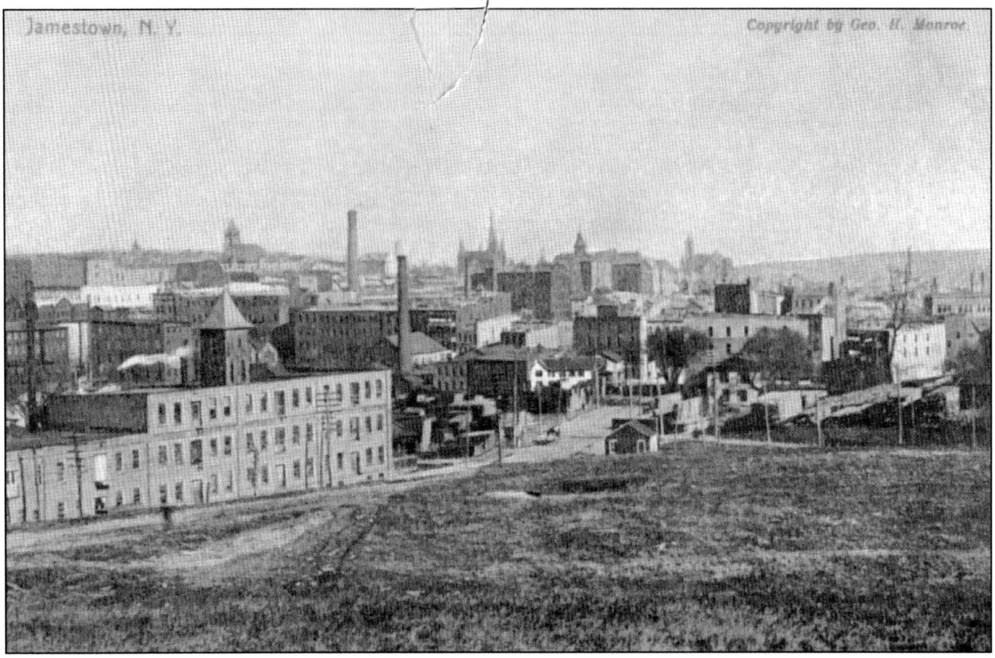

This early overview of Jamestown was taken from Jones Hill. The road in the foreground is Steele Street, or Market Street, as it enters Brooklyn Square. The two tall chimneys are at the textile mills. The near chimney is Hall and Company, and the farther one is at Broadhead Mills. The church in the back center is First Methodist Church. (Courtesy of the author's collection.)

Contents

Acknowledgments

Again, we must express our thanks to Dottie's mother, Alice Levin, who collected many of these postcards during her lifetime. They are now a part of the family's extensive postcard collection. Dottie has spent many hours (and dollars) in the pursuit of a very enjoyable hobby. Karen has begun her own collection. Also, we need to thank all of the people in the past who created the postcards, bought the postcards, and most importantly, saved the postcards.

There are many who have gone before us and recorded history in one form or another. To these people, we say, "Thank you." Just what is in a picture is sometimes a mystery. The recorded history, whether it is in a book, a letter, a newspaper story, a diary, a photograph (labeled, of course), or a recorded oral history, can help pull the pieces of a puzzle together.

We thank all the recorders of local history who have taken the time to share what they have recorded. Jamestown's Fenton History Center–Museum and Research Center, where Karen is the archivist, holds many printed books and booklets, along with manuscript material, that were consulted for this project. We thank the research center and all the staff for their support and cooperation during the creation of this volume.

We want to thank Marlin Casker, a fellow postcard collector, who lent postcards to help fill some of the gaps in our collections. Cards from this collection are indicated by MC. The Fenton History Center also lent some postcards to add more stories to the history of Jamestown. These are indicated by FHC. Unless otherwise indicated, all images are from our collections.

We hope you enjoy a visit to some of the homes, businesses, and events in Jamestown's history as you travel through the pages of this book.

Introduction

There were no photographers and few landscape artists when James Prendergast settled in Jamestown. There were few people in what became Chautauqua County. Luckily for Jamestown residents, there were people like Elial Todd Foote, who collected history, wrote history, and saved history for those who came after him. He wrote to early settlers and their families who moved away, asking them to write back about the time they came to Chautauqua County and Jamestown. He saved these letters and others, and they are still available. He wrote some of his reminiscences, collected newspapers and broadsides, and recorded events and activities. Jamestown has had a newspaper since 1826. Old-timers love to tell stories. All of this contributes to residents' ability to study the history of this area.

The main reason James Prendergast chose to settle in what became Jamestown was waterpower. The rapids in the outlet of Chautauqua Lake caught his attention as he was looking for horses that had strayed from the Prendergast family's settlement on Chautauqua Lake. His brother Matthew purchased 1,000 acres from the Holland Land Company, which James was then able to buy from him. This land included most of Jamestown, west of what is now Prendergast Avenue. This included the area around the outlet of Chautauqua Lake, which had become known as the Rapids, where James chose to locate a sawmill, a gristmill, and his home. He encouraged others to settle around him. Soon, there was a tavern, a doctor, a potter, and farmers. The lumbermen came to tame the forest, which was extensive. More sawmills started to handle the lumbering that began to dominate the industry of the area. Lumber was rafted down the waterways from Chautauqua Lake to the Mississippi River, finding markets in the growing towns along the rivers. The Rapids became Jamestown by 1816 and was incorporated as a village in 1827.

The village grew, and the surrounding hills above the outlet were soon dotted with dwellings and businesses. Wood was readily available for building, and soon, the main streets of Jamestown filled in with sturdy wooden buildings. Photographers came to town and began to chronicle Jamestown as it was in the 1860s. Later, these photographs were put on postcards and started the postcard history of Jamestown. The great fire of 1861 destroyed the sturdy wooden buildings that lined Main Street between Second Street and Third Street, but photographs survived to show what had been there. These were replaced by brick buildings, yet some of them would burn later.

Manufacturing flourished, and wood furniture was an early industry in Jamestown. Swedish immigrants with woodworking skills began arriving in the 1850s. Textile mills began in the 1870s. Metal furniture and tools were produced from the 1880s. The railroad came to Jamestown in 1860, and products found new markets along the railroad. Industry and jobs brought workers to the factories and provided the services needed in the growing village.

Today, photographs that lasted through Jamestown's history record its past. In the late 1800s, photographers found a new avenue for their pictures using a new communications device—the postcard. It was quick and cost only a penny to send. Photographers began looking for more subjects that could lend themselves to the new postcard trade. As Jamestown and other cities developed, places of interest began showing up on postcards. Travelers sent them to friends to show where they had been. Businesses caught on to the potential of the postcard for advertising their newest products or the new building in which they were located.

Early postcards were government issued. Private mailing cards were allowed beginning on May 19, 1898, but only the address was permitted on the back. Often, there was a message written across or around the picture on the front. In 1901, the designation "post card" was allowed for use by private publishers, but the undivided back was still only for the address. March 1, 1907, marked the change to a divided back, allowing writing on the left and the address on the right. These restrictions help date the cards today if there is no postmark. These cards, besides being mailed to family and friends, were collected as mementos of trips and often put in albums. These albums, when found today, may have postcards of the original owners' trips, or the postcards may be of the many places visited by friends and relatives.

Photographs of any building, home, event, activity, or landscape could be on a postcard. Today, these postcards are still collected by later generations to enjoy a bygone era. Some places on the cards still exist; others have disappeared or changed greatly. Family historians like to find postcards or photographs depicting places that were part of their family's history. Postcards are still produced, sent, and collected today.

The images chosen for this book are postcards showing Jamestown from the 1880s through the 1920s, with a few included from earlier times. As always, not everything was photographed and put on a postcard, and not every postcard is in the authors' collection. Many of the places remain today, but some are gone. People marvel at what was in Jamestown in the time period represented in this collection. Postcards always seem to capture the nice things in life, such as pretty landscapes, beautiful homes, or pleasant activities. Therefore, there are not many postcards of factories; thus, the industry that made Jamestown is underrepresented in this collection.

Hopefully, the images will either bring back memories for readers who lived in Jamestown when some of these places and people were here or help readers who have not lived here gain an understanding of Jamestown's history.

One

Early History

Jamestown, like many frontier towns, grew from the land, with hard work, natural resources, and adventurous men and women. When John Blowers built the first log cabin for his family near the outlet of Chautauqua Lake, he knew he would soon be joined by his employer James Prendergast and his wife. He also knew the plan was to build a sawmill at the water's edge and begin lumbering the hillsides. Prendergast and his wife, Agnes, arrived the next spring and went to work. Agnes became known as Aunt Nancy and opened her home to many early settlers until they found or built a place to live.

Prendergast was able to attract settlers to what became the village of Jamestown in 1827. Soon, there was a tavern, which functioned as an early hotel for travelers or new residents. The mechanics who produced goods and services found a place in the "West" where they were needed and found work to support themselves.

Not much of this history is recorded in pictures for the postcard trade. Postcards of early Jamestown are limited to photographs taken in the 1860s and to drawings. The drawings were based on the written descriptions of early Jamestown. Some photographs from the 1860s did, at a later time, find their way to postcards. There are other photographs of early Jamestown from the 1860s and 1870s, but no one published postcards from the photographs.

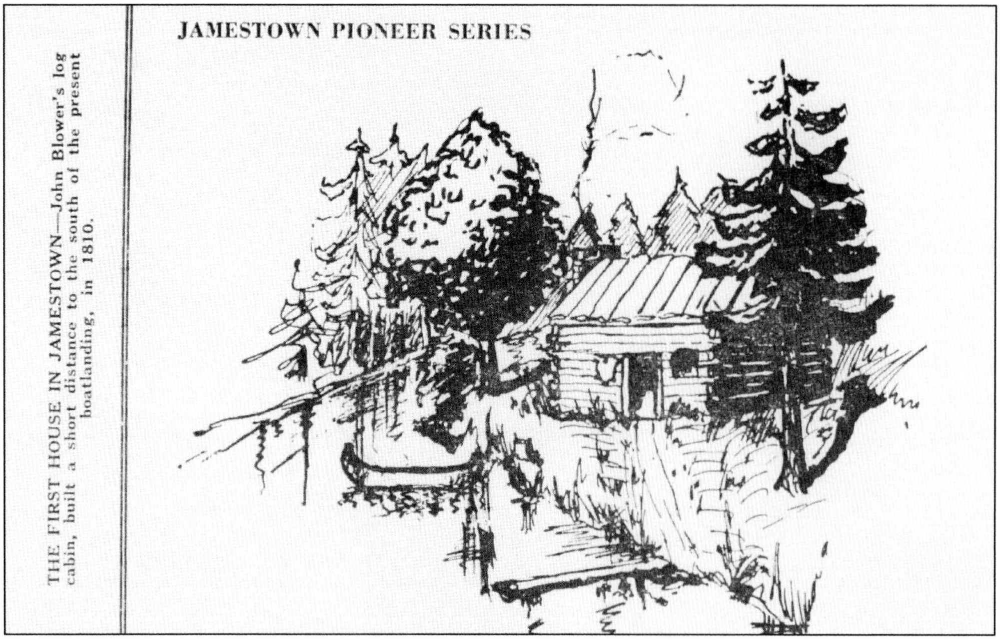

In 1927, to celebrate the centennial of the village of Jamestown, city historian Arthur Wellington Anderson made drawings based on descriptions of many of the village's early buildings. These drawings were used for postcards and other products. The first house was a log cabin near the outlet built by John Blowers, an employee of James Prendergast. (Courtesy of FHC.)

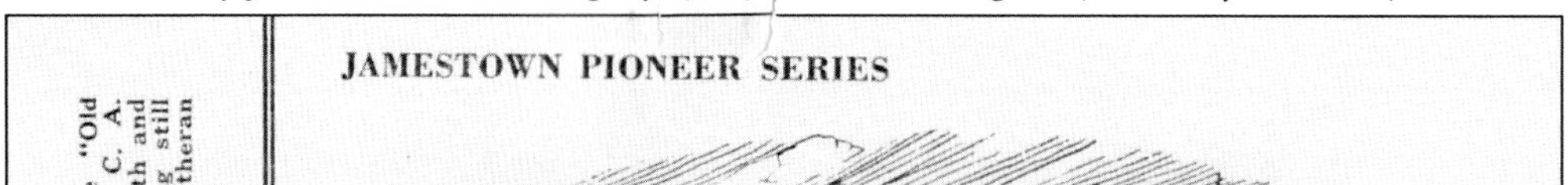

Another of Anderson's drawings was of the first school, called Prendergast's Academy, which was built on the southwest corner of Main and Fifth Streets. Classes began in 1816. It was also used as a multidenominational place of worship. In 1829, it was moved to the corner of Fourth and Cherry Streets, and it finished its days as the parsonage for the English Lutheran Church. (Courtesy of FHC.)

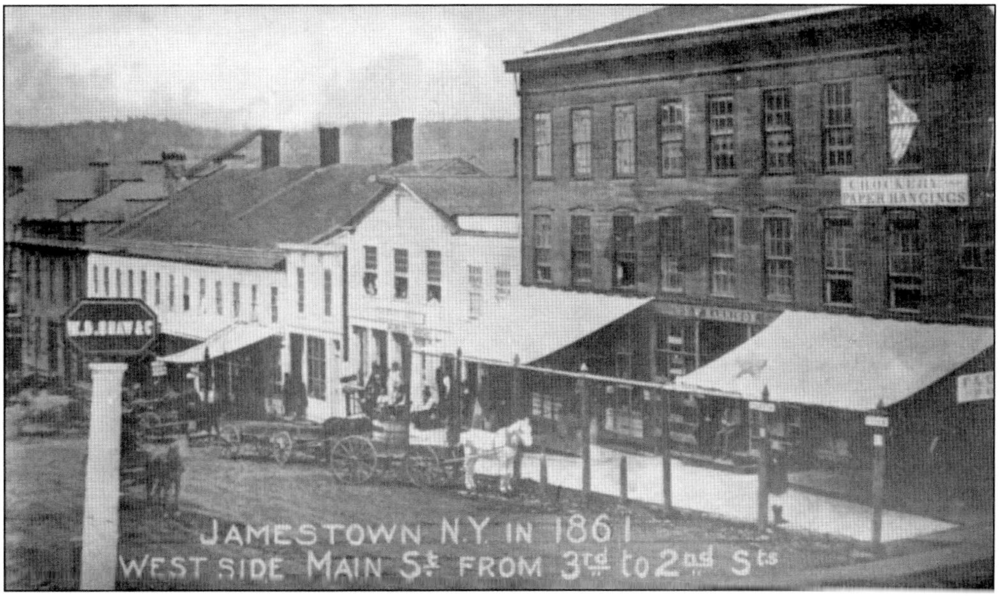

These buildings burned in the great fire of January 1861. After the fire, Jamestown rebuilt, but the eastside buildings burned again in 1871. Replacement buildings were brick and were erected gradually, with many three-story brick buildings on both sides of North Main Street by the turn of the century. Businesses continued to include various retail establishments with offices occupying the upper floors.

Jamestown, N. Y. on July 9, 1864. No. 1.—Albert Smith's Sash and Door Factory. No. 2.—Ford & Wood's Furniture Factory. No. 3.—Sprague, Steele & Co.'s Foundry Shop. No. 4.—Dan Rice's Circus. No. 5.—Gov. Fenton's Home.

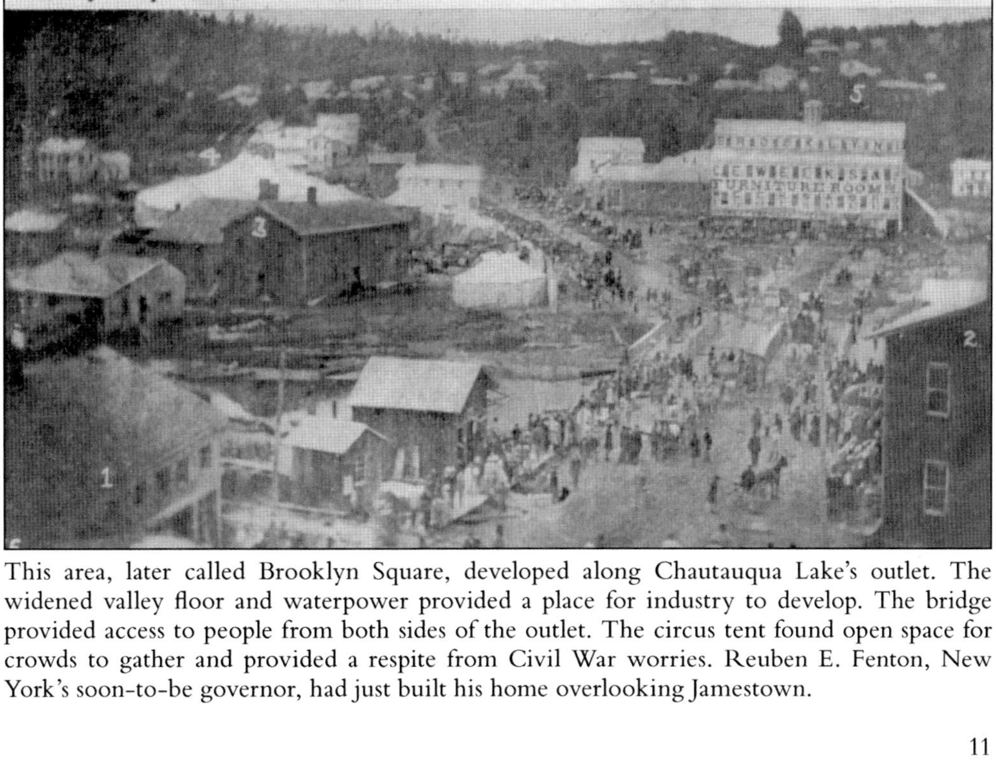

This area, later called Brooklyn Square, developed along Chautauqua Lake's outlet. The widened valley floor and waterpower provided a place for industry to develop. The bridge provided access to people from both sides of the outlet. The circus tent found open space for crowds to gather and provided a respite from Civil War worries. Reuben E. Fenton, New York's soon-to-be governor, had just built his home overlooking Jamestown.

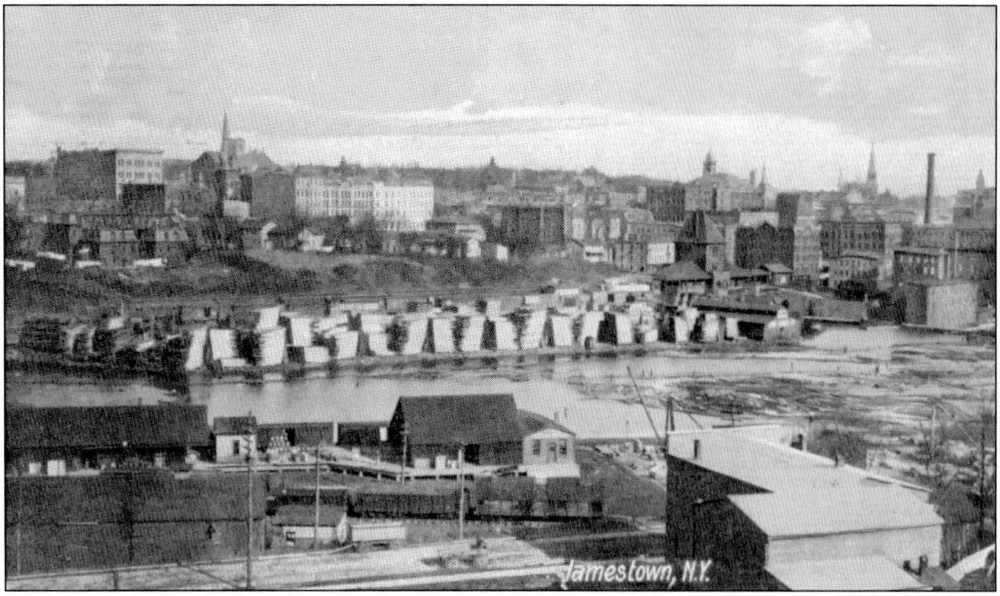

The expanding city of Jamestown is climbing the hills north of the Chadakoin River. Along the river is evidence of the lumber industry on which Jamestown's prosperity grew. Logs were harvested, and when the ice left the lake, they were floated to the sawmills in Jamestown. The lumber supplied the furniture industry, and Jamestown wood products were shipped around the country and, eventually, the world.

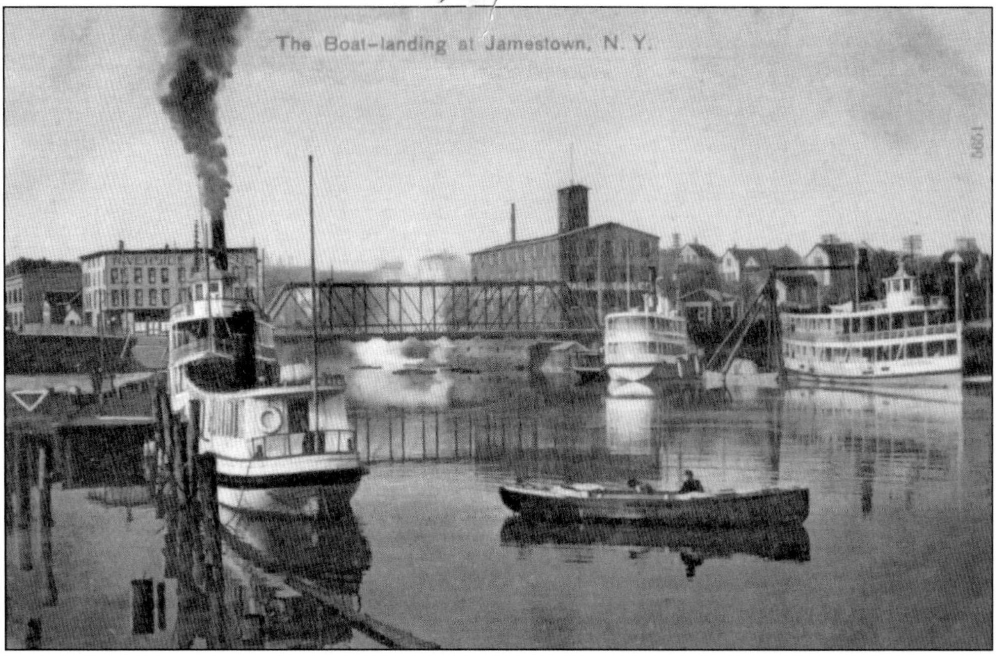

The boat landing for steamers was established where the Chadakoin River widened above the rapids. A bridge at river level gave access from both riverbanks. The Riverside Hotel can be seen to the left. The large brick building was originally the Morgan Manufacturing Company, which could produce over 25,000 tables a year. An addition was built in 1891, and in 1906, the name was changed to the Jamestown Table Company.

Two

Brooklyn Square

Why the name *Brooklyn Square* was chosen and when it came into use is unknown, but a number of theories have been proposed. Reference to Brooklyn can be found as early as the 1860s in the local newspapers. Brooklyn Square resembles a triangle more than a square and has changed many times. The latest significant change was in the 1970s, as urban renewal swept through, taking the old and leaving some new. Newcomers to the city soon learn where Brooklyn Square is and probably hear many stories about what it was.

In the early days, the Brooklyn Square area was flat, wet, and swampy, with a river running through it. It was a place to unload boats near some businesses as the village grew and a flat space where the militia could drill or where the circus could set up a large tent. This area was subject to flooding in the early days. Some claim that fill was added to raise the level of the land high enough to stay dry. The early homes and the tavern were just up the hill, as was the first store when it started. The flat land did provide a place to build some industry. As time went on, more was built in the area, and the river was bridged. People had more reasons to go to the area, and what was there increased.

Roads coming from many directions ended in Brooklyn Square, making it a destination. Hotels and stores were built, and Brooklyn Square became an important commercial and industrial area. Homes and businesses continued to develop on the higher ground above Brooklyn Square. Soon, large buildings lined the streets, and these are the subjects of the postcards from the turn of the century. Activities in the square were photographed occasionally, and a few appear as postcards.

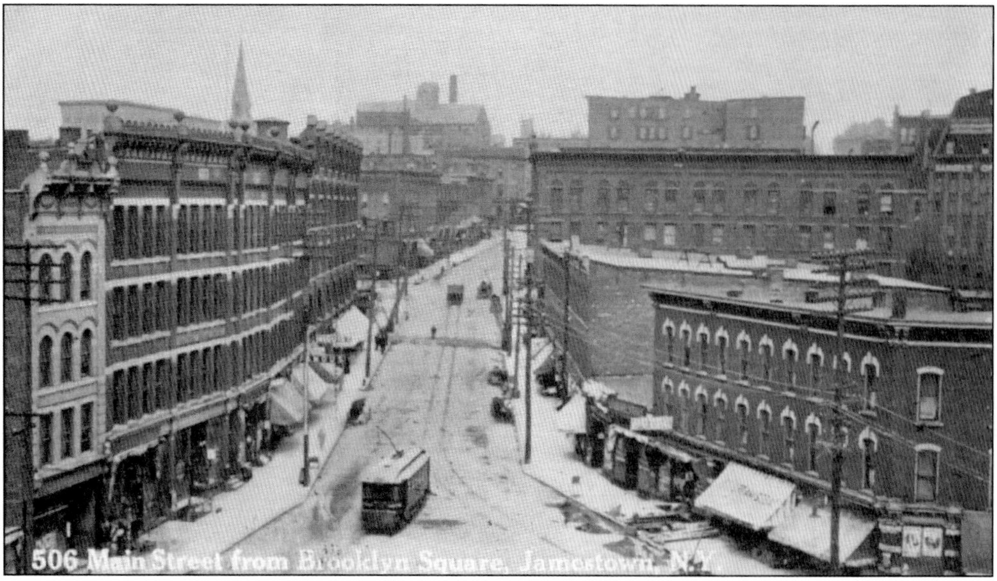

By the 1890s, Brooklyn Square developed into a hub of business activity. Retail establishments, hotels, restaurants, and a trolley line transfer point all crowded into the square. Businesses climbed the hill to the north, developing a second cluster of businesses around Third and North Main Streets. The train tracks crossed partially up the hill, making both business areas convenient for travelers.

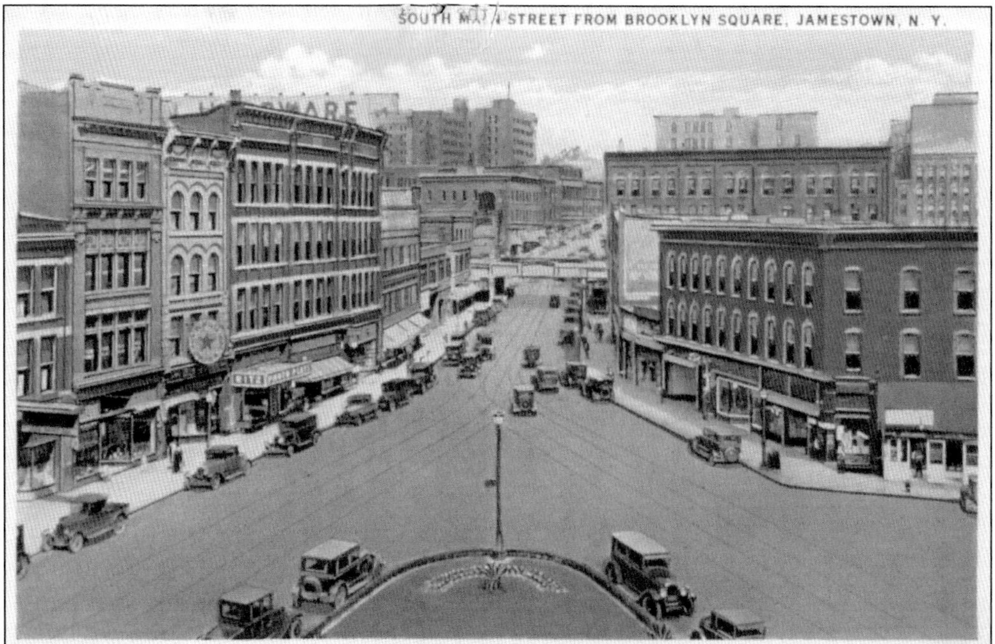

Some 20–30 years later, Brooklyn Square continued as a hub of business activity. Automobiles were replacing the horse and wagon. Streets were paved with bricks, and the four movie theaters in the area of the square were popular entertainments. Trolleys were electrified and brought customers from farther distances. The formal garden area funneled the traffic to the outflowing streets. Each year, a community Christmas tree was located there.

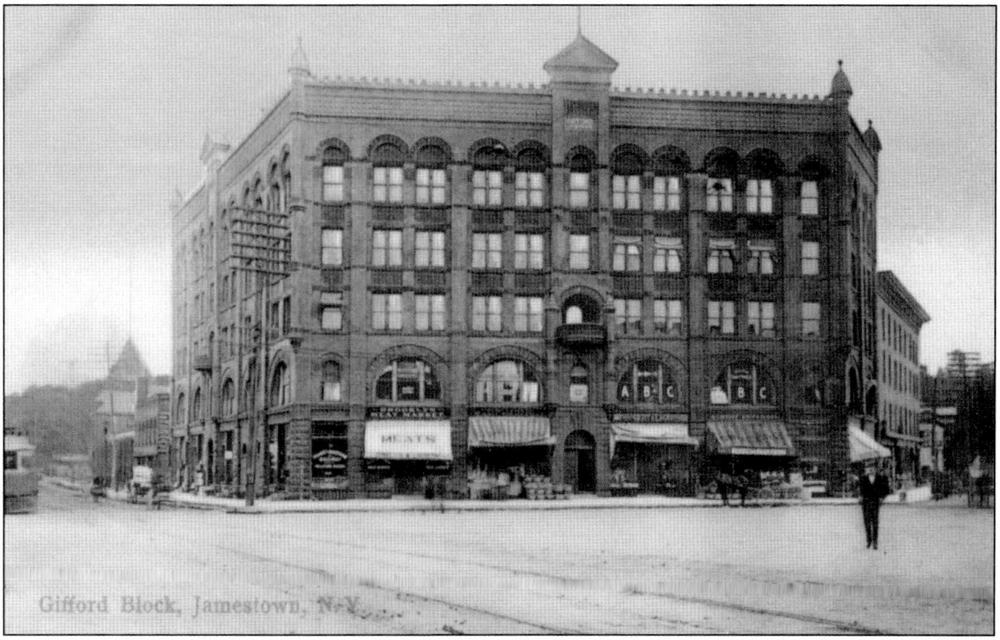

The Gifford Building, a multiuse building with retail space on the ground floor and offices and apartments on the upper floors, anchored Brooklyn Square's south side. Built in 1890 to replace an earlier furniture company, it was razed in 1968 during the urban renewal initiative. New York State's armory was behind on the left, and the Kent Apartments were on the right side of the Gifford Building. Trolleys from Warren approached on South Main Street.

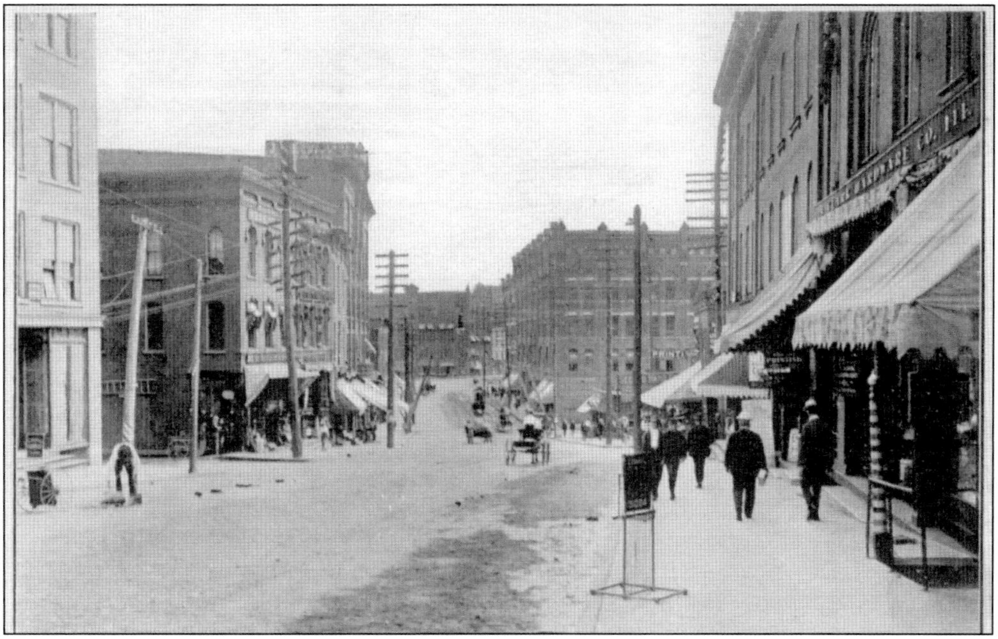

Looking south on Main Street into Brooklyn Square, the Gifford Building is at the south side of the area. The street to the left is First Street. The front of the Arcade Building is just visible on the left, and the Hotel Everett is the large building in the middle of the right side. A street sweeper is on the left. This photograph was taken before 1906.

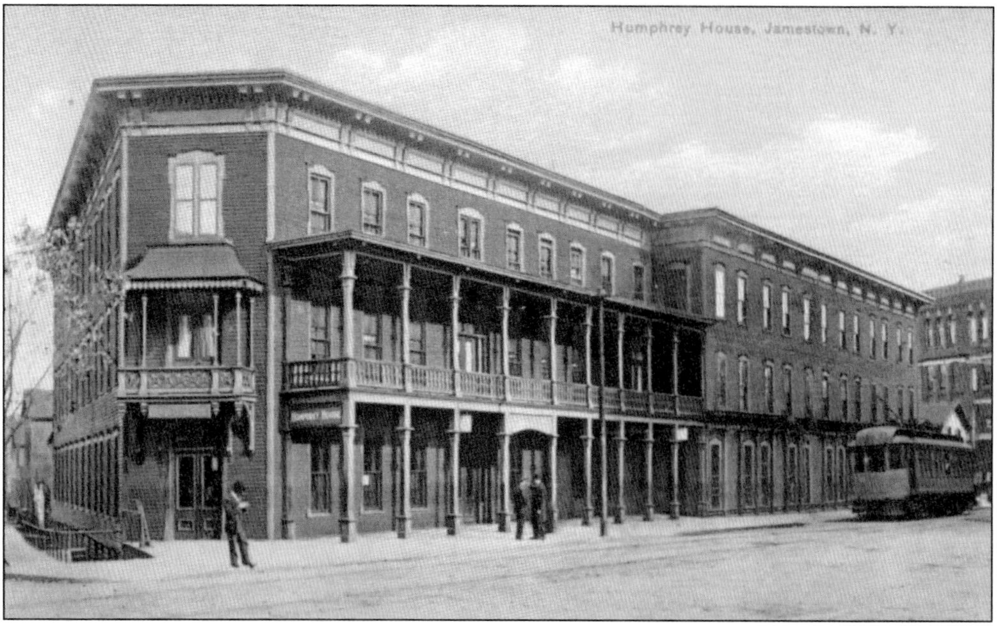

The Humphrey House in Brooklyn Square began in 1872 as the Weeks House. John W. Humphrey Jr. was the proprietor from 1883 until his death in 1911. The dining room had an excellent reputation and was well known to travelers. This postcard was published between October 1919, when the city council changed Brooklyn Square's name to Roosevelt Square, and November 1925, when public outcry forced the return to Brooklyn Square.

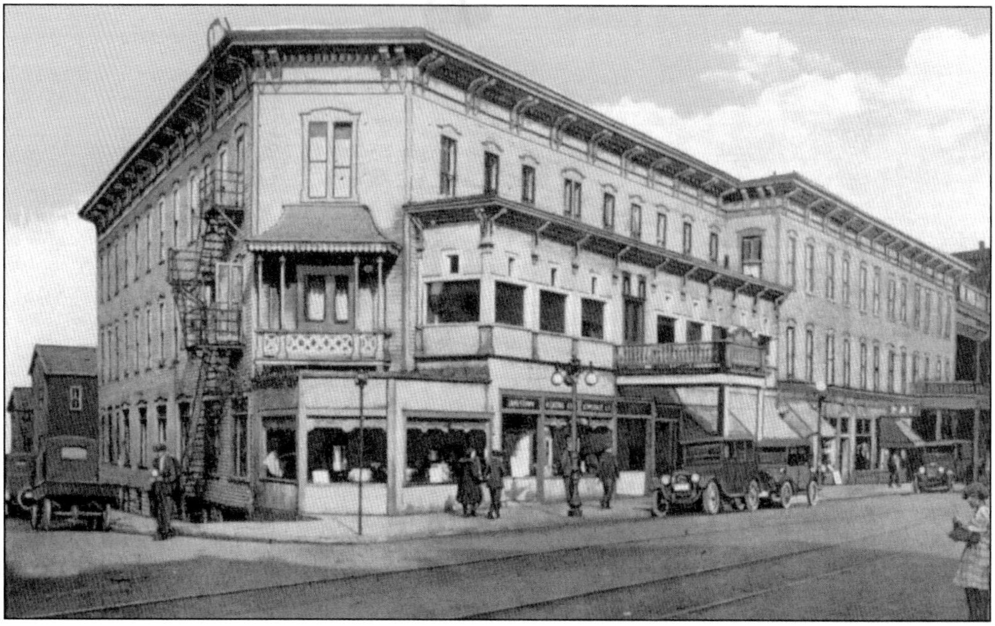

By the late 1920s, the Humphrey House had been renovated by enclosing the upper and lower porches and covering an entrance. Fire escapes were added near the corner. From 1905 to 1929, the terminal for the Jamestown–Warren trolley line was located at the Humphrey House. In its final years, it existed as a one-story structure, and it closed in November 1932, just short of its 60th anniversary as a hotel.

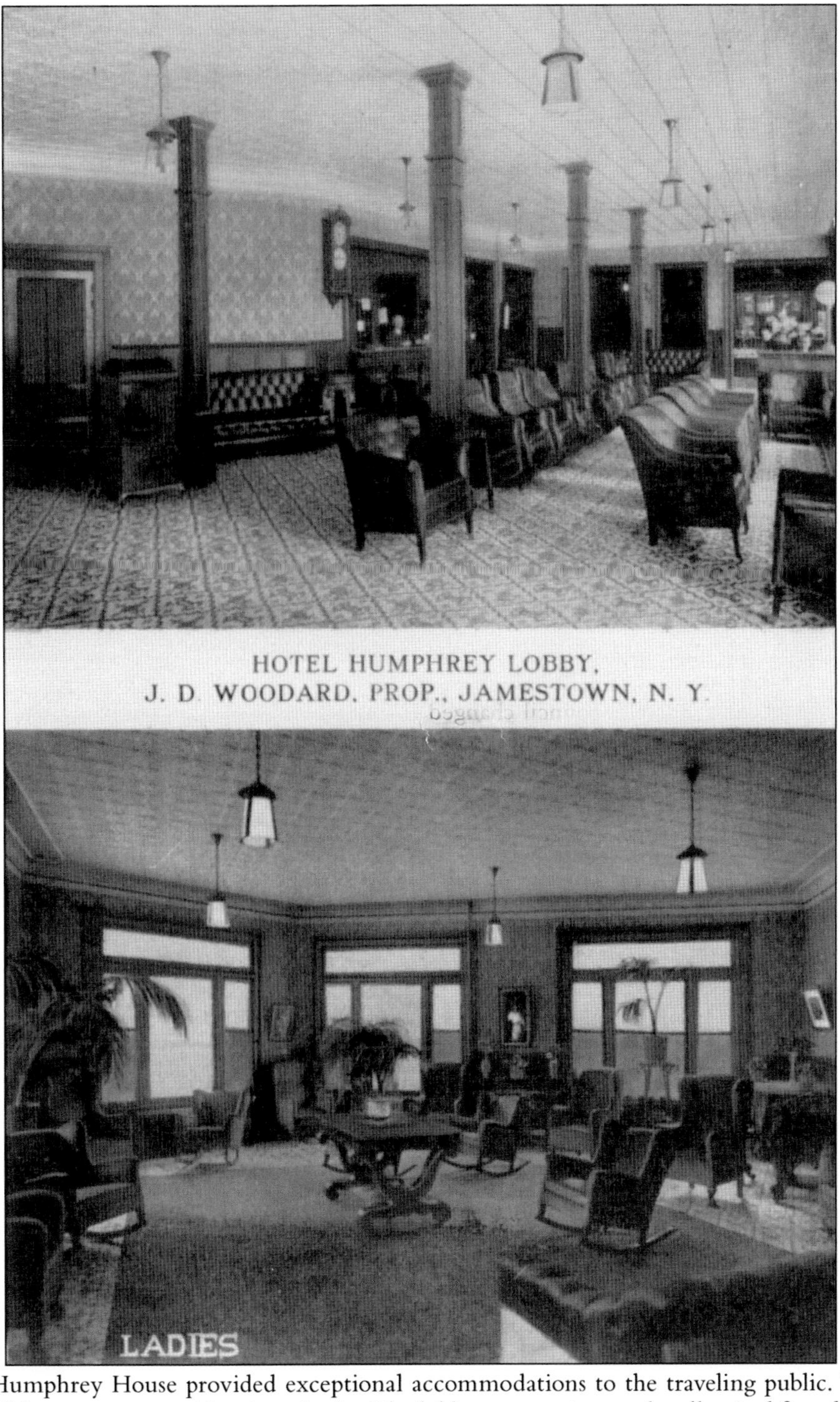

The Humphrey House provided exceptional accommodations to the traveling public. There were 100 rooms, some with private baths. The lobby was spacious and well-suited for relaxing. A separate ladies area gave the women a place of their own, probably without cigar smoke. Notice the women had rocking chairs in conversation groupings, while the lobby chairs were lined up in straight rows.

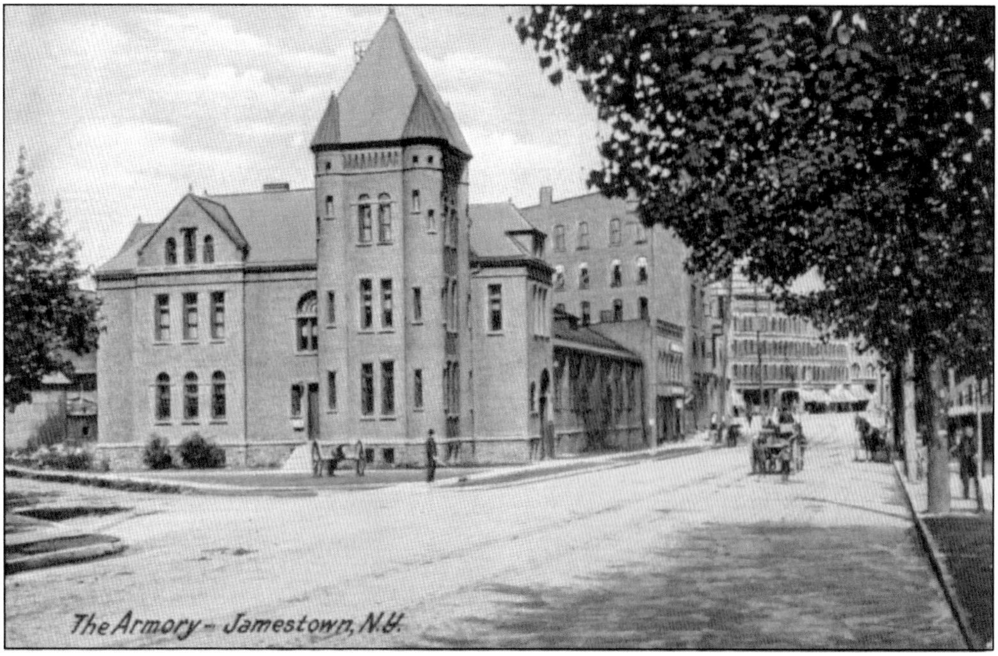

Located just south of Brooklyn Square, at the corner of Fenton Place and South Main Street, the New York State Armory served from 1898 to 1932, when a new armory was built. The Fenton Guards met and drilled at various halls in Jamestown before the armory was built. The armory burned in 1942, and the site was used to deposit all of the metal collected during World War II scrap drives in Jamestown.

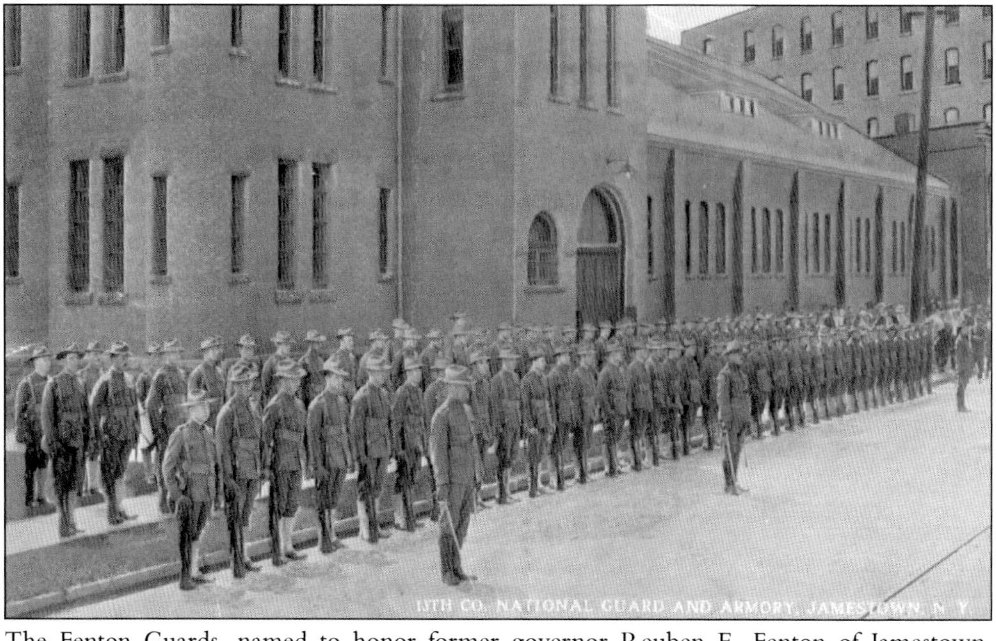

The Fenton Guards, named to honor former governor Reuben E. Fenton of Jamestown, organized in 1875. Most early members were Swedish. As part of the National Guard, they were called up a few times; they reported for the Spanish-American War and saw duty on the Mexican border in 1910, and many served during World War I.

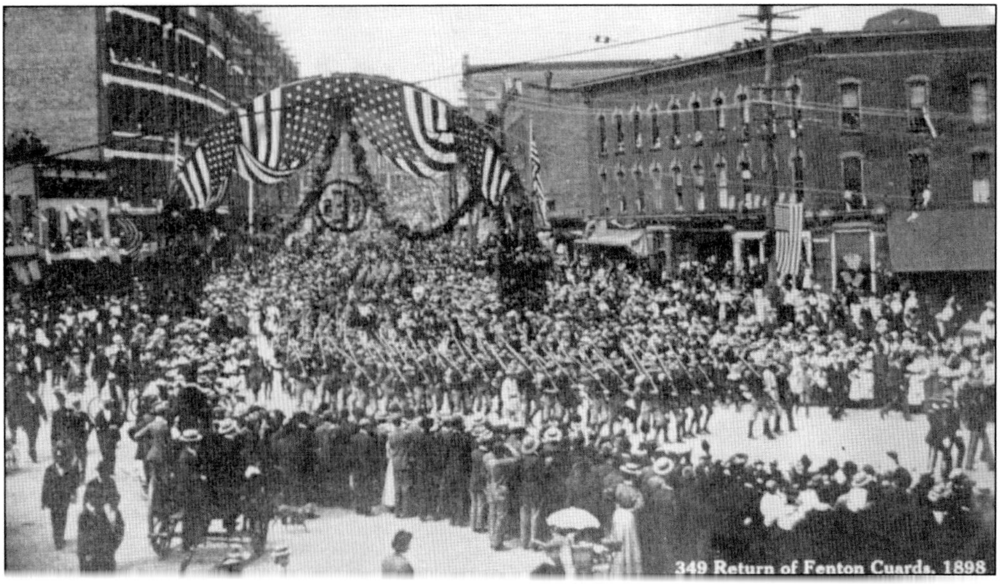

The Fenton Guards were called up for service in May 1898, during the Spanish-American War. When they left and returned, they marched between their armory and the train station on First Street. Here, they are returning from the train station on Main Street, coming into Brooklyn Square. They had been in Long Island, Virginia, and Buffalo, returning in November 1898. (Courtesy of MC.)

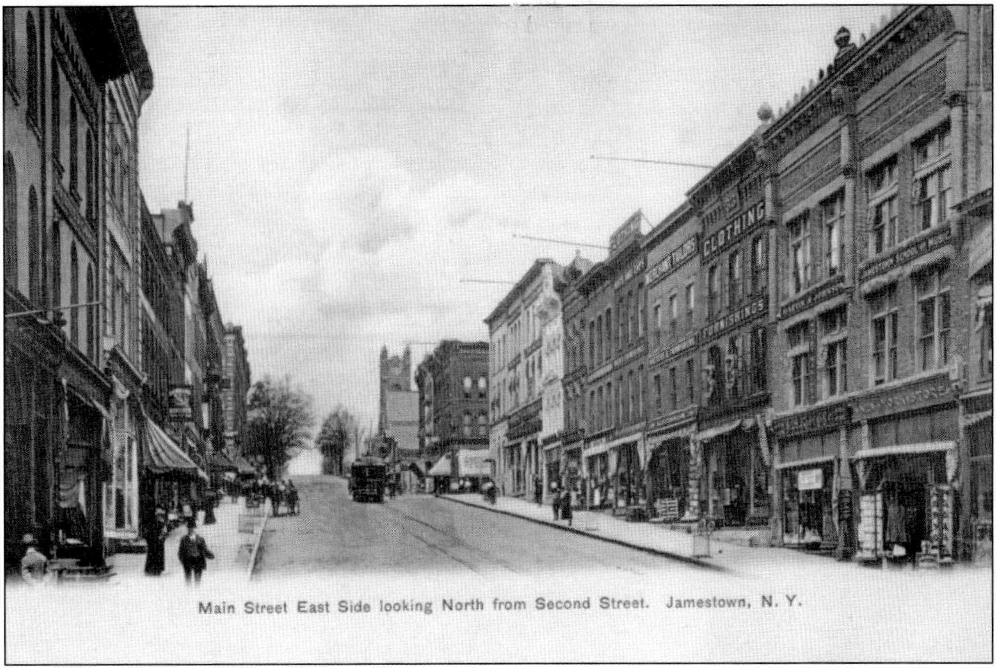

Leaving Brooklyn Square and heading up the hill to another business district, substantial brick buildings greeted the shoppers. Along North Main Street, between Second and Third Streets, were many clothing stores, each with their own tailor for men's clothing. St. Luke's Episcopal Church is at the crest of the hill at Fourth Street. By the mid-1920s, banks occupied three of the four corners between Second and Third Streets. (Courtesy of FHC.)

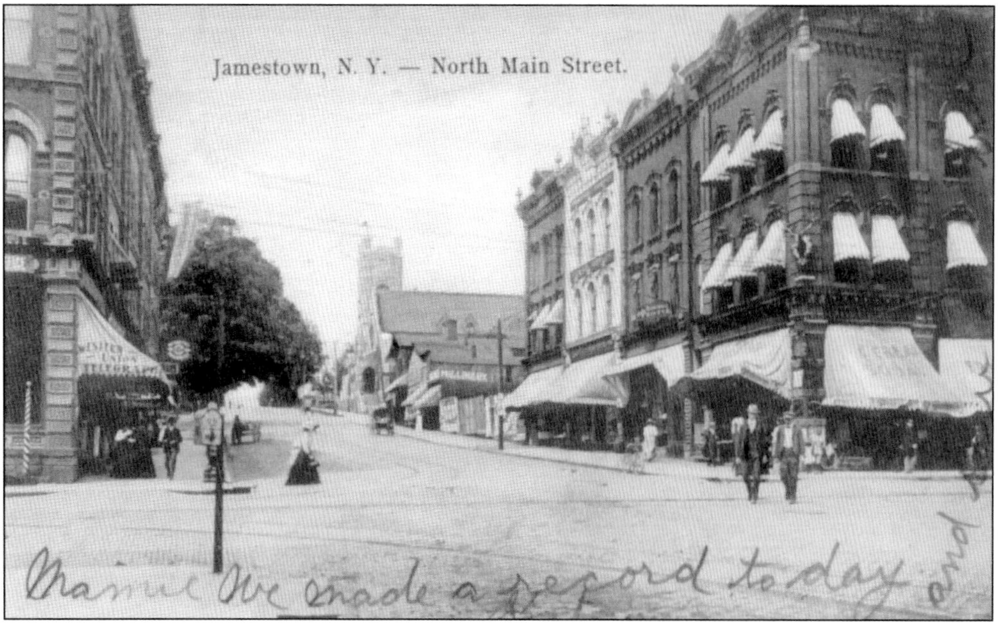

Continuing up Main Street from Third Street, looking north, the building on the left is the Prendergast Block. The income from it supports the James Prendergast Free Library. Clark's Drugstore is on the other corner. The next three buildings north still exist. The wooden building on the corner, across from St. Luke's, survived a 1931 fire and is still used today. The other smaller buildings have been replaced.

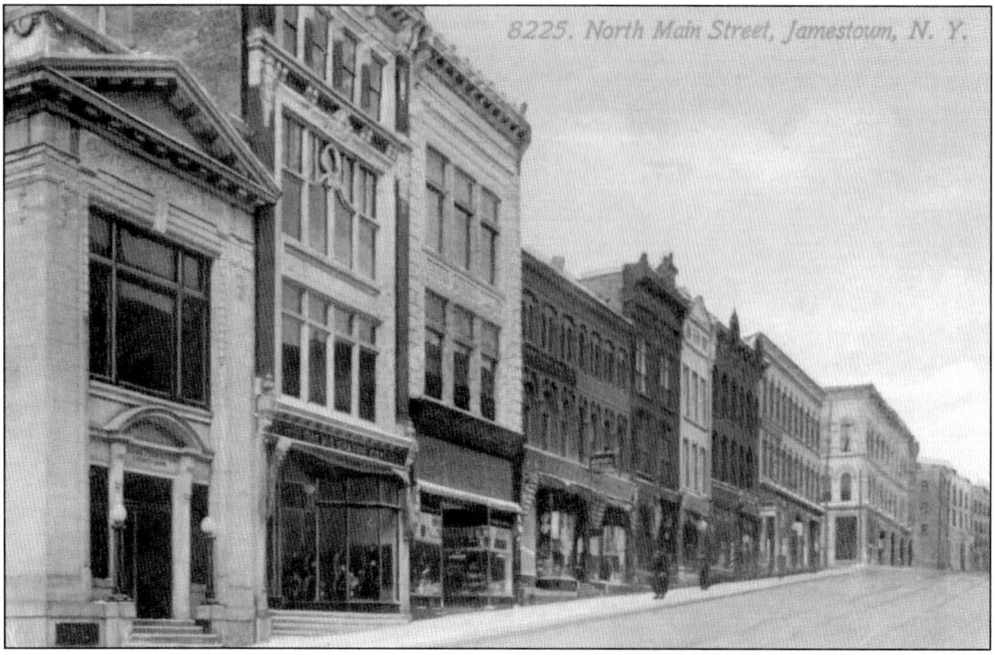

This is the west side of Main Street from Second Street to Third Street about 100 years ago. On this side of the street, residents could get cigars or stationery, go to the bank, attend a lodge meeting, visit the dentist, have a photograph taken, buy almost anything in a dry goods store, and more. Most of these buildings continue to house businesses and offices.

Three

Second and Third Streets

As Brooklyn Square was developing along the river, the area on higher ground was becoming dotted with homes and businesses. James Prendergast used a grid pattern when he laid out the plan for the village. The blocks created by the grid were all the same size and designed to have buildings fronting along the streets and an alley bisecting each block from north to south. First Street was still near the river and apparently not as favorable as the next couple of street to the north. James Prendergast's home was one lot north of the corner of Main and Second Streets. Around this area of Main Street and Second and Third Streets, new settlers chose to build dwellings and open businesses.

After the great fire of 1861, the village trustees declared new buildings in the business district would have to be brick or stone. But 10 years later, some of these buildings burned also. It is possible to trace the building history along some of the streets by looking at the pictures in the postcards. Wooden buildings are replaced by brick buildings; brick buildings are replaced by larger brick buildings. The occupants of these buildings changed over time, and that history is not always evident from the postcard. City directories can be guides to the dating of the pictures, because the signs on the buildings are legible, and the directories can help determine what years those signs would have been in use. Postcards from different publishers may be the same photograph taken by a photographer, but there may be a person or people added to the sidewalk, a bicycle, a horse and buggy, or a car added to the picture. In general, postcards can be used to trace the evolution of a street or a building if it was of enough interest to the postcard-buying public. Thus begins the journey through the history of two streets in downtown Jamestown.

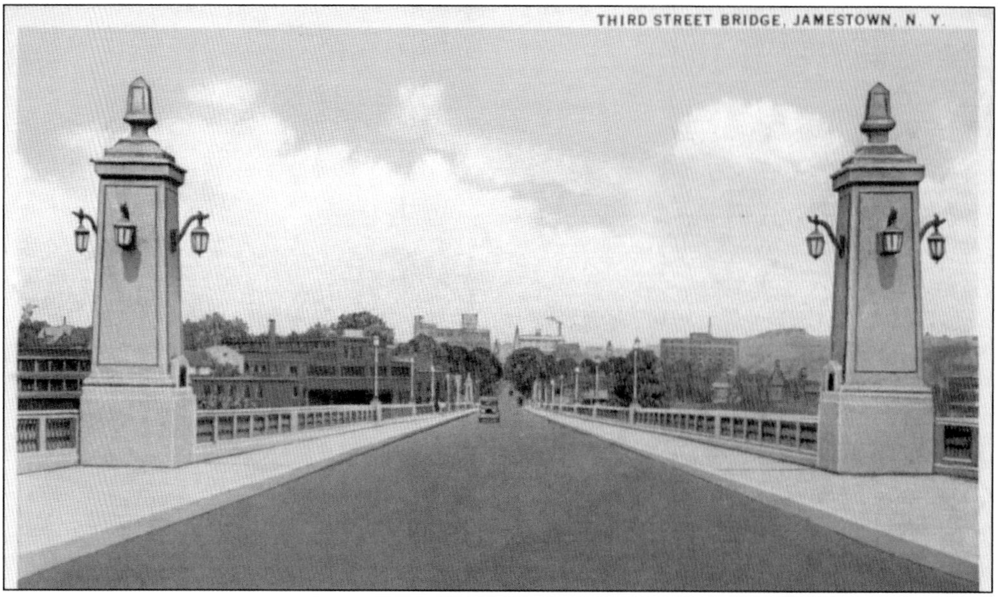

Constructed in the mid-1920s, the Third Street Bridge gave quick and easy access to the business district for west-side residents. Visible from the west end of the bridge are the car barns of the Jamestown Street Railway just to the left, the Furniture Exposition Building to the far right, and the many buildings along Third Street. The bridge has been replaced twice since the first was built.

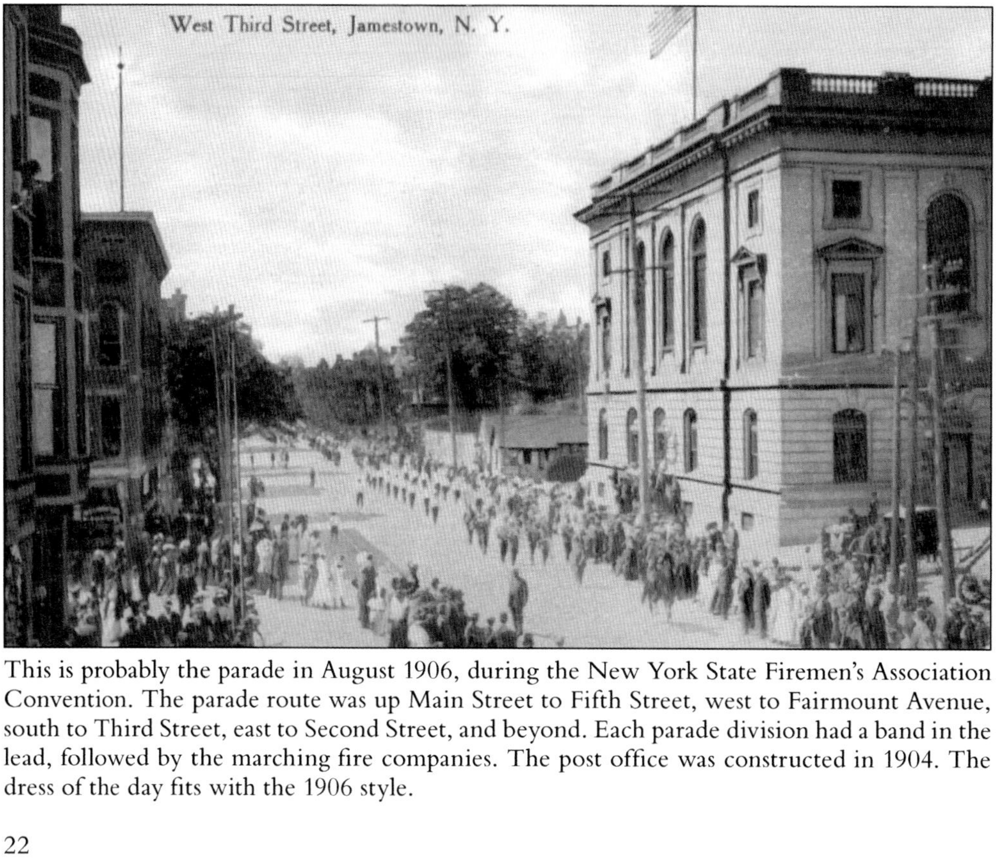

This is probably the parade in August 1906, during the New York State Firemen's Association Convention. The parade route was up Main Street to Fifth Street, west to Fairmount Avenue, south to Third Street, east to Second Street, and beyond. Each parade division had a band in the lead, followed by the marching fire companies. The post office was constructed in 1904. The dress of the day fits with the 1906 style.

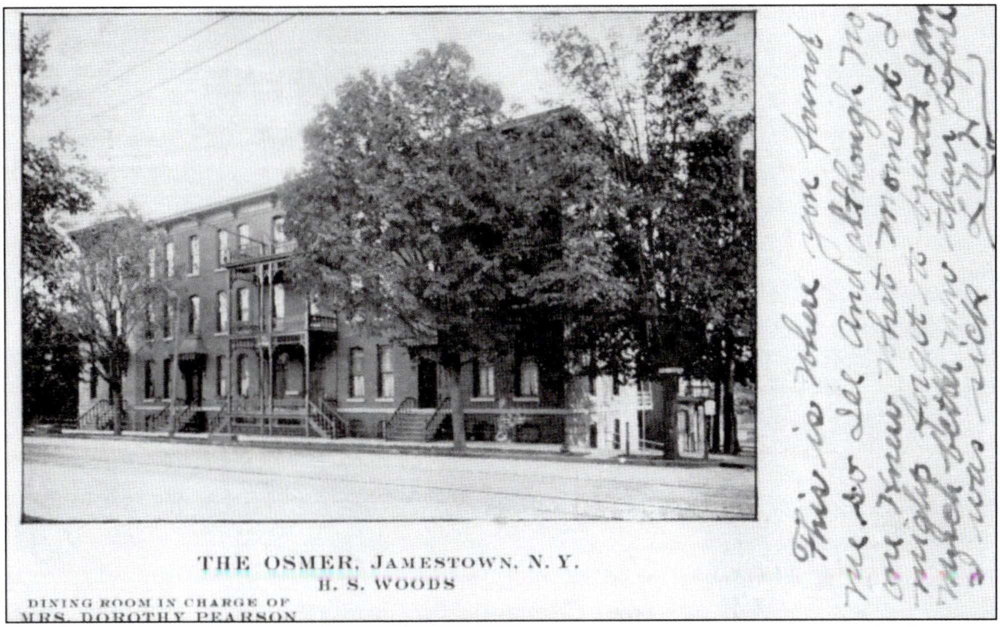

The Osmer, a private boardinghouse, was located along Third Street, a few blocks from the business district. Henry S. and Celia E. Woods opened the Osmer around 1884. Since Woods's job required travel, his wife managed the boardinghouse. The dining room, open to the public, enjoyed a reputation of excellence. The four-story brick building had 45 rooms and took two years to build.

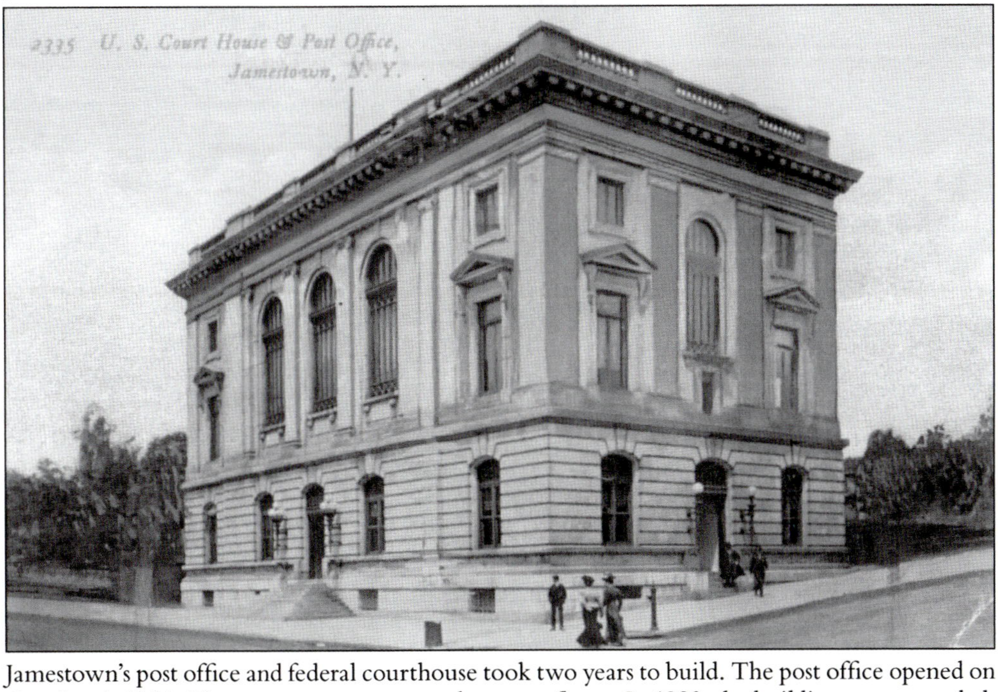

Jamestown's post office and federal courthouse took two years to build. The post office opened on October 1, 1904. The courtrooms were on the upper floors. In 1923, the building was expanded. For many years, the city had mail delivery twice a day. The post office moved to the new Federal Building in December 1960. It took two months to tear down the old building in 1963.

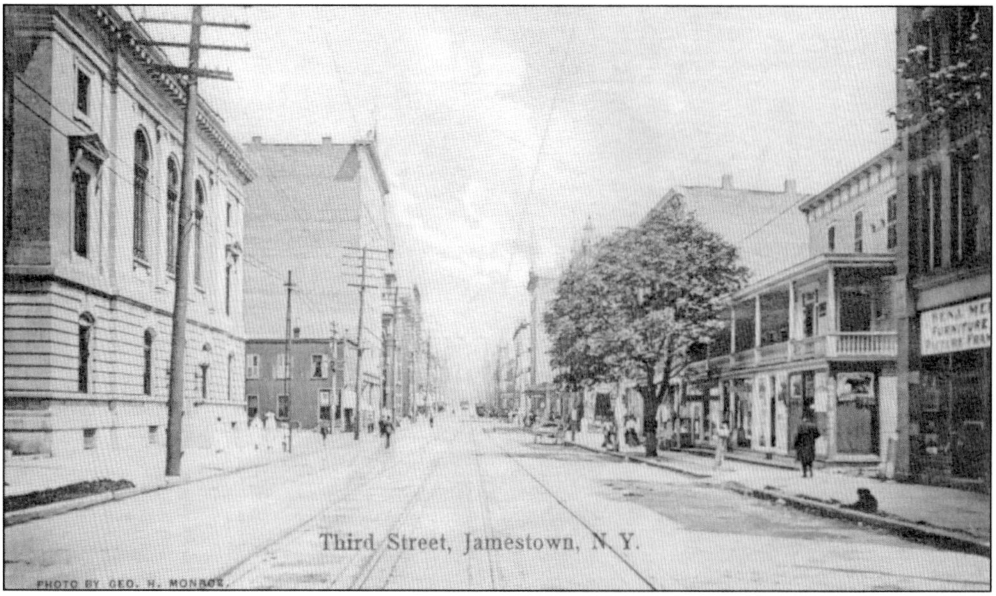

Looking east along Third Street, the older two- and three-story buildings are beginning to be replaced by taller, larger brick buildings. Along the north side is the post office, the Chadakoin Building, the Gokey Block, and more beyond. On the right side, hidden by the tree, would be the Tribune Building, with the Wellman Building and the New Sherman House in the distance.

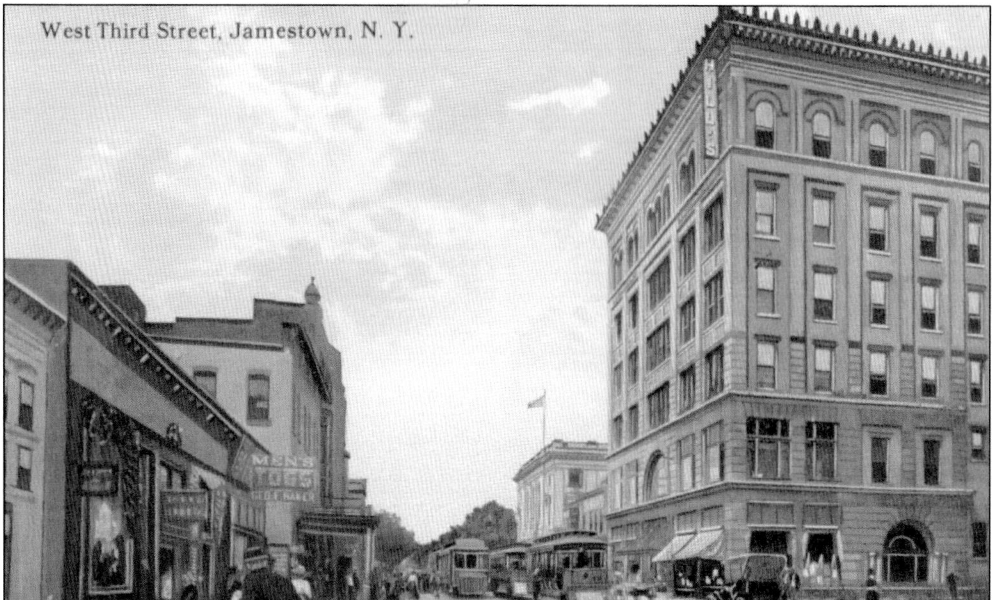

The six-story Chadakoin Building is the prominent structure on the right. In 1894, Charles Abrahamson was working in the dry goods business on Main Street. After partnering with Reuben Bigelow in 1900, Abrahamson was sure Third Street would be the place for their store. Built in 1906 by Charles Abrahamson, the Chadakoin Building housed the Abrahamson-Bigelow department store, using only the first two floors initially.

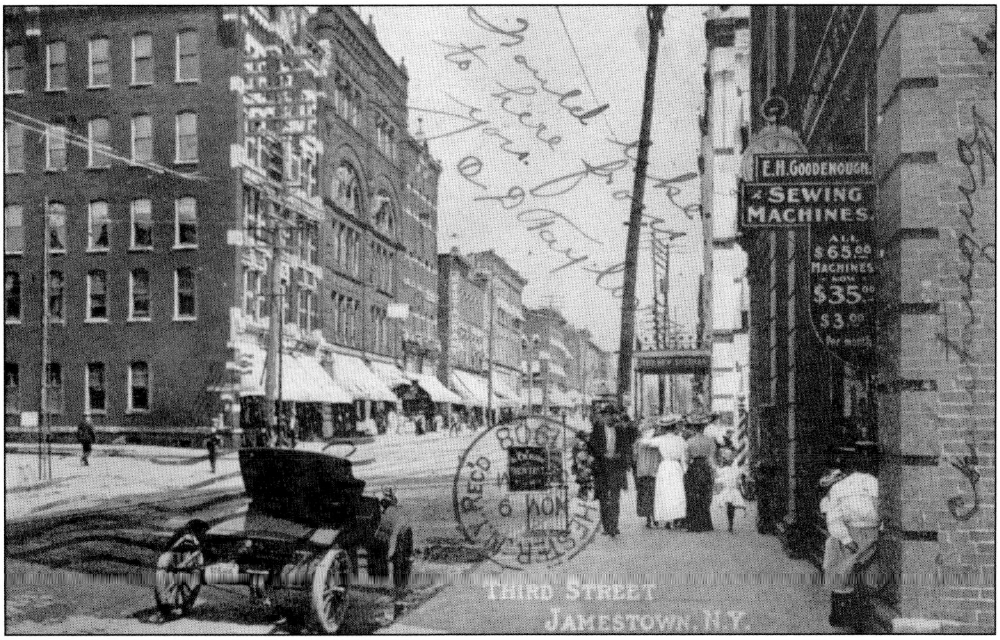

West of Cherry Street is the large Gokey Block, along with the Hall and Fenton Block and the Briggs Block on Third Street. In the foreground is the Wellman Building, where E.H. Goodenough sold sewing machines and other businesses filled three-room suites, each of which had a lavatory and toilet. There was a modern electric elevator in the building. The New Sherman House is the white building beyond the Wellman Building.

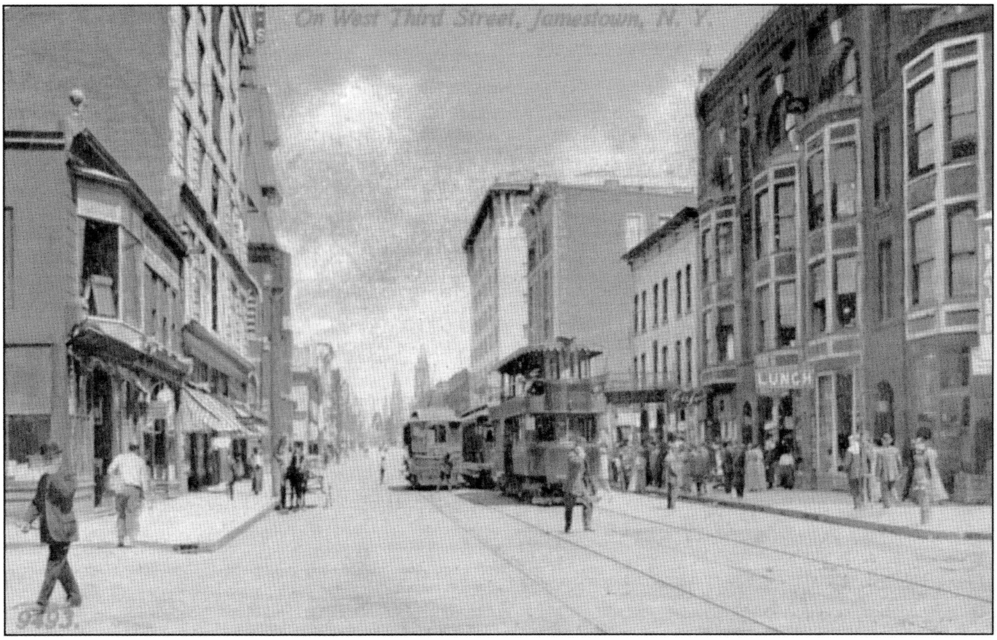

Looking east from Washington Street, a crowd has gathered on the sidewalk to the right of the trolley cars. After the 1910 Gokey fire, the trolley line's waiting room and ticket office moved to the Russell Block, the smaller building in the middle of the block. On the far right is the Hayward Block. Celoron Park was the usual destination of the double-decker streetcar.

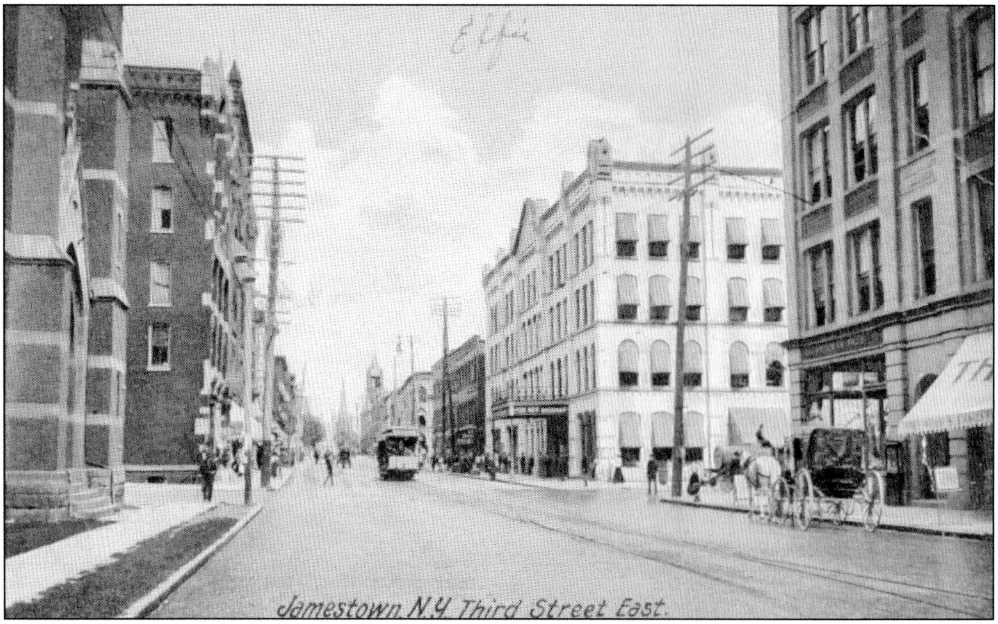

Prominent along West Third Street is the New Sherman House. Manager George F. Hurlbut refurbished all 100 rooms in 1899. The four-story brick structure was considered fireproof. Brass bedsteads, steam radiators, and a locking writing desk were included in each room. A smoker's emporium in the lobby, long-distance telephone service, a competent stenographer, and manicure parlors were available. Clothes could also be pressed while guests rested.

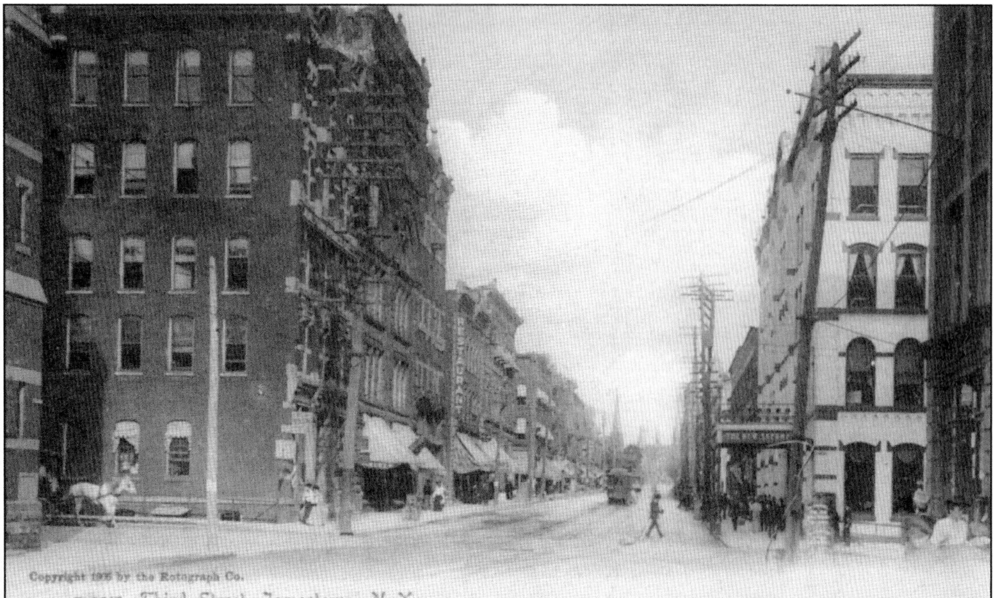

Across Third Street from the New Sherman House was the large Gokey Block. Businesses in the Gokey Block included a dry goods store, a barbershop, the chamber of commerce, the Jamestown Business College, insurance companies, lawyers, and other professionals. The trolley office and waiting room in the New Sherman House was convenient for Gokey tenants. Other smaller buildings along Third Street had retail stores and offices.

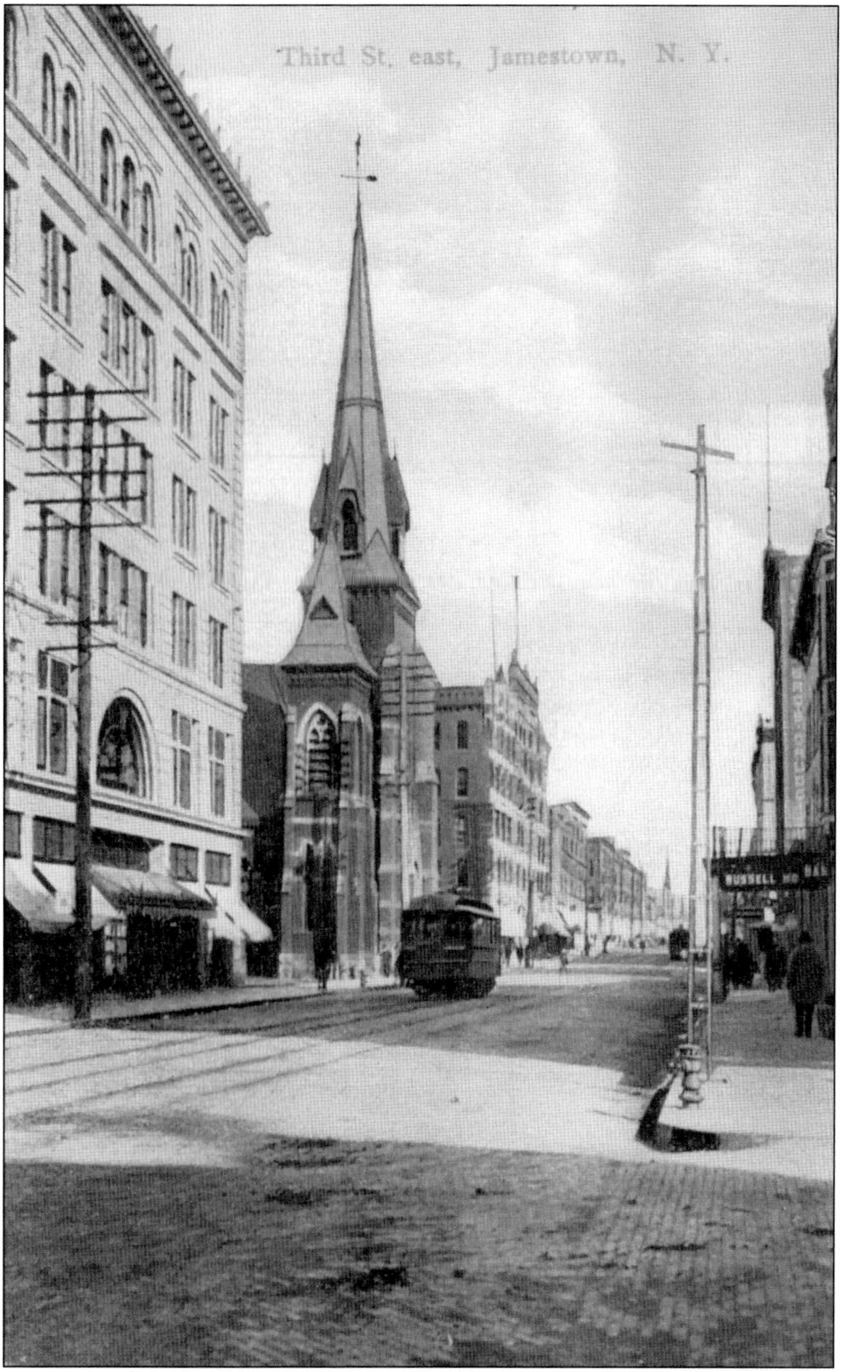

The large brick First Presbyterian Church, constructed in 1879, towered over the smaller buildings scattered along Third and Cherry Streets. By the 1890s, the Wellman Building and the Sherman House across Third Street had been built. The neighboring Chadakoin Building overlooked the church. The three buildings that were connected to make the Gokey Block were completed. Progress and prosperity were changing Third Street into a bustling business district.

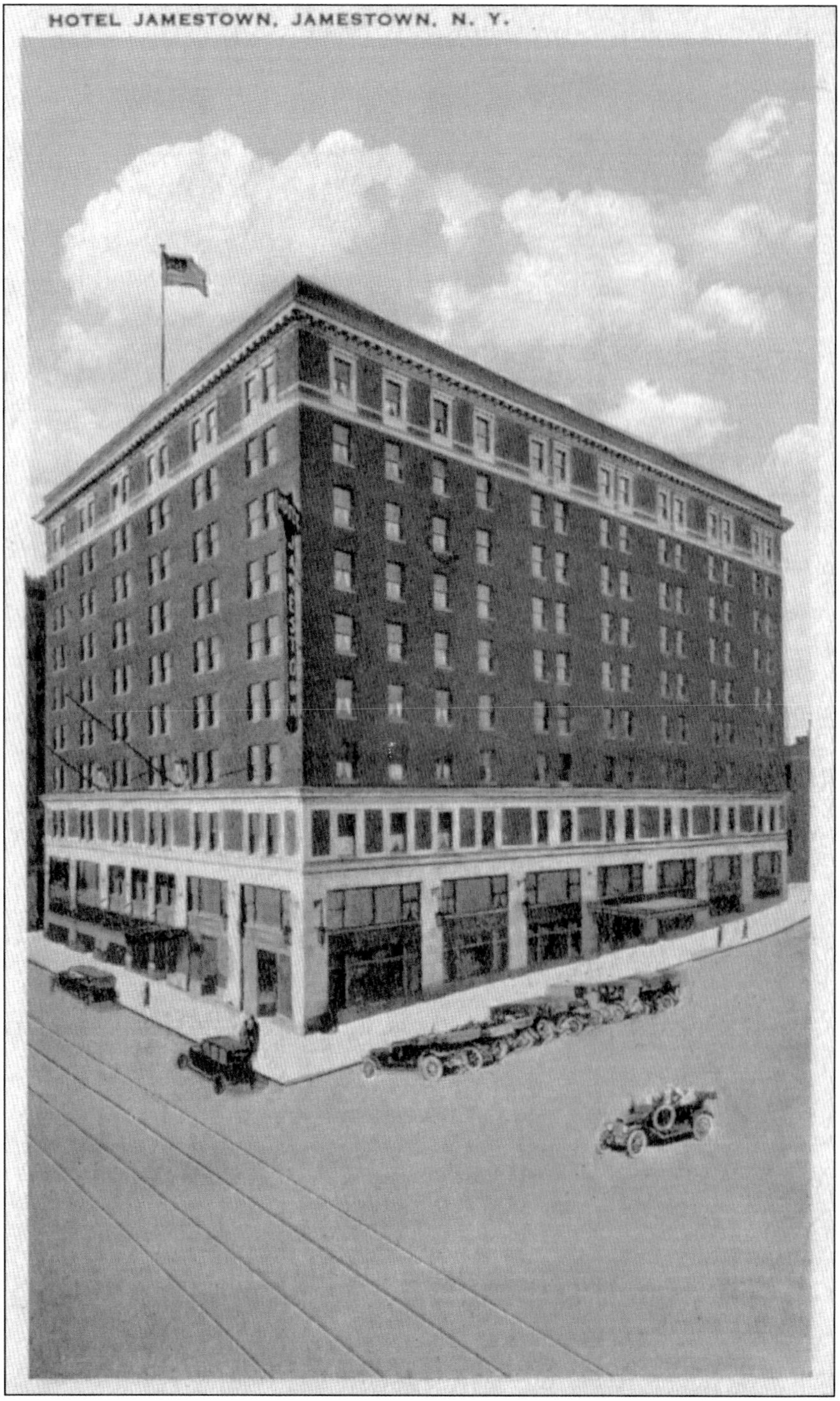

By 1925, Third Street changed again. The First Presbyterian Church, with its tall steeple and towers, was no longer there. In its place was the nine-story Hotel Jamestown, built to provide first-class hotel rooms close to the Furniture Exposition Building. Successful furniture companies attracted national store buyers to Jamestown, and they needed hotel rooms. Along with hotel rooms, some professional offices, restaurants, and services were included in the building.

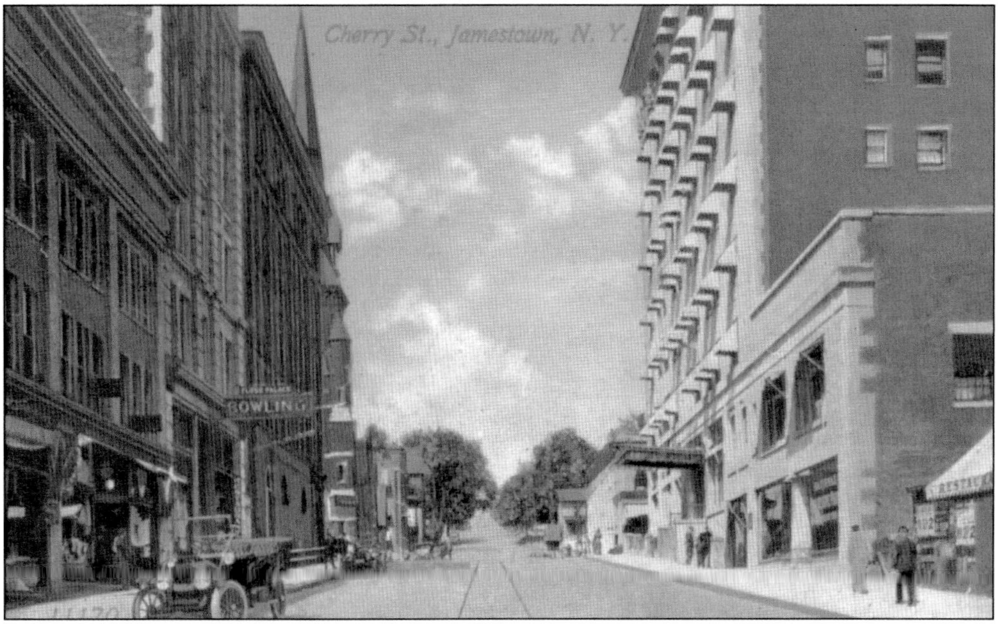

Looking north on Cherry Street from Second Street, one can see the Samuels Hotel, built where the New Sherman House was before the fire. Across Third Street, a few smaller two-story buildings fill the space of the burned Gokey Block and Gokey Shoe Factory. The First Presbyterian Church and the Wellman Building anchor the other corners of Third and Cherry Streets. Along Cherry Street are retail shops, a restaurant, and a bowling alley.

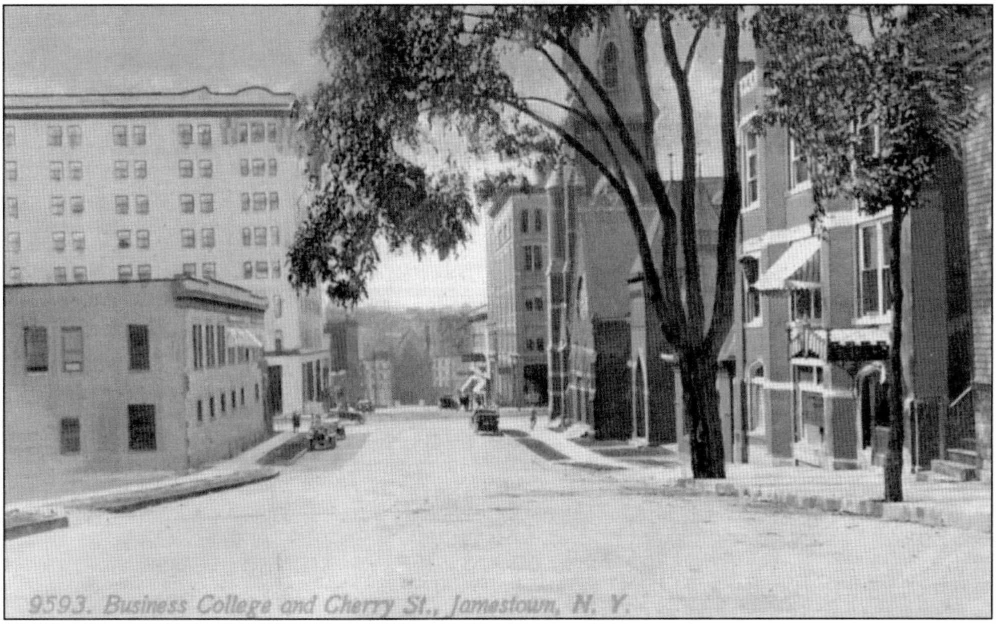

Jamestown Business College and the First Presbyterian Church fill Cherry Street between Fourth and Third Streets. Farther south is the Wellman Building, and the pointed roofline of the train station can be seen across the south end of Cherry Street. It was only a two-block, uphill walk from the trains to the Samuels Hotel at the corner of East Third and Cherry Streets. (Courtesy of FHC.)

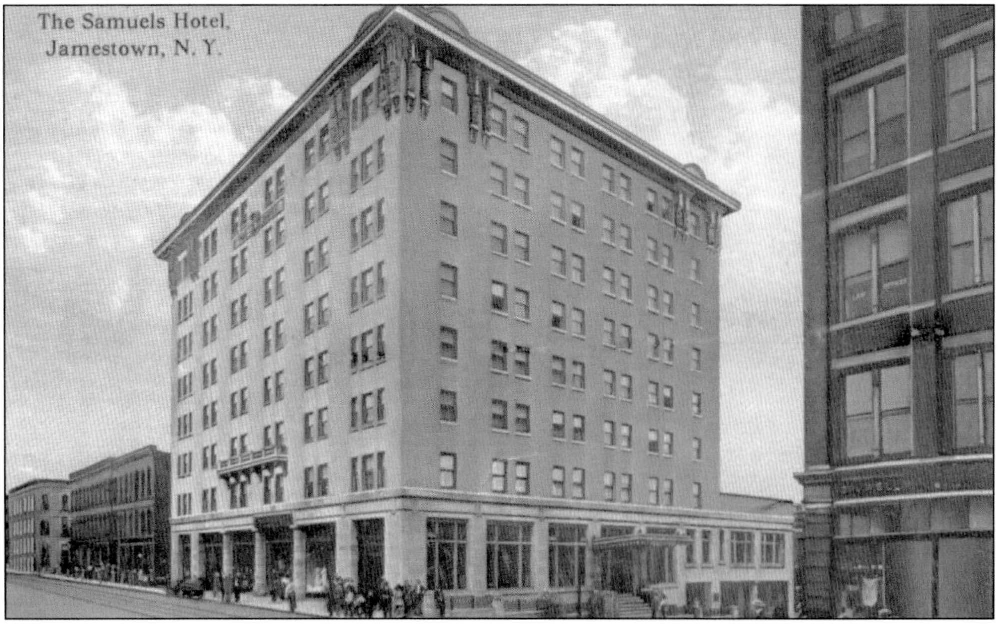

The New Sherman House burned in March 1910. Charles Samuels began construction, and in June 1912, the new Samuels Hotel opened on the same site at the southwest corner of West Third and Cherry Streets. It was an eight-story, Renaissance Revival–style brick building with retail shops at the street level. All of the conveniences of a first-class hotel were available. Today, it is a senior housing complex.

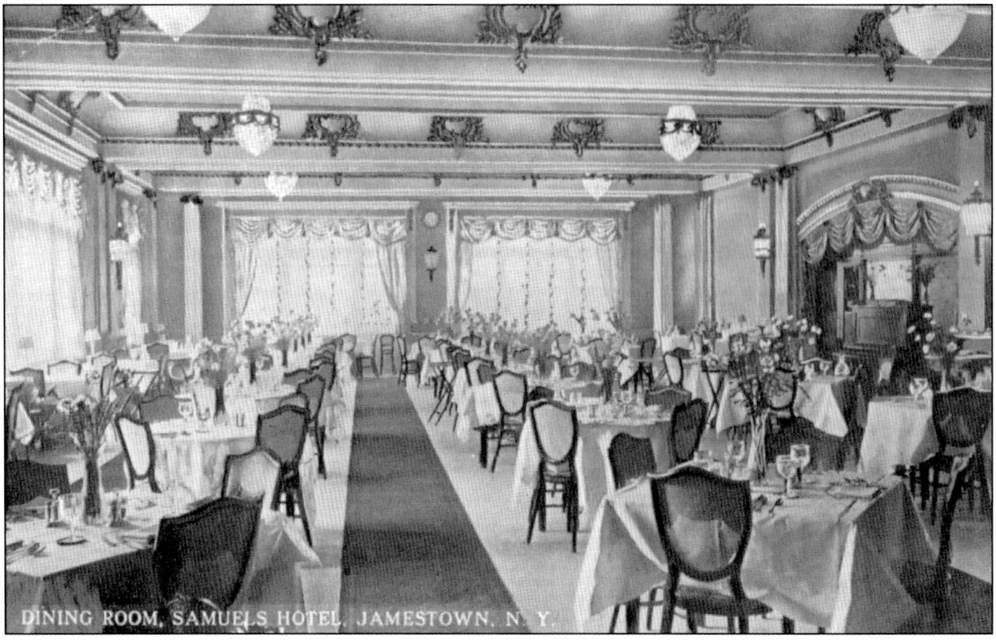

When the Samuels Hotel opened, this elegant dining room catered to travelers and locals looking for fine dining. The dining room and the adjacent kitchen were located on the second floor of the rear two-story section. The hotel also had a café adjacent to a billiards room.

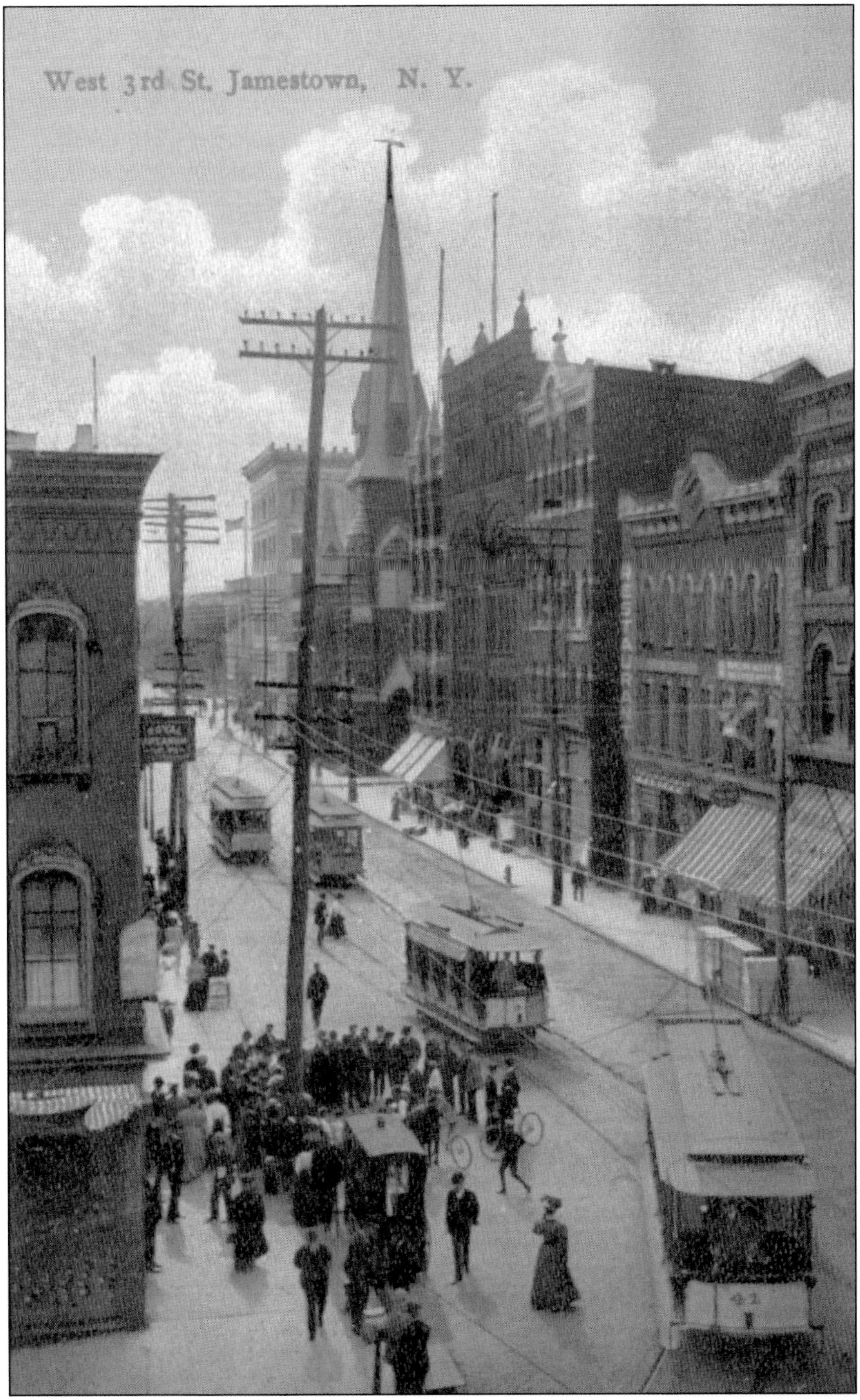

The southwest corner of West Third and North Main Streets is crowded with a line for the trolley cars. The car turning down Main Street is car No. 41, which, like the others, is an open car, used since 1894. The vendor at the corner may be the popcorn man who, for a time, had his popcorn wagon at Third and Main Streets.

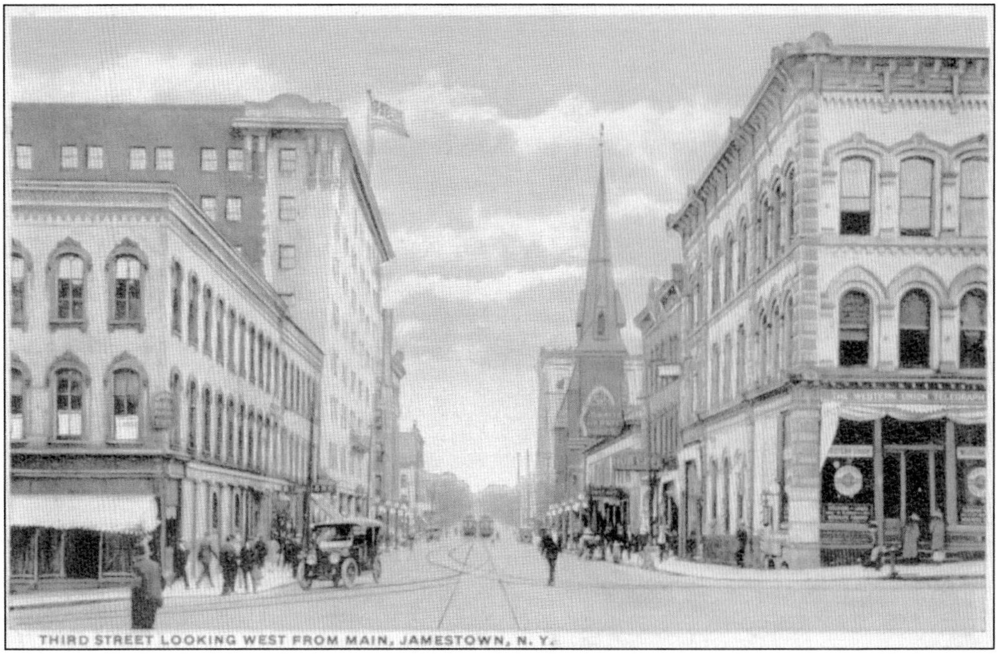

The corner of Third and North Main Streets was the center of the uptown business district. Trolley tracks can be seen going in all four directions. The large building on the right is the Prendergast Block. The income from that building funded the James Prendergast Free Library. Retail stores with offices above, and some with lodge halls on the upper floors, lined the street. (Courtesy of FHC.)

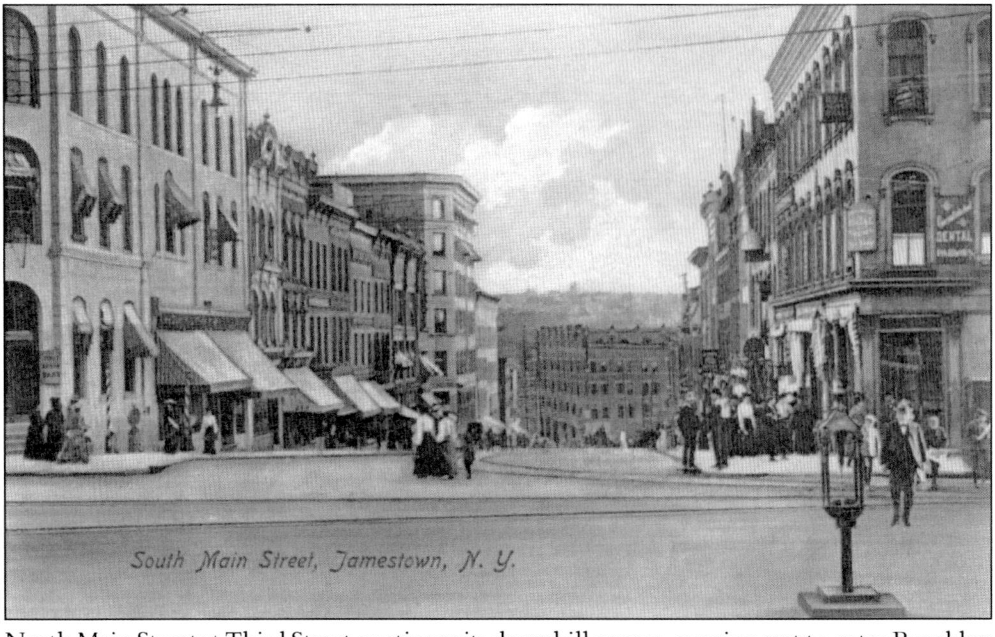

North Main Street at Third Street continues its downhill course, curving east to enter Brooklyn Square. This section to Second Street had at least six banks at one time. The corner building on the left housed the National Bank. The bank's successor is still there. Many of the brick buildings seen here still line the street. The corner building on the right has since been replaced.

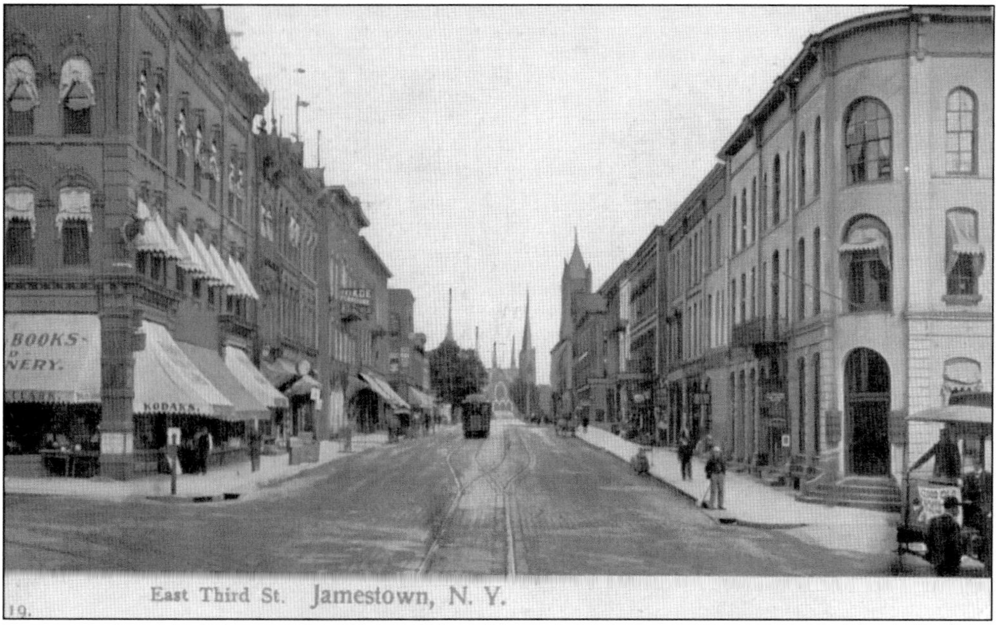

East Third Street continues to the First Methodist Episcopal Church, where the street turns south, meeting East Second Street near the high school. The church is in the center of this picture. The tower to the right of the church is the city hall. The Clark Drugstore is in the corner building on the left. Besides shops and offices, some buildings had garages with automobile sales offices.

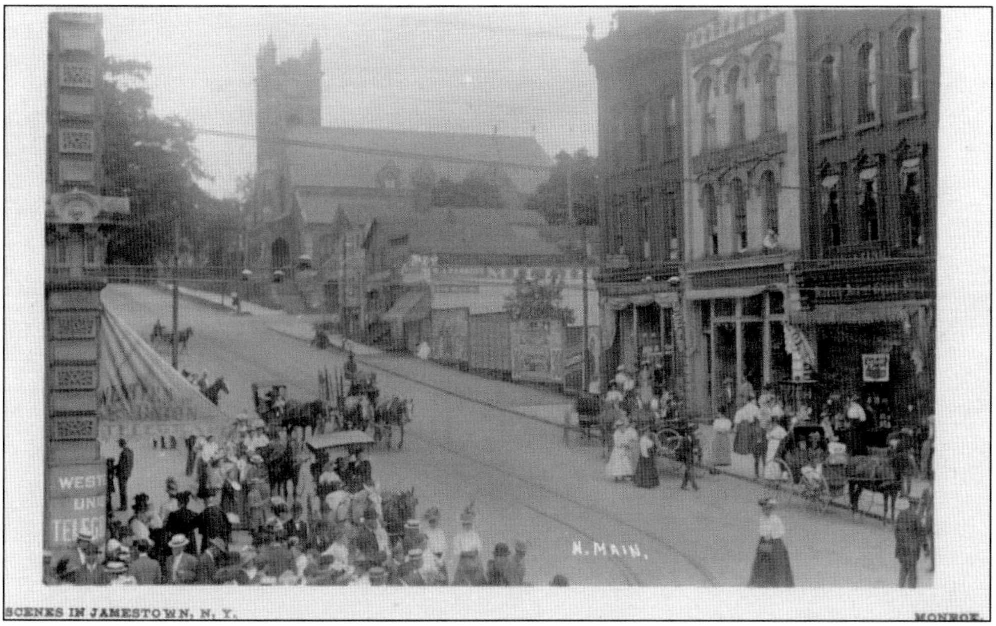

North Main Street continues up the hill. The Prendergast Building, occupied by Western Union, is on the left. The three brick buildings on the right still stand on North Main Street. The wooden building on the corner, across from St. Luke's Church, survived a 1931 fire and is occupied today. The other wooden buildings burned and have been replaced. (Courtesy of FHC.)

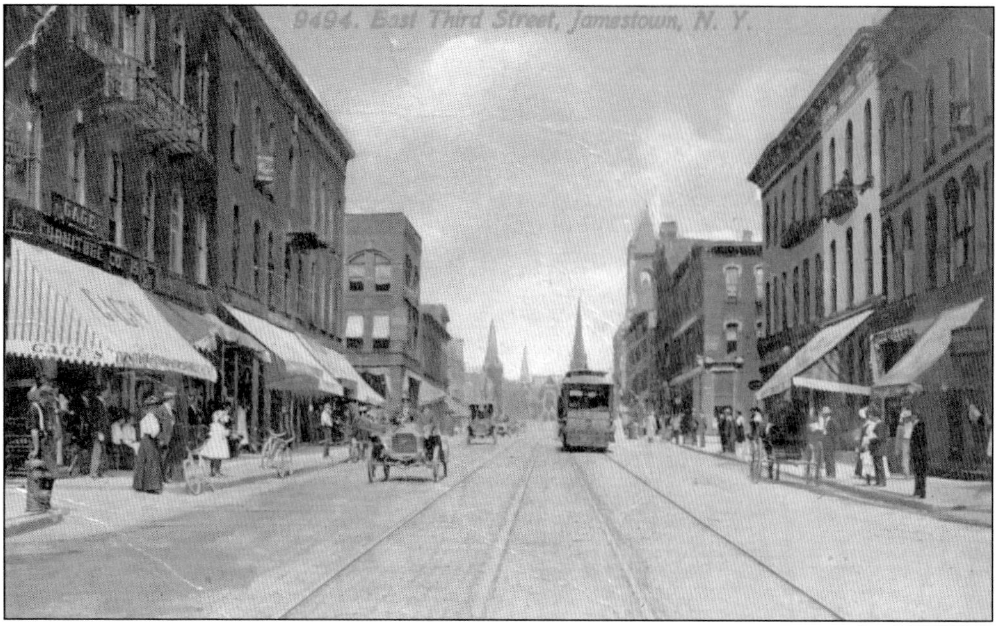

On the left, on East Third Street, is the Jones Block, which housed the Gage Furniture store on two floors and included an Independent Order of Odd Fellows (IOOF) hall. A meat market and a fish market were in the next building. Across the street, at the corner of Pine Street, is the Ellicott Building, with a brick veneer that hid an 1878 Buffalo Bill billboard rediscovered at the end of the 20th century. (Courtesy of FHC.)

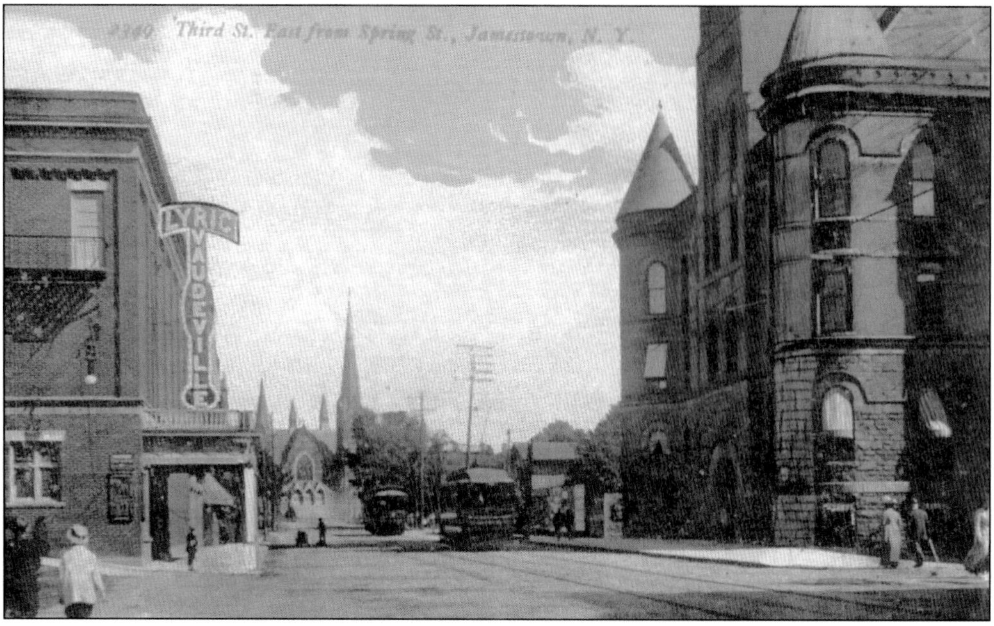

At the corner of Spring and East Third Streets was the Lyric Theater, featuring vaudeville acts. Like many buildings downtown, by the 1920s, it had a garage and automobile sales in part of the building. Across the street is city hall, built in 1895. The First Methodist Episcopal Church can be seen at the end of East Third Street before the roadway turned south to meet East Second Street.

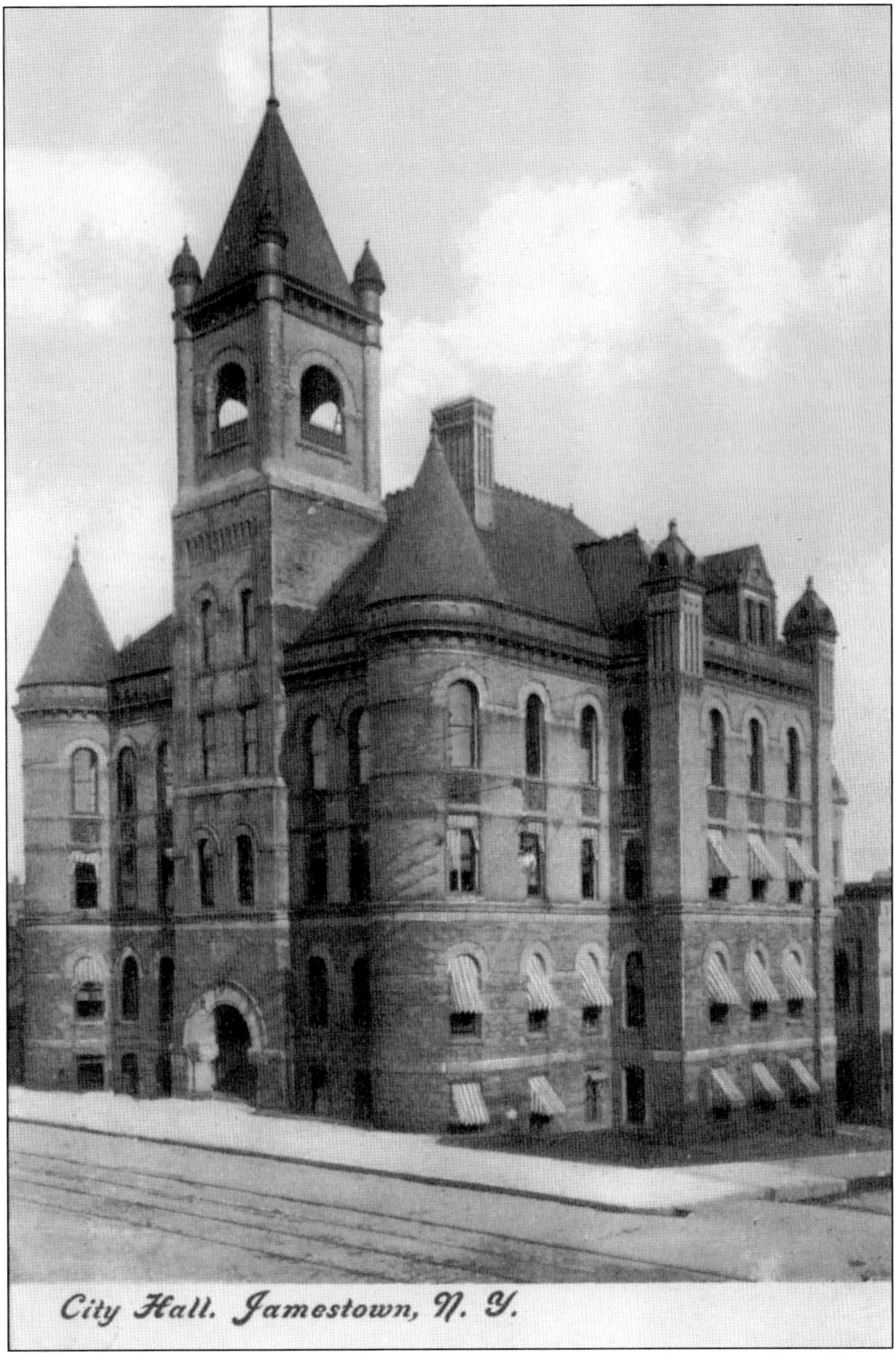

City hall was built in 1895, nine years after Jamestown was incorporated as a city. City offices filled the first two floors, with council chambers on the third floor. It was constructed with Medina sandstone and pressed brick for $65,000 in a style similar to the Richardsonian Romanesque Prendergast Library. The police department was in city hall, and the fire department was located behind city hall.

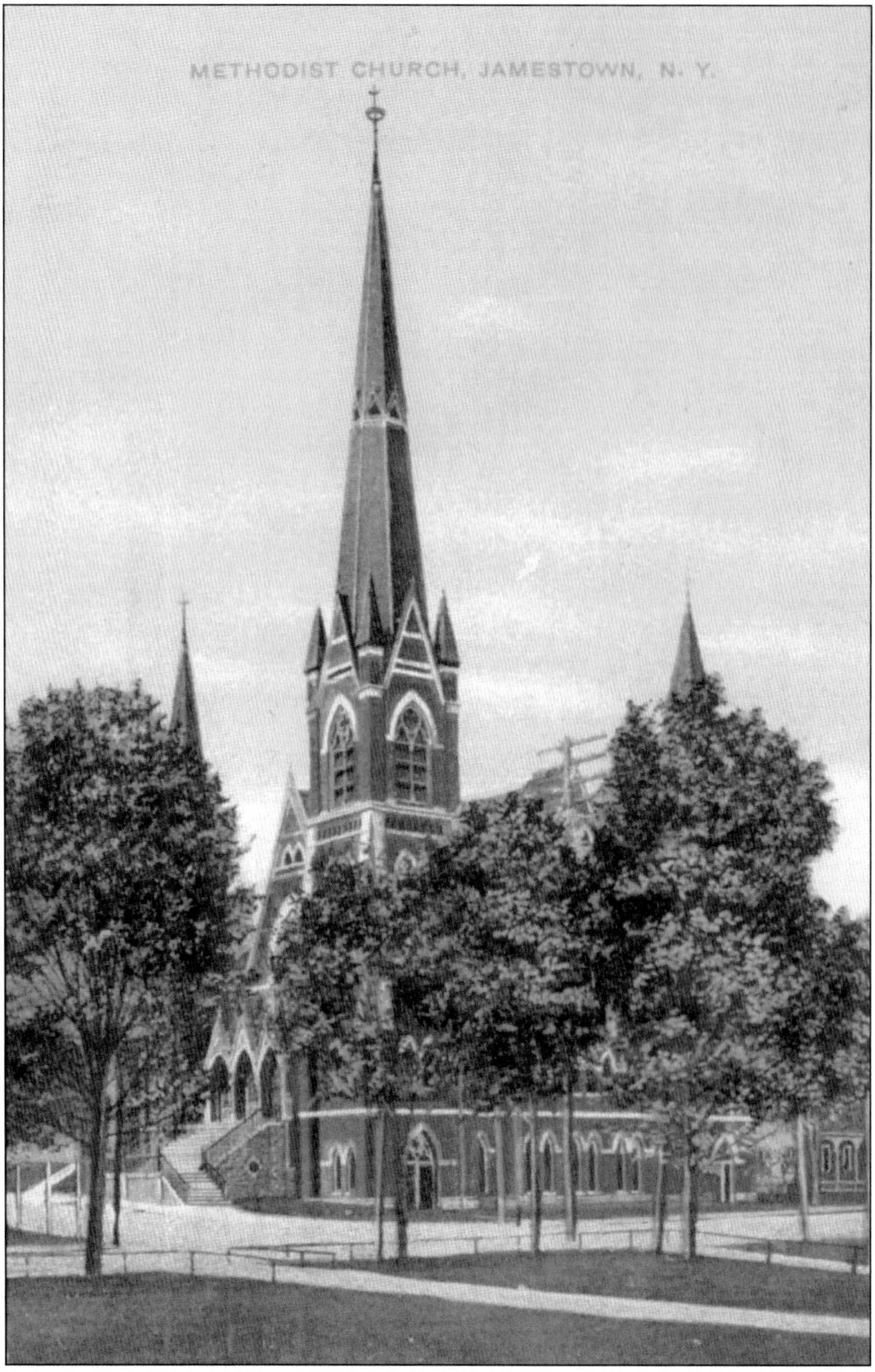

The First Methodist Episcopal Church moved from a small wooden church, located at the intersection of East Second and Chandler Streets, to the corner of East Third and East Second Streets. An early land ownership dispute turned Third Street south to intersect with Second Street. The church was built to face the length of Third Street, with Second Street passing along the south side of the church.

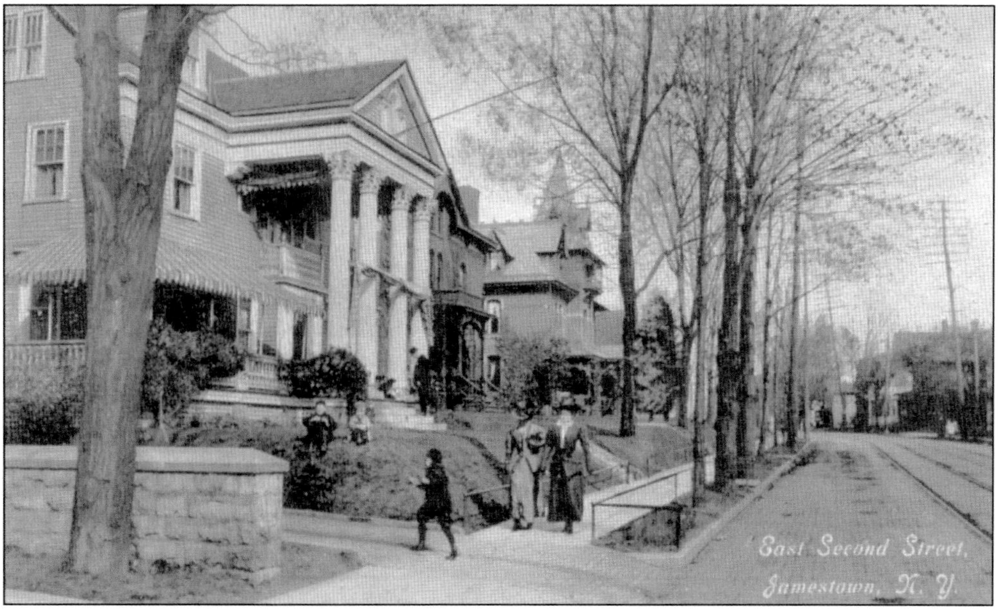

Leaving the business district, East Second Street continues east to the city limits. These homes are the next three after the First Methodist Church, just before East Second Street bears to the left. There are residences along the street with pockets of commercial enterprises. In East Jamestown, factories are located on Second Street and adjacent streets, where neighborhoods for the workers developed. The trolley lines helped move laborers from home to work.

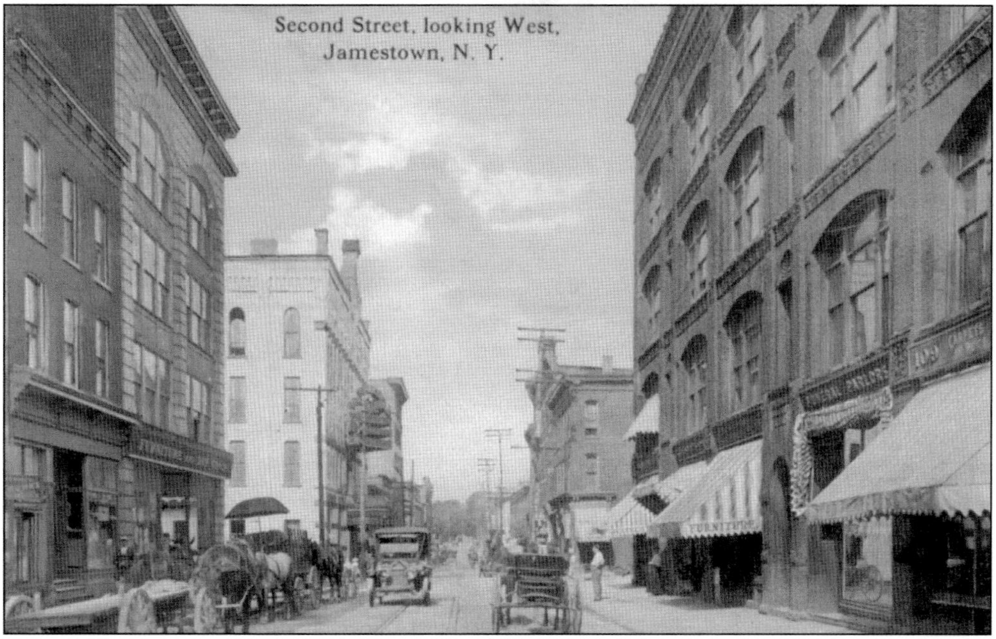

Back in the business district, East Second Street resembled East Third Street. The light-colored building with the marquee is Samuels Opera House. It had been Allen's Opera House, would become Shea's movie theater, and is today the Lucille Ball Little Theater. The Vandergrif Block on the right, located at the corner of Pine Street, housed numerous businesses, including the Henderson and Lincoln Funeral Parlors.

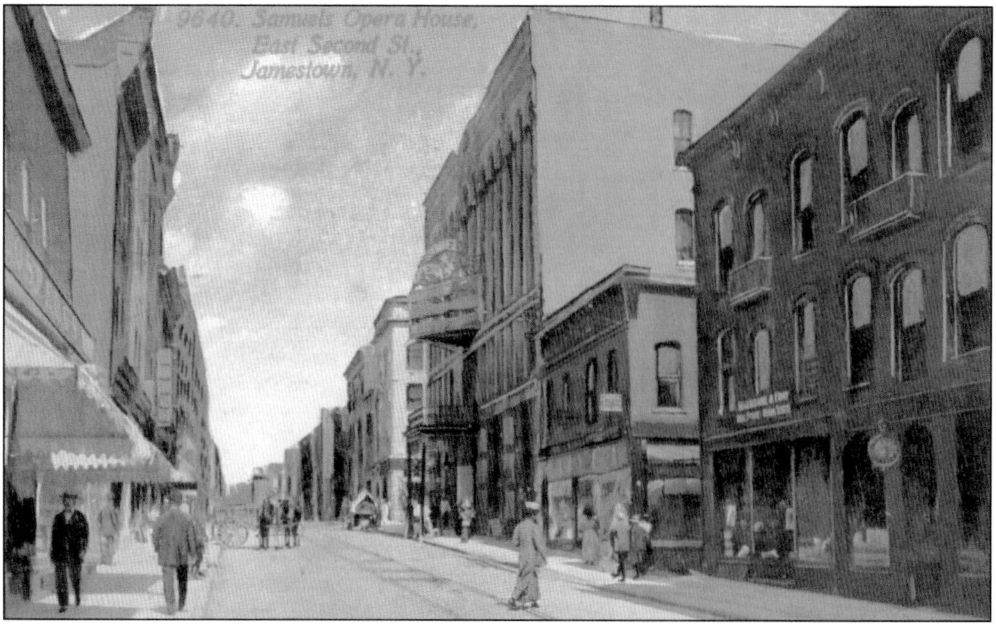

Looking east along East Second Street, Samuels Opera House is in the middle of the buildings on the right. The building in the foreground on the right still stands. The store on the left with the awning is Slosberg's furniture store in the Burtch Block. More furniture stores, garage facilities, automobile sales offices, and small hotels were included in the next few blocks.

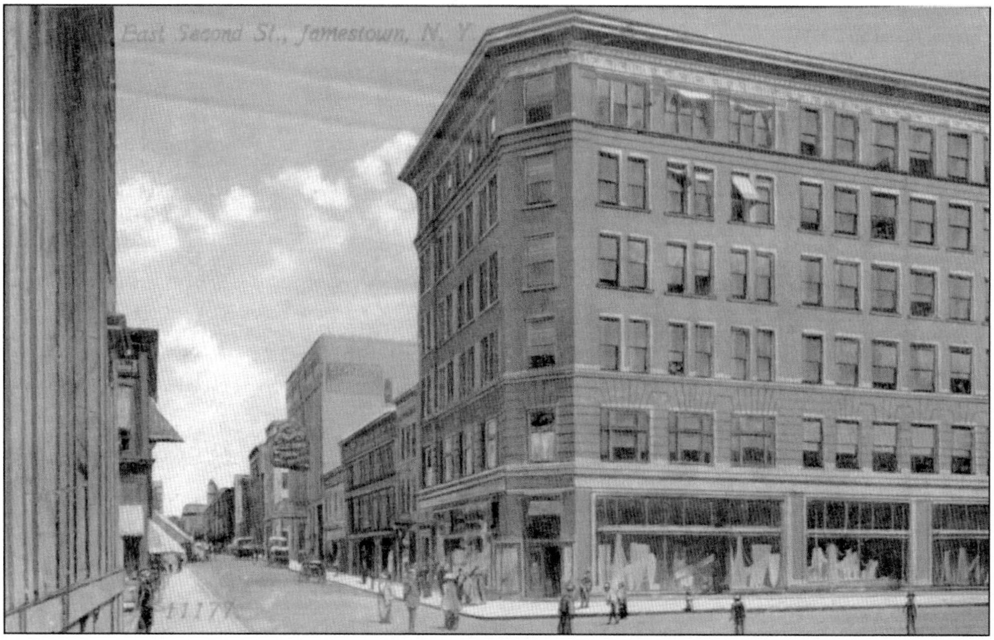

The New Fenton Building at the corner of Second and North Main Streets was built in the 1890s. Jones and Audette, a dry goods department store, filled the first floor and extended south into the Broadhead Block. Many lawyers had offices in the New Fenton Building, including Ernest Cawcroft, Benjamin S. Dean, and Robert H. Jackson, whose career would include the United States Supreme Court and the Nuremberg Military Tribunal.

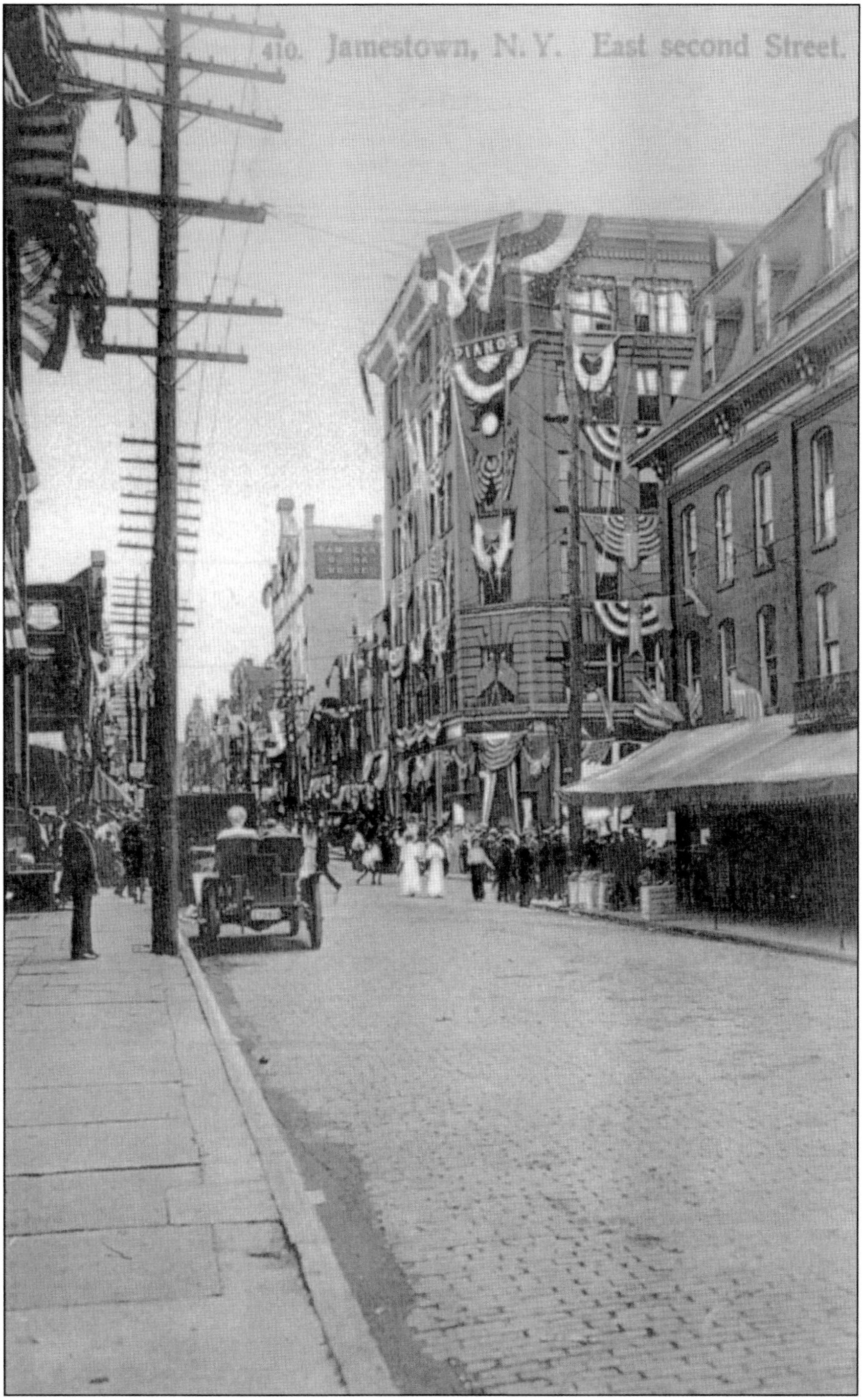

The New Fenton Building and its neighbors are decorated for an event, celebration, or parade. The building at the right with the mansard roof is the Allen Square, which burned in 1923. The left edge shows just a little of the bank building, located on the northwest corner of North Main and West Second Streets. Also visible is a line of utility poles with many crossbars.

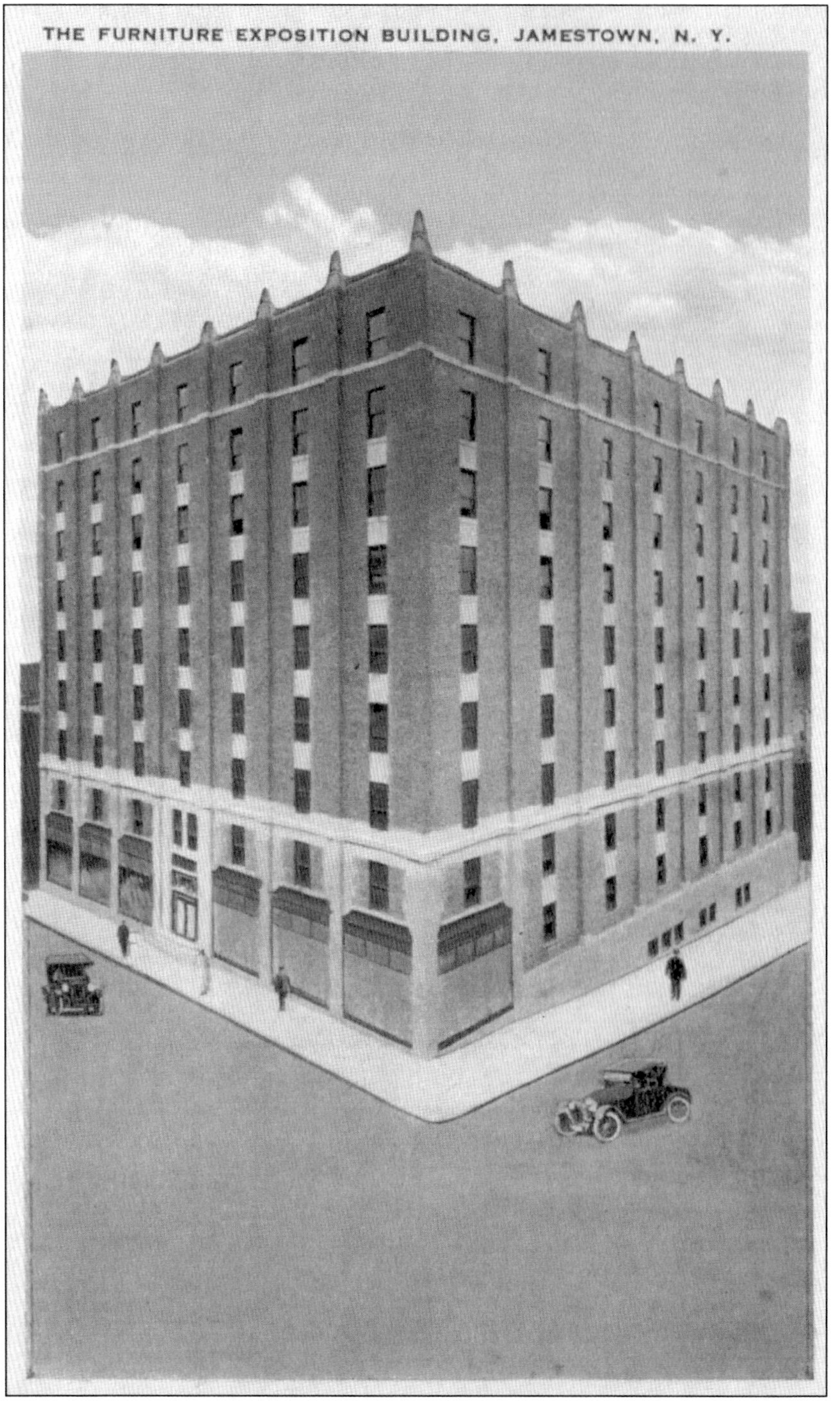

The Furniture Exposition Building, more commonly called the Furniture Mart, was constructed in 1917. Jamestown's furniture companies desired a permanent place where they could display their products. Twice a year, special markets were held to showcase their new lines of furniture, bringing many buyers for the days-long occasion. Jamestown was a convenient stopover by train, because it was halfway between New York City and Chicago.

Four

Residences

Beginning in 1810 with a log cabin, homes have been erected, rebuilt, remodeled, vacated, and moved into by the changing population. Ordinary homes and homes that were the newest style at the time have been built. Homes have been burned and torn down, but the land refills with other homes or with buildings for other purposes. Homes can be single-family, duplexes, multifamily, row houses, apartments, flats, or even temporary structures. Occupants can own or rent, but wherever they reside is home—at least for a while.

Jamestown's homes have been photographed and published as postcards. The early-20th-century photographers and postcard publishers often concentrated on the homes of prominent families. The ordinary family often had a photograph taken and postcards produced to share with family and friends.

Streetscapes included more than one home and sometimes captured more of the street and trees than the homes. Some of the homes on these postcards are gone now, while some have been altered, remodeled, or added on to, making some homes unrecognizable. Sometimes, the approximate date a neighborhood was built can be identified based on home styles. Similar homes may have been constructed by the same builder at the same time. The areas built by the prominent businessmen are varied, as each one hired a different architect and builder and chose which style they wanted.

Jamestown's first industry was wood, and many skilled woodworkers lived in Jamestown. Many homes have woodwork and built-in features that demonstrate the handiwork of these skilled craftsmen. Here are just a few of the many homes from Jamestown.

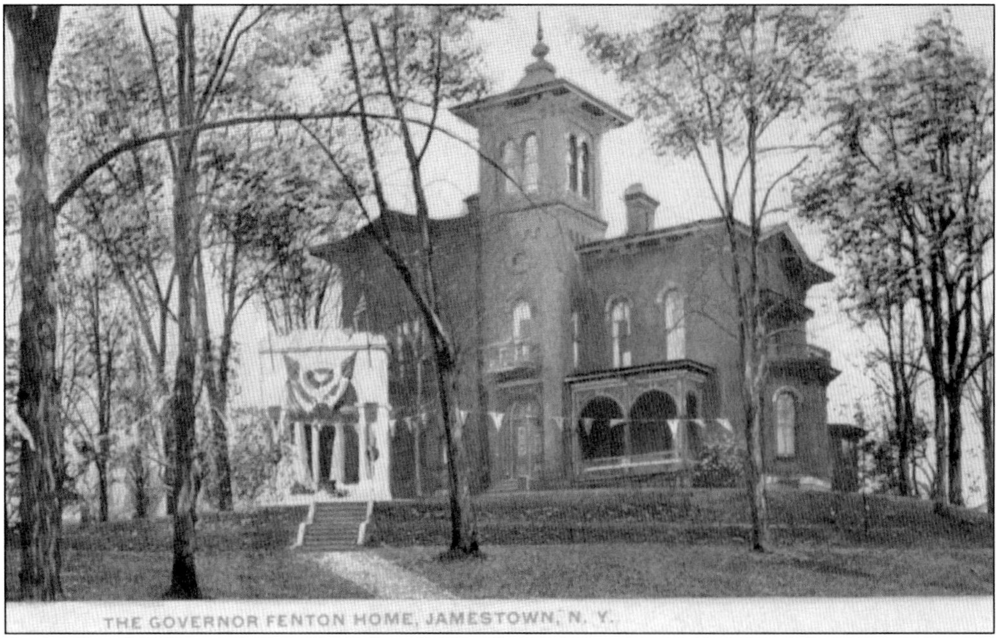

In 1863, Reuben E. Fenton built this home overlooking Jamestown. The next year, he was elected New York State governor and served two two-year terms. After his widow's death, the city purchased the home and grounds. Numerous veterans groups met at the home. The large board is the World War I honor roll. The Fenton History Center–Museum and Research Center occupies the home today.

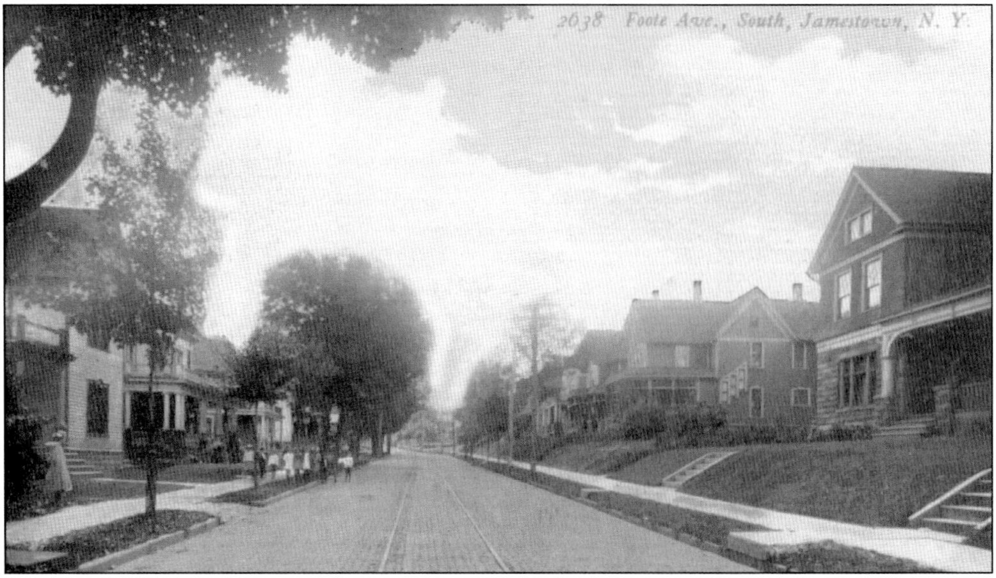

Foote Avenue, beginning at Second Street, runs south past the Woman's Christian Association (WCA) Hospital and toward the southeast outskirts of Jamestown. Many homes lined the street beyond the business area. The Warren-Jamestown trolley line followed Foote Avenue to Harrison Street and Brooklyn Square beginning in 1905. Foote Avenue-area residents used the Warren-Jamestown line to get to Brooklyn Square, where they could transfer to the Jamestown trolleys.

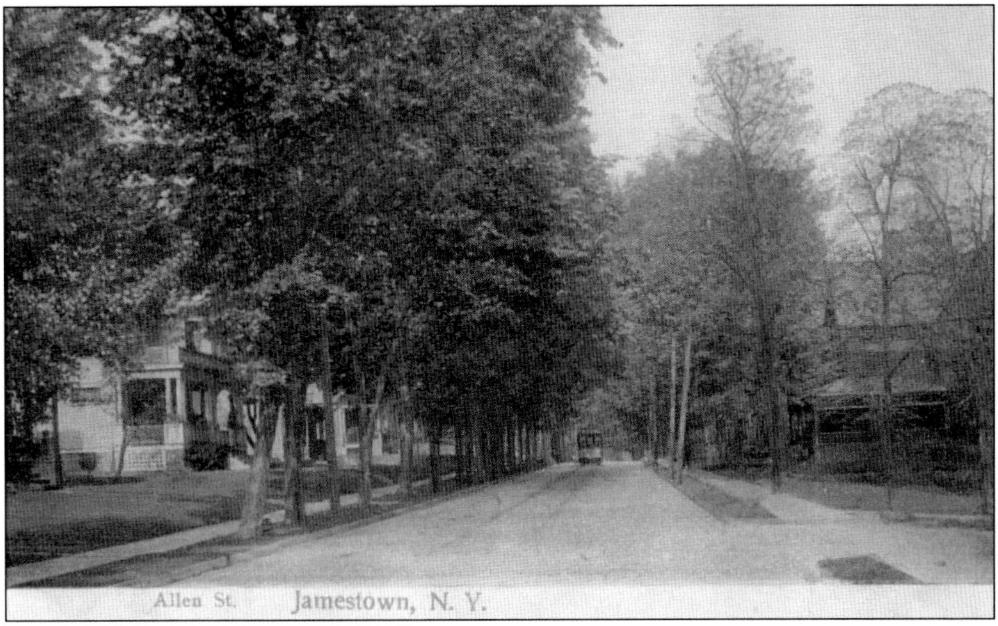

Allen Street connected the area south of Brooklyn Square, the residential areas on the southeast side of Jamestown, and the factories on the way to Falconer. Between the WCA Hospital and Willard Street, tree-lined Allen Street had many homes along the way. From Brooklyn Square and South Main Street, the trolley line followed Allen Street on the south loop to Windsor Street and back along East Second Street.

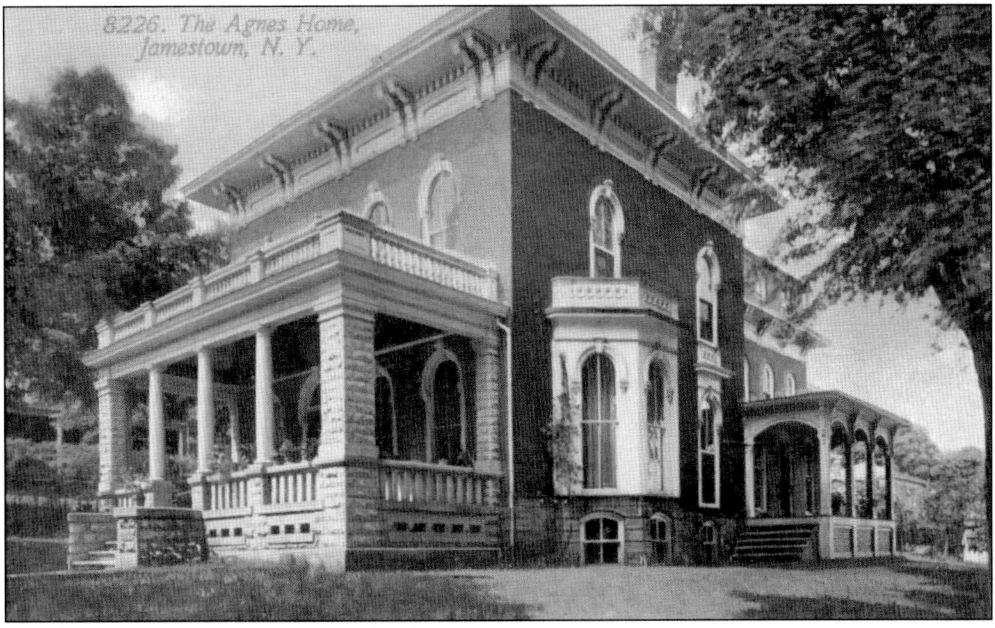

This home was built in 1875 in the Italianate style at 6 Broadhead Avenue for John J. and Agnes Reynolds Whitney. Donated by Mrs. Whitney in 1905 to the Boarding Association of the Woman's Christian Association, it became a boardinghouse for girls who worked in the mills and factories. Called the Agnes Home in honor of the donor it filled a need expressed by the employers of girls from rural areas.

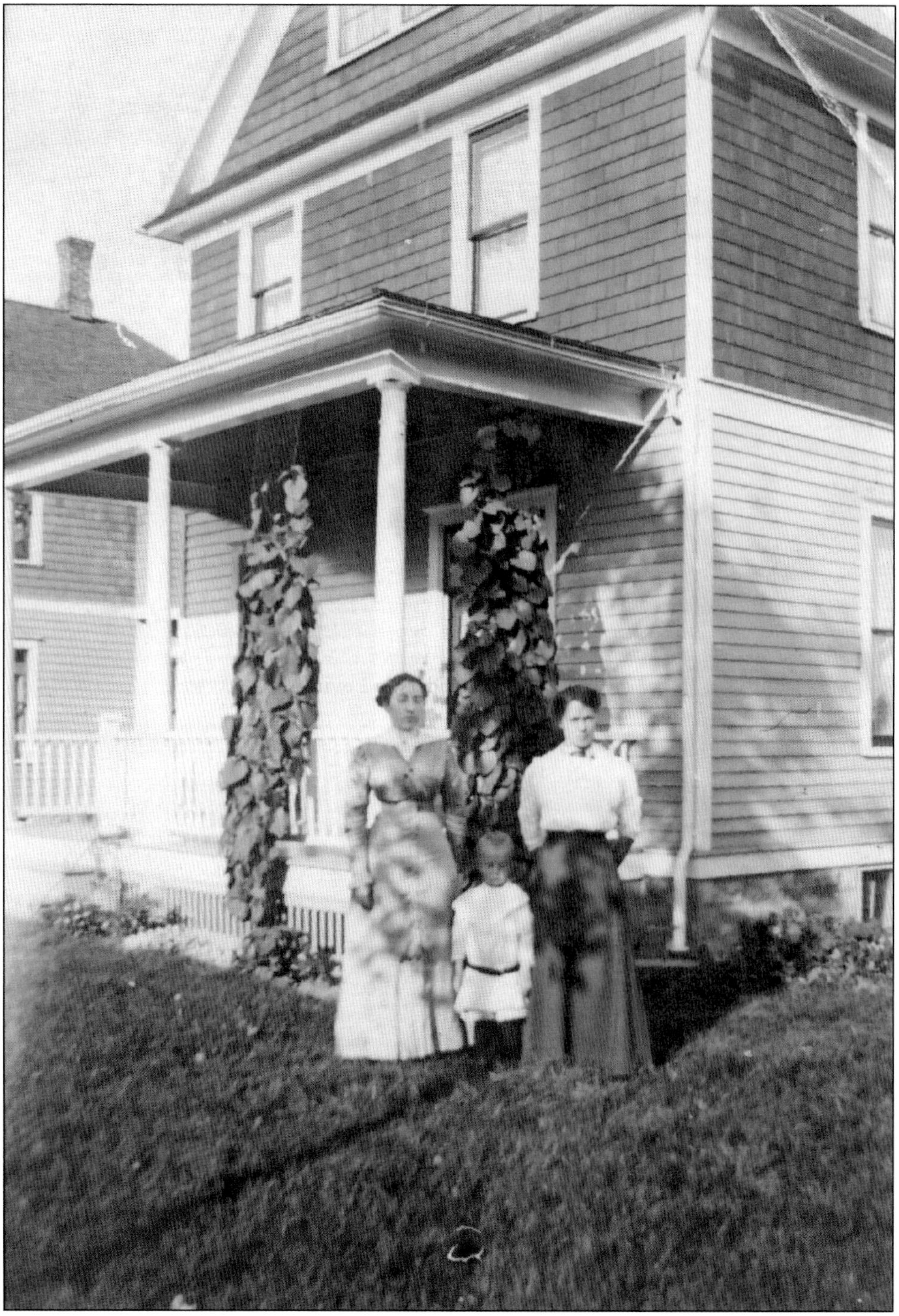

Standing in front of her home is Amanda Engstrom (left), her son Carlton, and cousin Minnie. Amanda is the grandmother of one of the authors. The two-story, three-bedroom home on Genesee Street is typical for the west-side neighborhoods along Fairmount Avenue. Included on the city lot were a garage and a lovely garden. Like many Jamestown homes, the interior had beautiful oak woodwork made by the local craftsmen.

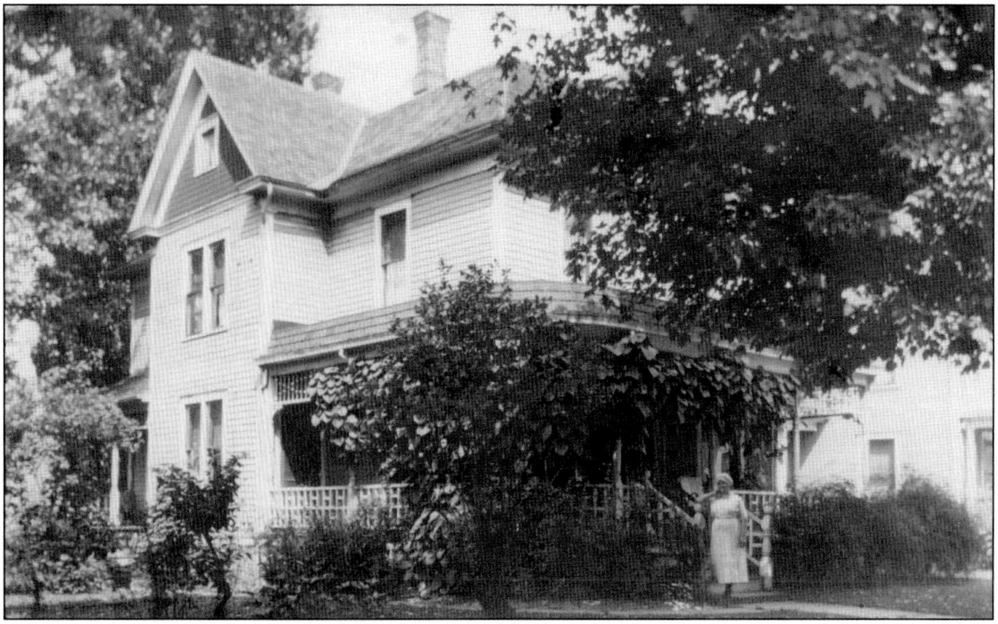

Mary Peterson, great-aunt of one of the authors, is outside her Chapin Street home on "Swede Hill." It was a four-bedroom home with front and back stairways and a double-door front entrance. Her husband was a druggist, which may explain why this home was one of the larger homes in the neighborhood. Her niece Doris Anderson Levin, 94 years old in 2011, remembers the tin bathtub and the wraparound porch.

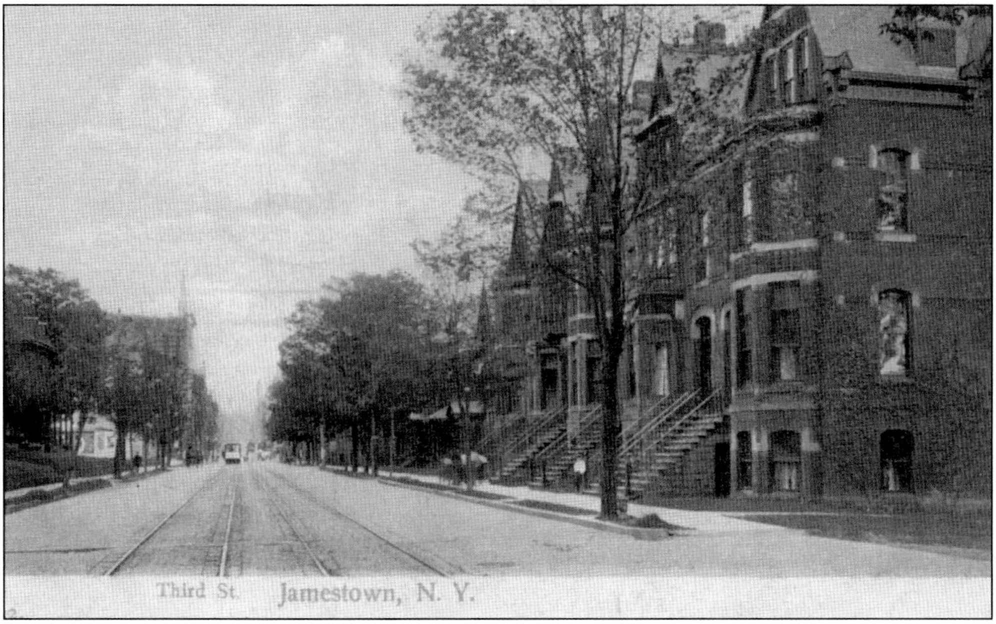

The Hoyt Block was built about 1885 on West Third Street between Jefferson and Lafayette Streets. How the interiors of these row houses were laid out is unknown. In some years, the city directories list one person or household per address, and in other years, many people were listed at an address, as if it were a boardinghouse. The Hoyt Block was occupied until 1939 and was replaced by a gas station during World War II.

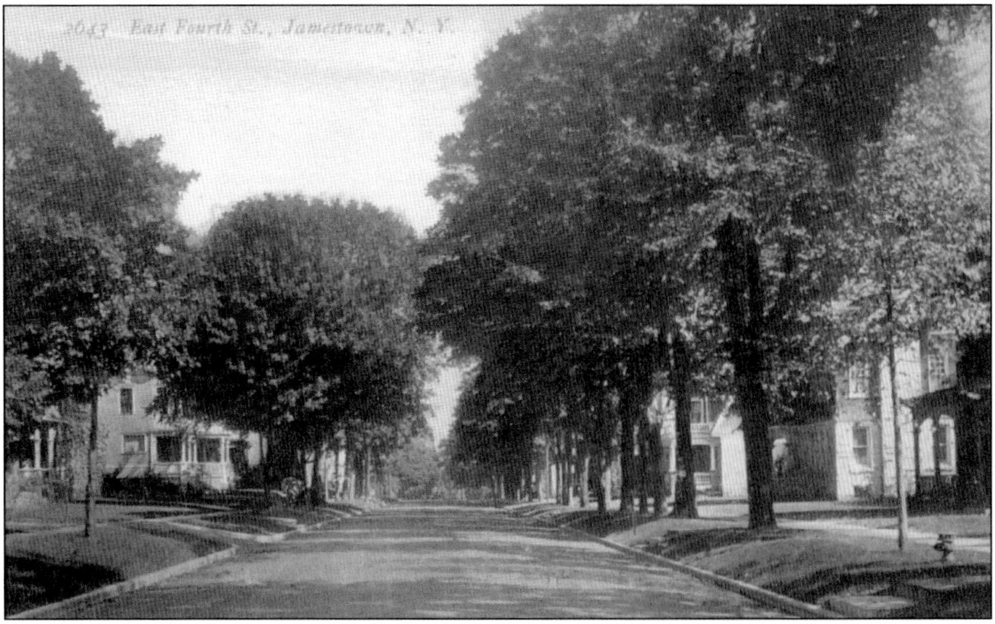

East Fourth Street from Prendergast Avenue to East Second Street is a residential area close to the business district. Substantial homes, built by 1900, still line the street. With the trees in this view obscuring details, it is difficult to identify which houses they are today. The street is brick, and with a slight downhill appearance at the end of the street, this could be looking east toward East Second Street.

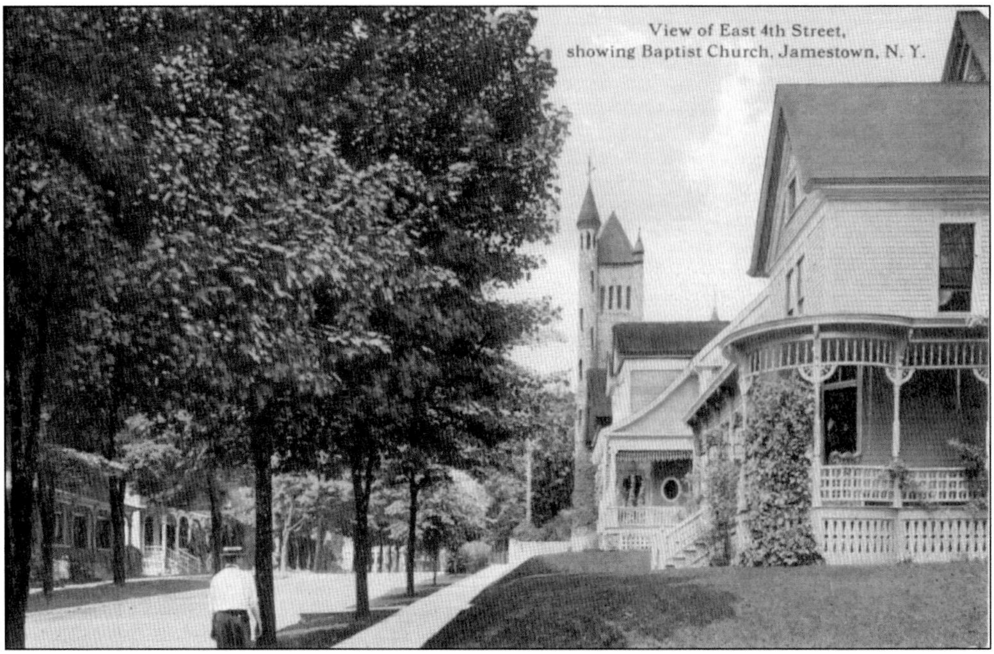

Just past First Baptist Church at Church Street, East Fourth Street descends to meet East Second Street. The first house lost its pretty porch by 1930. The second house, built in 1905, had its porch replaced in 2011. In 1912, Samuel Thorstenberg, organist at First Lutheran Church, lived in the first house. A. Harrison Reynolds, treasurer of Barrett Realty, lived in the second house.

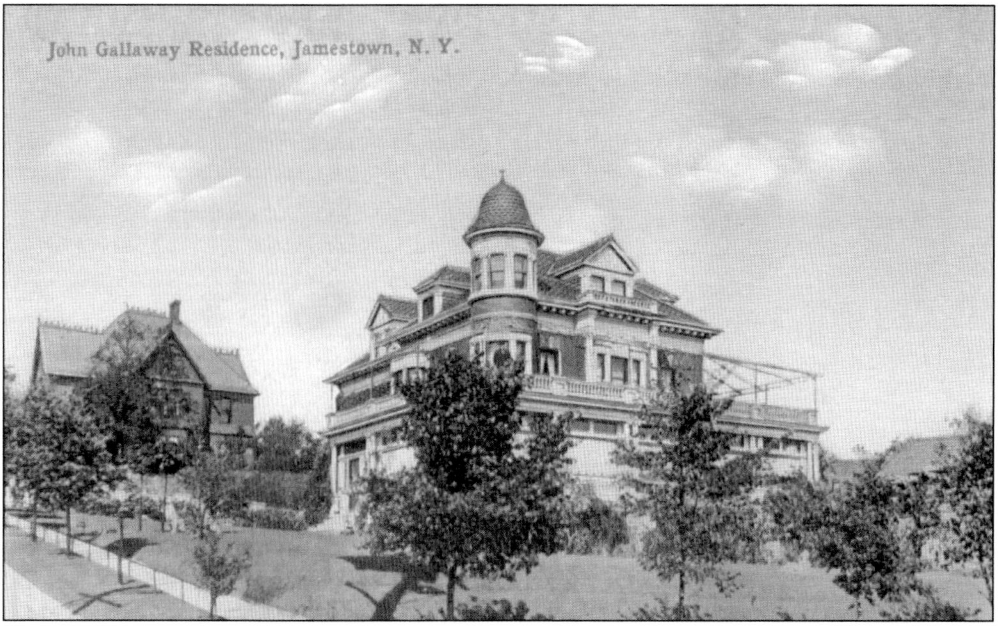

In the foreground is the East Fifth Street home of John Galloway, an oil producer. His daughter Grace died of tuberculosis. Her grave in Lake View Cemetery has an Italian marble statue of her referred to as the "girl in glass," because it is in a protective glass enclosure. The home in the background on East Sixth Street belonged to Thomas H. Smith, owner of the Jamestown Cotton Mill.

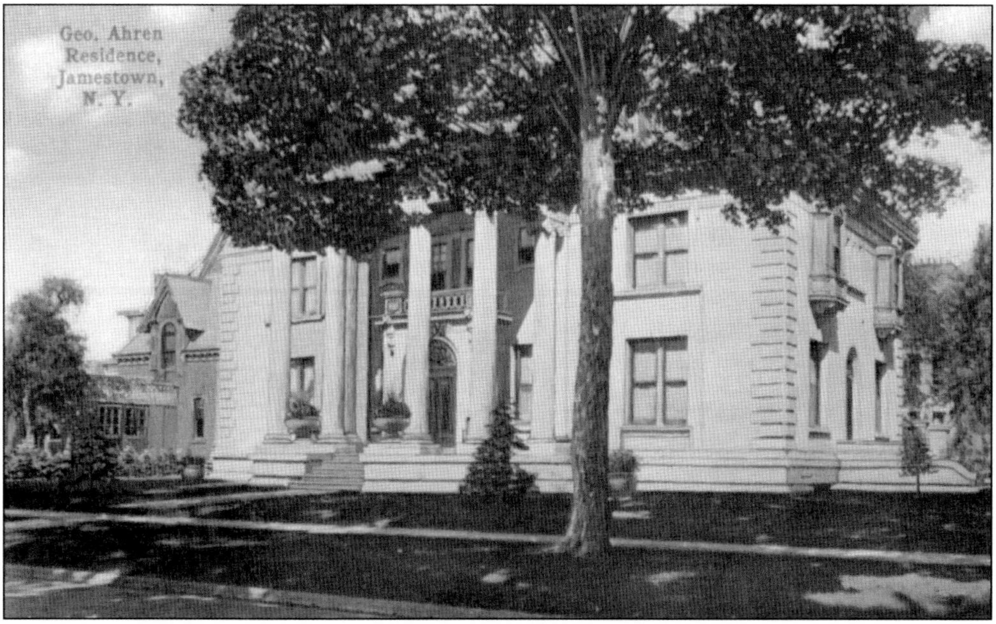

Built in the Beaux Arts style, the George Ahrens home reflects the owner's affluence when it was built in 1898. Ahrens, an oil producer, was one of Jamestown's successful businessmen at the turn of the century. Not used often for private residences, the Beaux Arts style was typically reserved for public or institutional buildings. The interior continued the style with wood ornamentation of excellent design and craftsmanship.

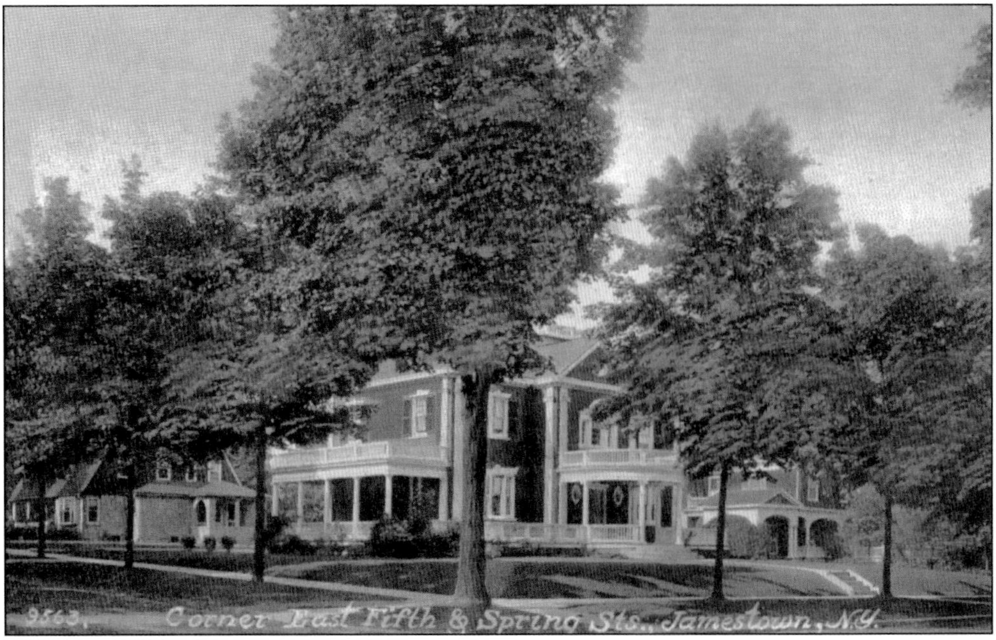

After consulting maps, this is believed to be the northeast corner of East Fifth and Spring Streets. All houses are gone from the block, and it is now occupied by the First Covenant and First Presbyterian Churches. The *1888 Jamestown Atlas* indicates Norman K. Ransom lived there, but it is unknown if this is his home or a later one.

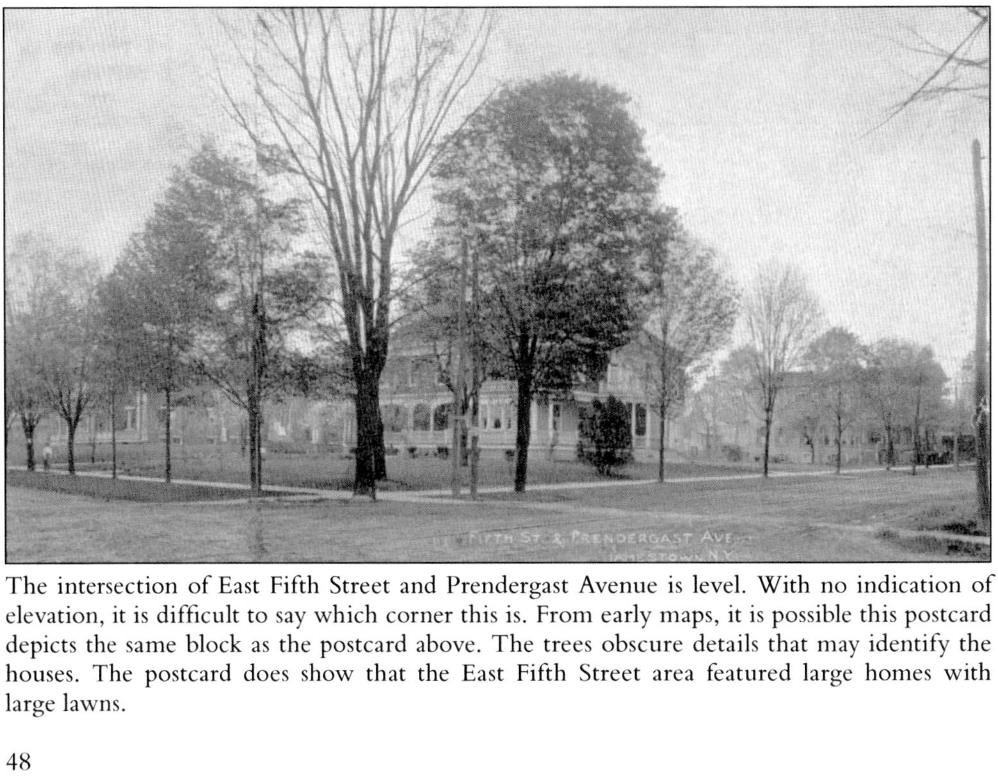

The intersection of East Fifth Street and Prendergast Avenue is level. With no indication of elevation, it is difficult to say which corner this is. From early maps, it is possible this postcard depicts the same block as the postcard above. The trees obscure details that may identify the houses. The postcard does show that the East Fifth Street area featured large homes with large lawns.

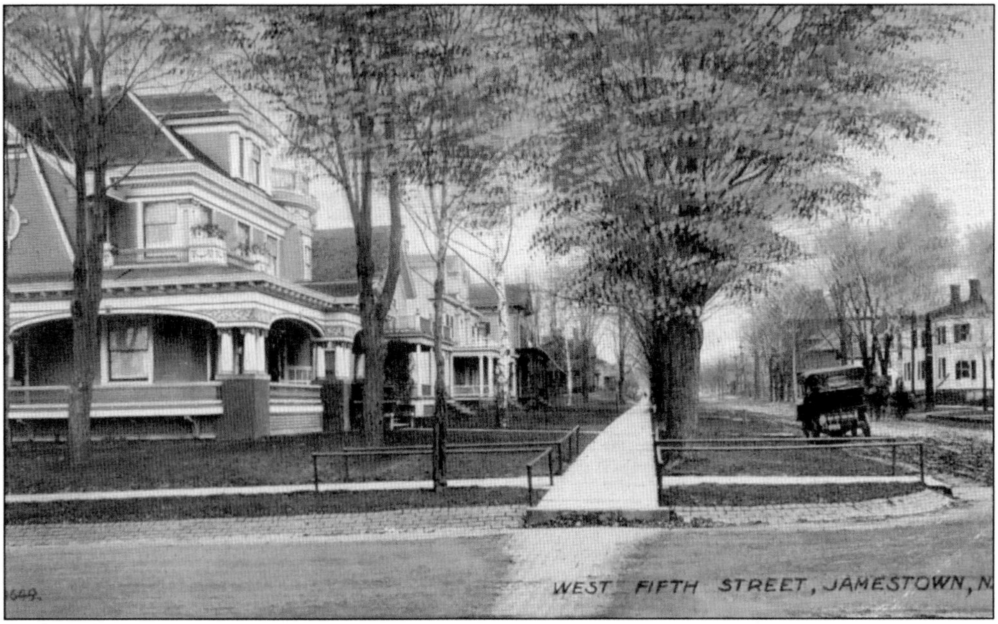

The house at the left was built by 1900 for Daniel A. Sullivan of the Union Lumber Company. Milton D. Stone, his next-door neighbor, was his business partner. Notice the sidewalks and the bricked curbing with the dirt streets. It also looks like the car has left ruts in a muddy part of West Fifth Street. The street in the foreground is Jefferson Street.

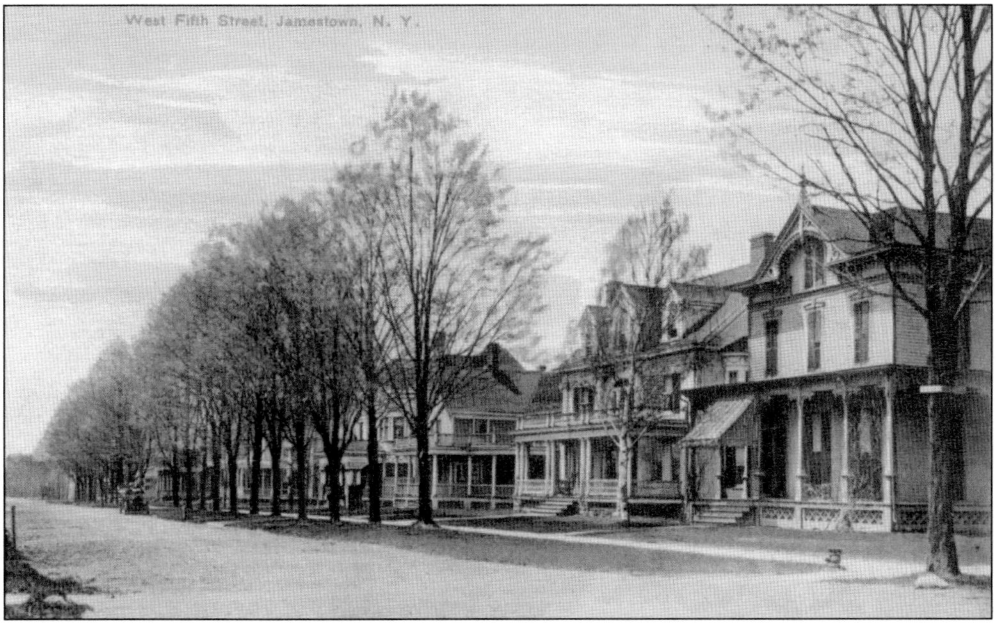

Still standing along West Fifth Street and built in the late 1890s, these houses represent different residential building styles. The first house belonged to George H. Coburn, manager of Standard Oil. The second home is a Colonial Revival style built in 1895 for William R. Reynolds, who was associated with Broadhead Mills. The next two homes belonged to the owners of the Union Lumber Company.

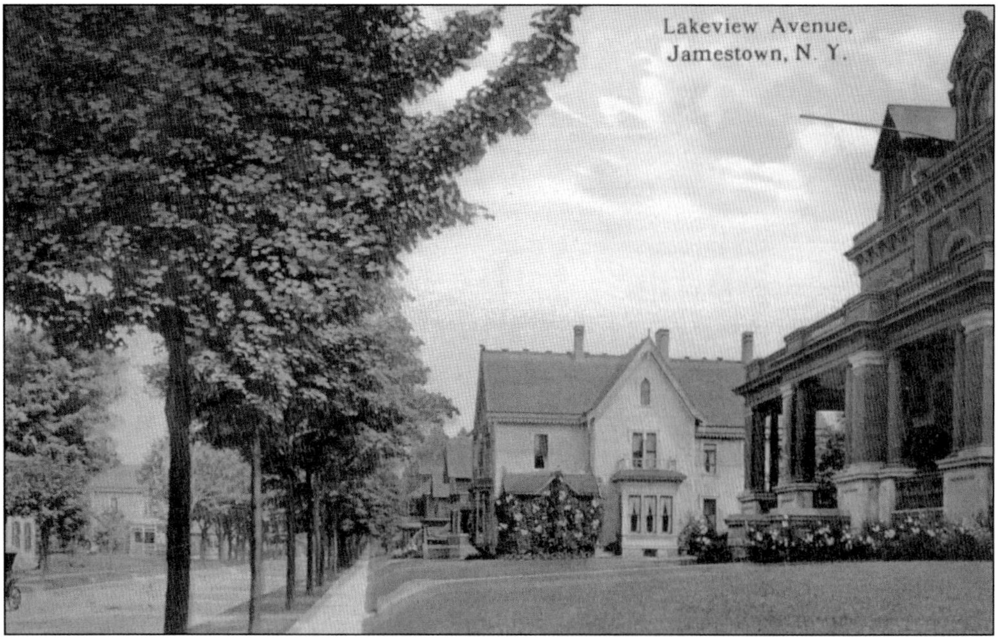

Located near Eighth Street on Lakeview Avenue, the Gokey homes joined the line of homes of successful businessmen along Lake View Avenue by the early 1890s. Noah W. Gokey, owner of the Gokey Shoe Factory, lived in the large brick home on the right. His son, William N. Gokey, lived next door. After his death, Noah Gokey's home was altered, and by 1915, Ralph Sheldon occupied the home.

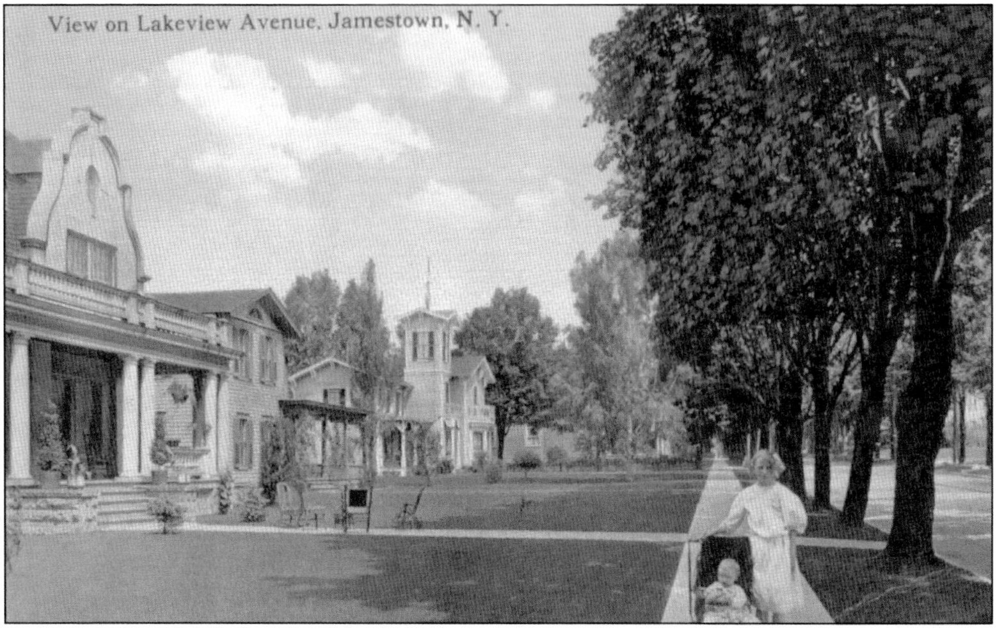

Many of Jamestown's businessmen lived on Lakeview Avenue. The Dutch Colonial at the left was built about 1908 for Fred. B. Tinkham. He and his brother Frank owned Tinkham Brothers, a wholesale house of cigars and notions. Next door is a typical wood-frame house from the 1880s. The third home is an Italianate-inspired home from the late 1860s.

Five

Churches

There were 25 churches in Jamestown a century after the first settlement. Rev. John Spencer, a circuit-riding minister sent by the Connecticut Missionary Society, traveled throughout Chautauqua County organizing classes and societies. The First Congregational Church in Jamestown was an outgrowth of his work. Methodist and Baptist circuit riders were active in Chautauqua County.

Often, a church began with only a few people meeting in homes or a rented space. With the growth of the population, the number of members increased for most churches. Soon, the need for individual churches was acknowledged. Many churches were built in that first century but were outgrown, burned, or both. As immigrants arrived, new churches were started. These churches continued to use the mother tongue of the immigrants and provided a social network for those who had just arrived. This was particularly evident with Swedish immigrants. Coming from a country where Lutheranism was the most prominent denomination, most Swedes first attended Lutheran churches in Jamestown. However, many joined other denominations and went on to organize a Swedish church within that denomination, retaining the language and other traditions. Similar paths were taken with other, smaller immigrant groups. The Irish started SS. Peter and Paul Roman Catholic Church, while Italians started the St. James Parish in 1910. English immigrants were absorbed into many churches because of the similar language. The Greek Orthodox church and the Albanian church were organized in Jamestown in the early 20th century as immigrants from those countries arrived.

Over the last 200 years, churches have come and gone, merged, split, or continued. This chapter includes some of the churches that have appeared on postcards.

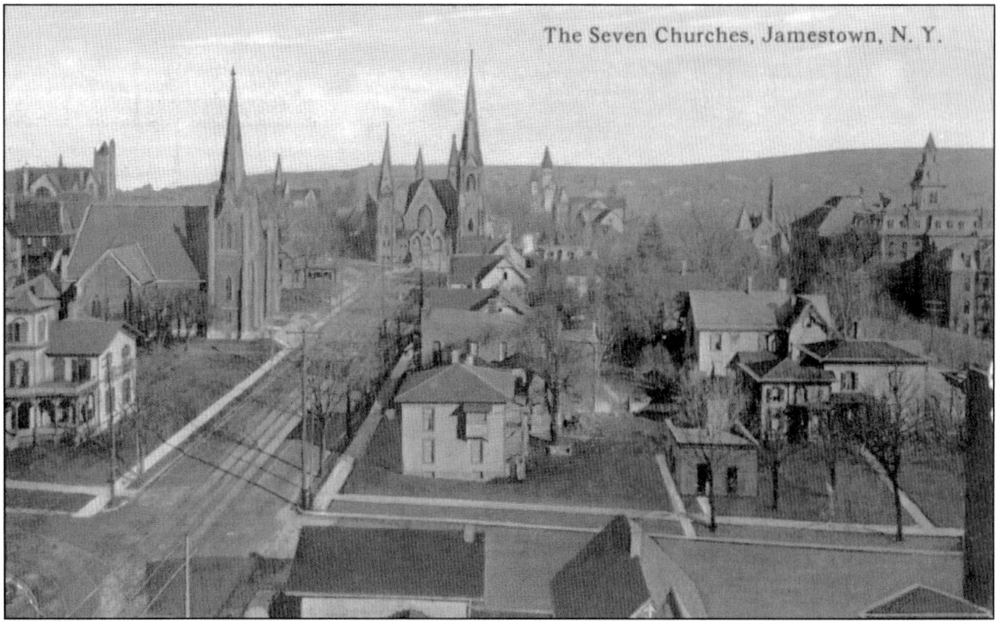

The classic picture of seven churches of Jamestown includes, from left to right, First Baptist Church, First Congregational Church, Immanuel Lutheran Church, First Methodist Church, First Lutheran Church, First Mission Church, and Zion Mission Church. On the far right is the clock tower of the old high school. The streets in the foreground are East Third Street and Prendergast Avenue. The photographer was probably in the city hall tower.

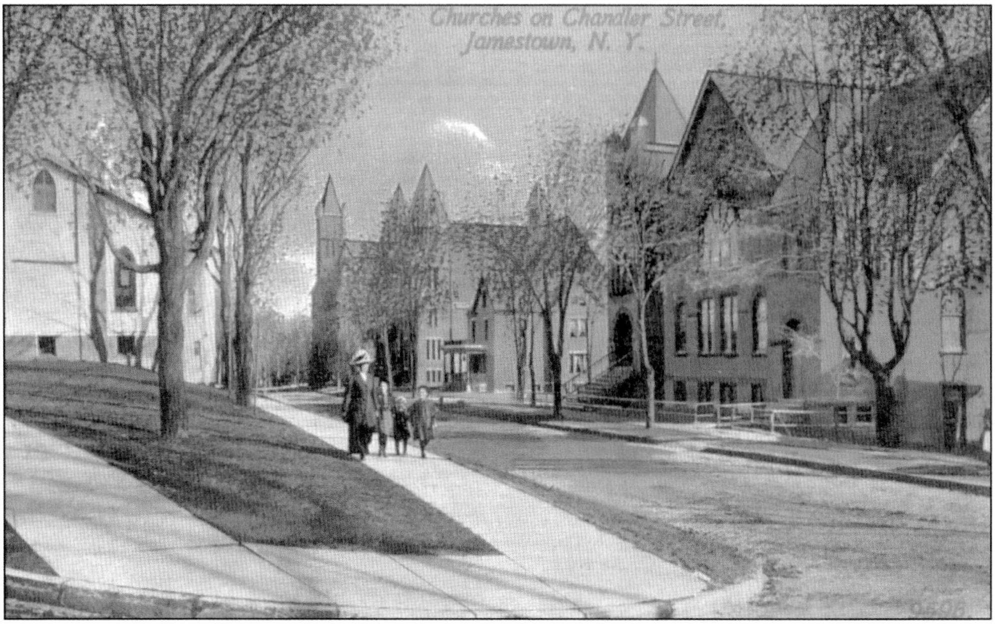

The churches on Chandler Street were clustered in a two-block area. The white church at the left was originally the First Methodist Church, but in 1886, it was purchased by the Unitarian church. The others on the right include, from front to back, the Swedish Methodist Episcopal Church (later Epworth Methodist), the Swedish Mission Church, and the First Lutheran Church. The Swedish Baptist Church is hidden behind the Unitarian church.

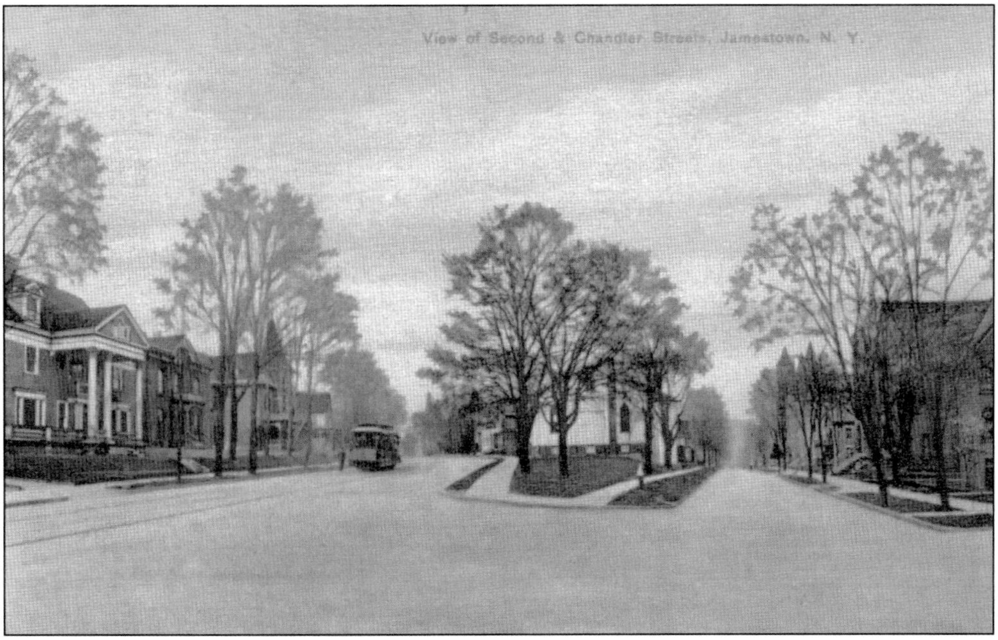

Second Street (to the left with the trolley), Chandler Street (on the right), and Foote Avenue (in the foreground) frame the white building in the center. Formerly the Methodist Episcopal church, it became the home of the Unitarian church in 1886. It was razed in 1975 when the streets were realigned. This area once had 10 churches and a Jewish Community Center within only a few blocks.

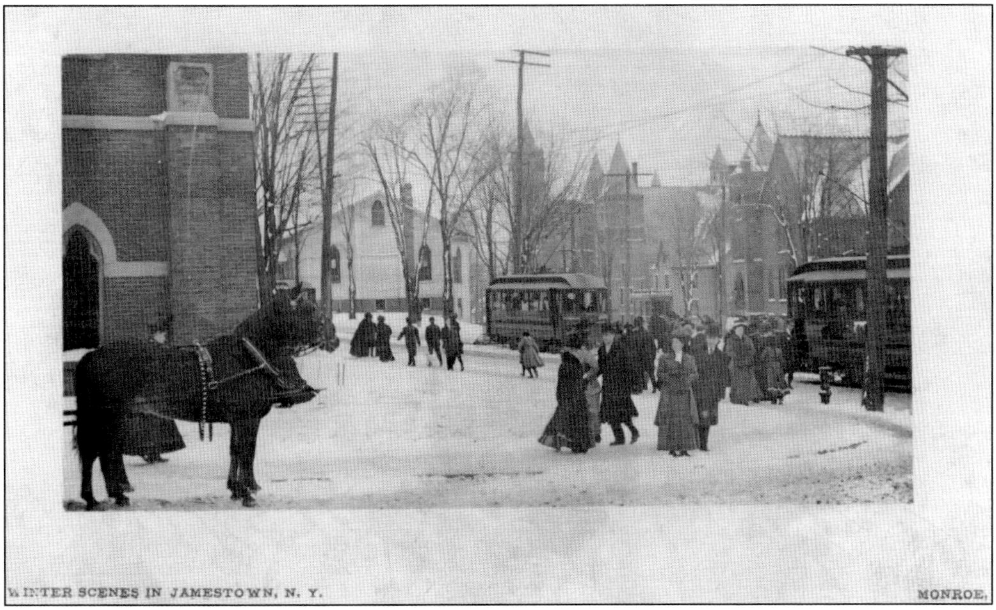

Trolleys brought thousands of worshipers to the east-side churches every Sunday. The First Methodist Church (on the left), the Unitarian church (in the center), and four other churches (on the south side of Chandler Street) can be seen in this postcard. Trolleys ran in the winter, and the line had a snowplow car in case the snow became too deep. Horse-drawn snowplows kept the sidewalks clear. (Courtesy of MC.)

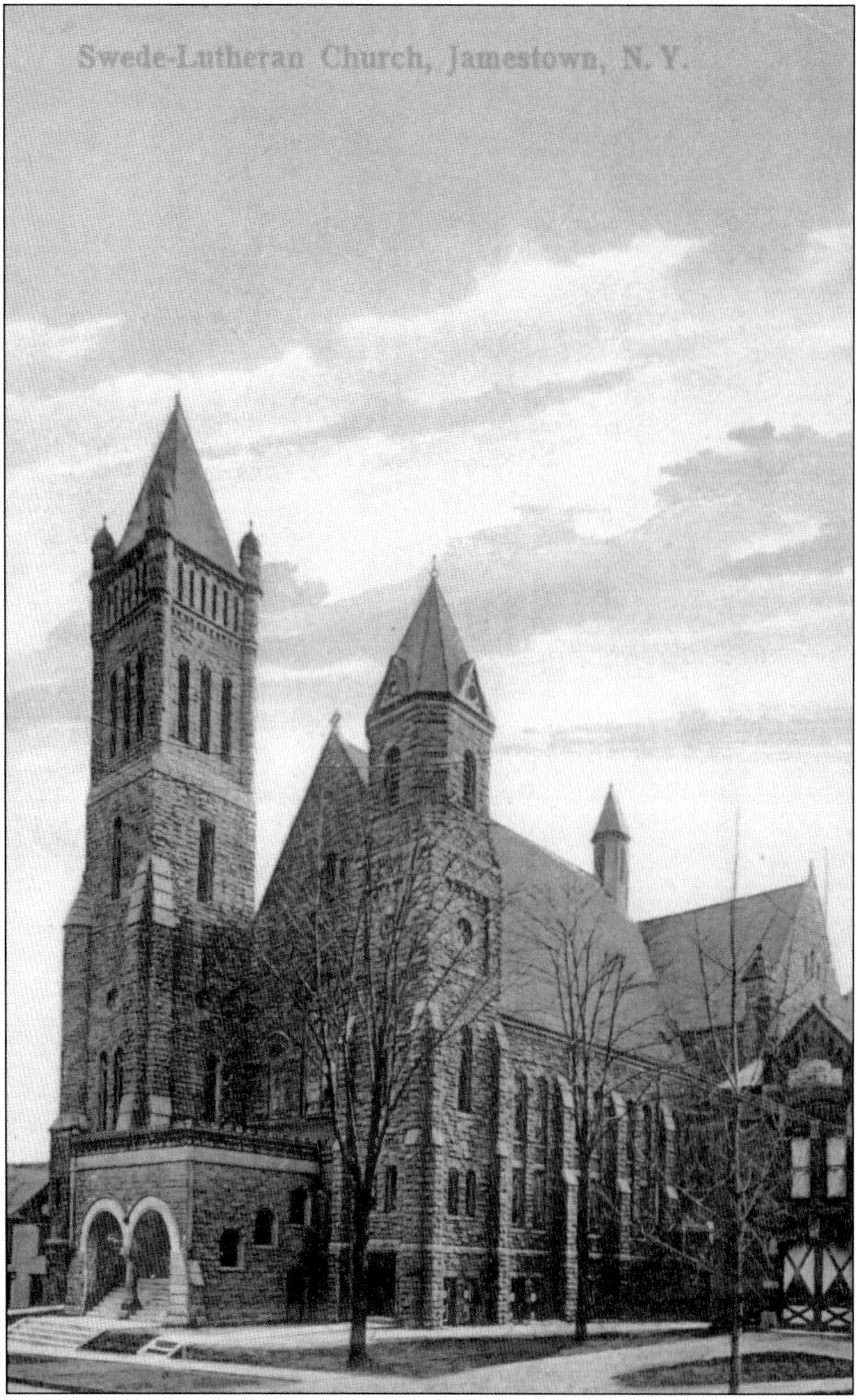

Organized in 1856 by Swedish immigrants, the First Lutheran congregation built a wooden church in 1866, expanded it several times, and in 1892, began construction on the large cathedral-style church. At the time of its construction, it was the largest Lutheran church in the country. The nave can seat almost 1,000. Designed by local architect Aaron Hall, it is built of Medina sandstone with woodwork of local hardwoods. (Courtesy of FHC.)

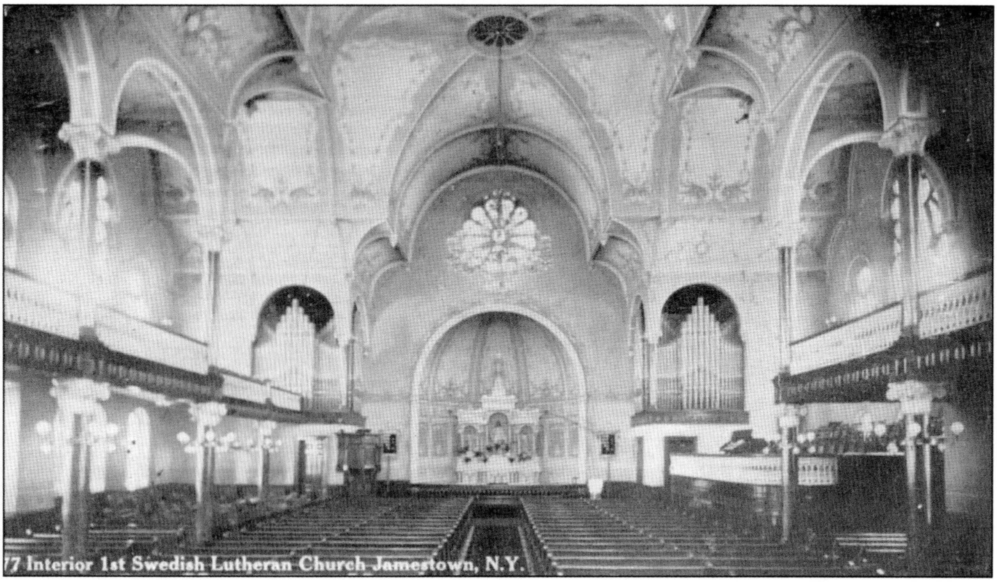

First Lutheran Church was built over a 10-year period. The pews and pulpit were made of golden and red oak, and other local hardwoods were used throughout the interior. A Hook and Hastings pipe organ was installed in 1901 and replaced in 1955. The original pipe organ from 1870 has been electrified and is still played occasionally in the church parlors.

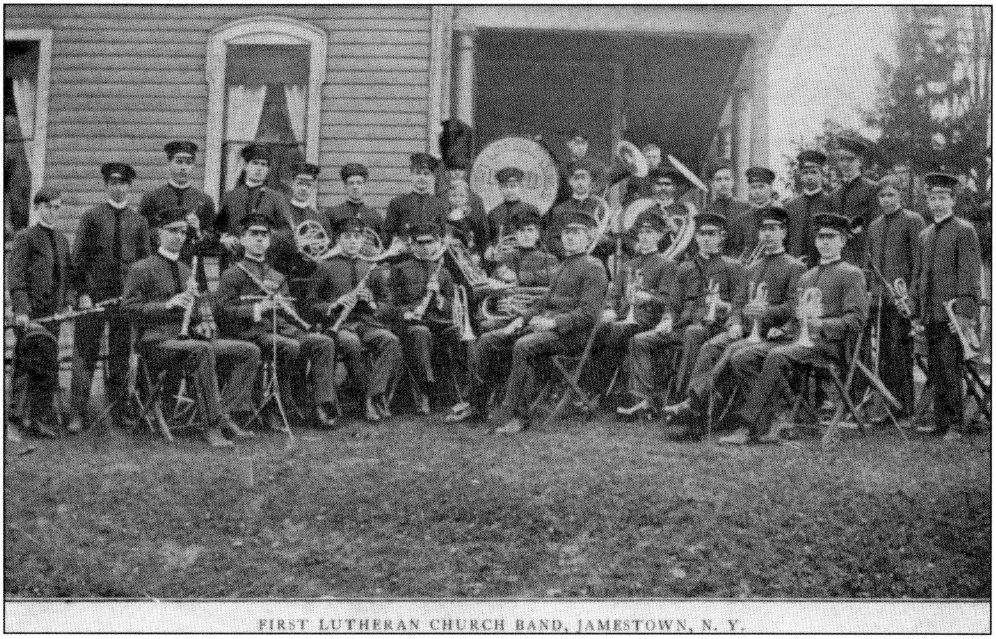

Churches and other organizations often had their own band in the early 1900s. The First Lutheran Church band was formed in 1904. Here, they are assembled on the lawn of the parsonage at 116 Chandler Street. The band played for activities at the church and at other locations, often as a fundraiser. In August 1907, it played during a moonlight excursion on one of the Chautauqua Lake steamboats. (Courtesy of FHC.)

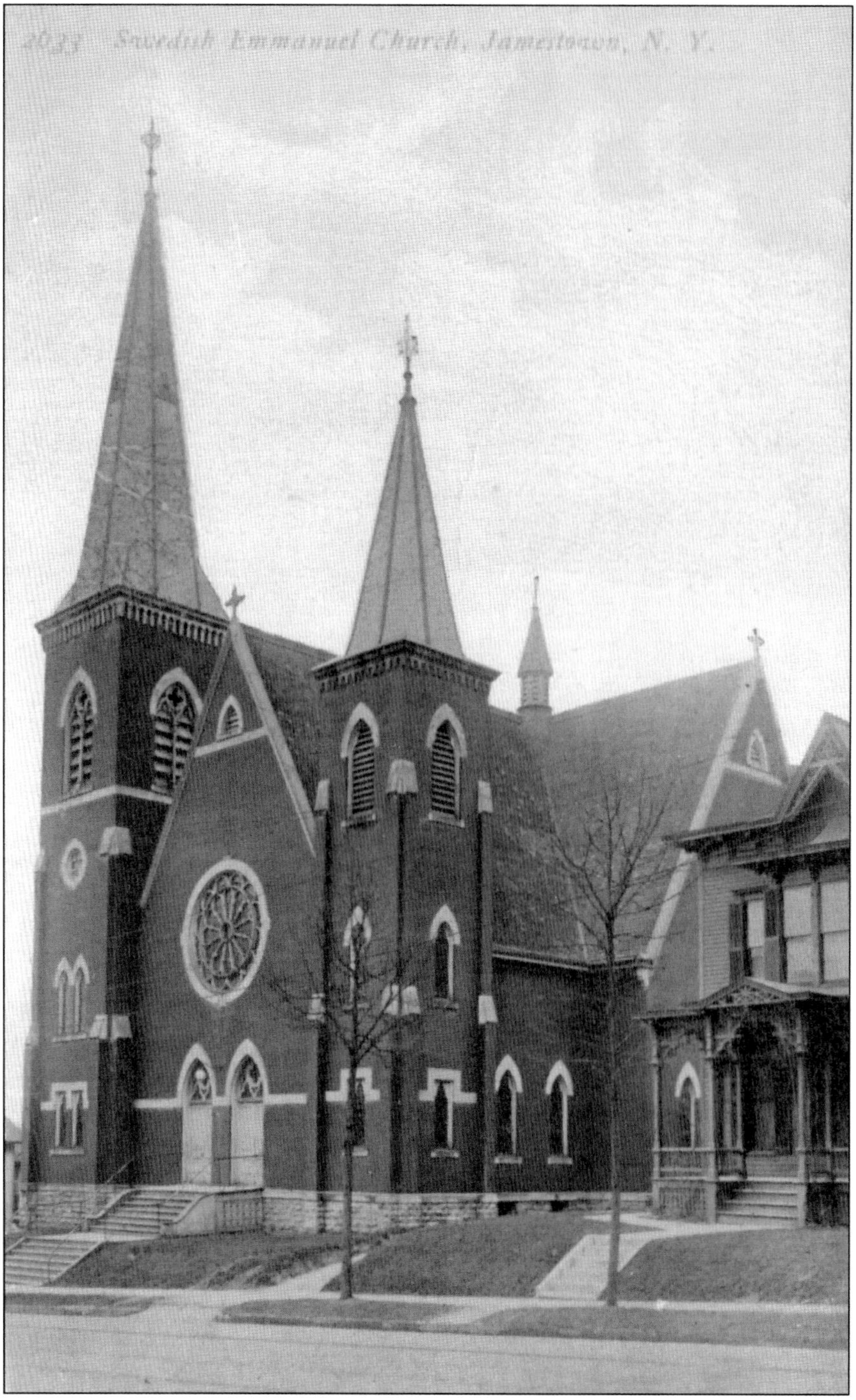

In 1887, some members of First Lutheran Church withdrew to organize Immanuel Lutheran Church. By 1889, their church was built on East Second Street. Work continued, and by 1895, the towers were completed, and the building was veneered with brick. By the 1930s, they owned three houses and three vacant lots near the church. Today's church replaced the earlier church on these properties.

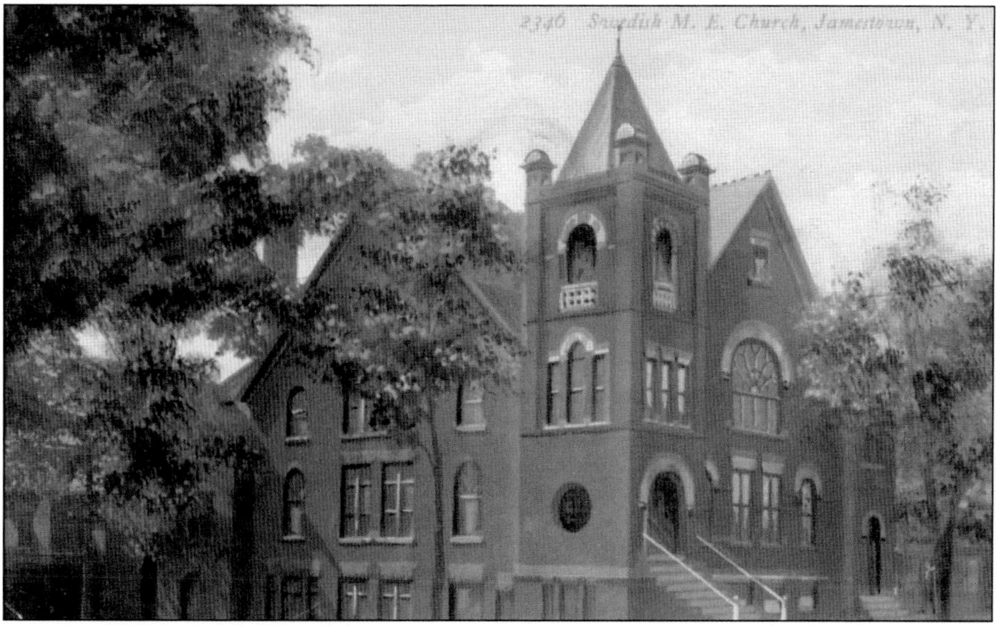

The first Swedish clergyman in Jamestown converted Samuel Johnson Sjostrand to Methodism. He joined the First Methodist Church; then, with 11 others, he started the Swedish Methodist Church in 1852. After meeting in various locations, this church was built at the corner of Foote Avenue and Chandler Street in 1891. Medina sandstone was used in this church for the entrance steps.

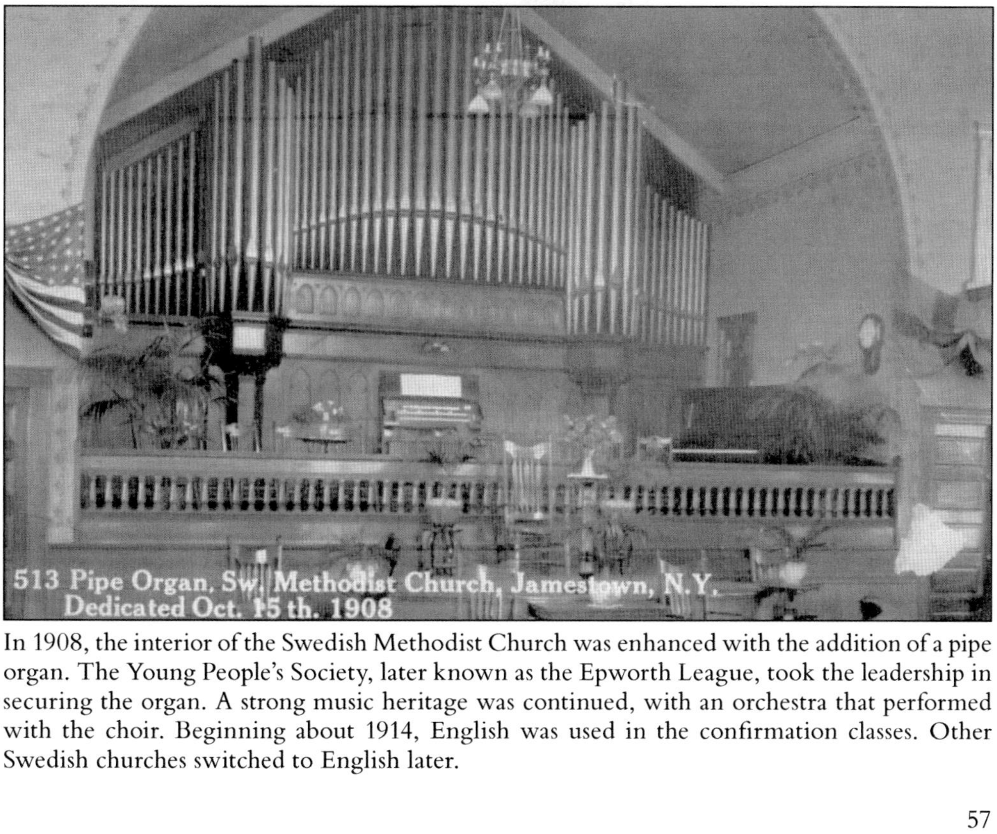

In 1908, the interior of the Swedish Methodist Church was enhanced with the addition of a pipe organ. The Young People's Society, later known as the Epworth League, took the leadership in securing the organ. A strong music heritage was continued, with an orchestra that performed with the choir. Beginning about 1914, English was used in the confirmation classes. Other Swedish churches switched to English later.

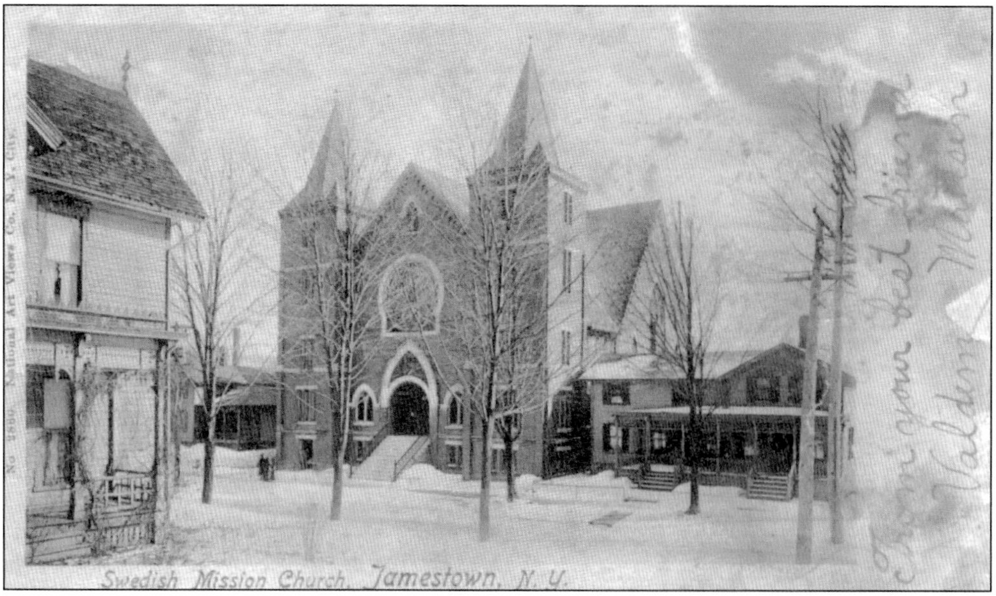

Founded by Swedish immigrants in 1879, the Swedish Mission Church built its third church on Chandler Street in 1897. In 1904, the neighboring home was replaced by a new parsonage. By 1916, there were 891 members, with 103 serving during World War I, including Pastor Frykman, as chaplain at New Jersey's Camp Dix. A new entrance was built in 1924. This church burned in 1950.

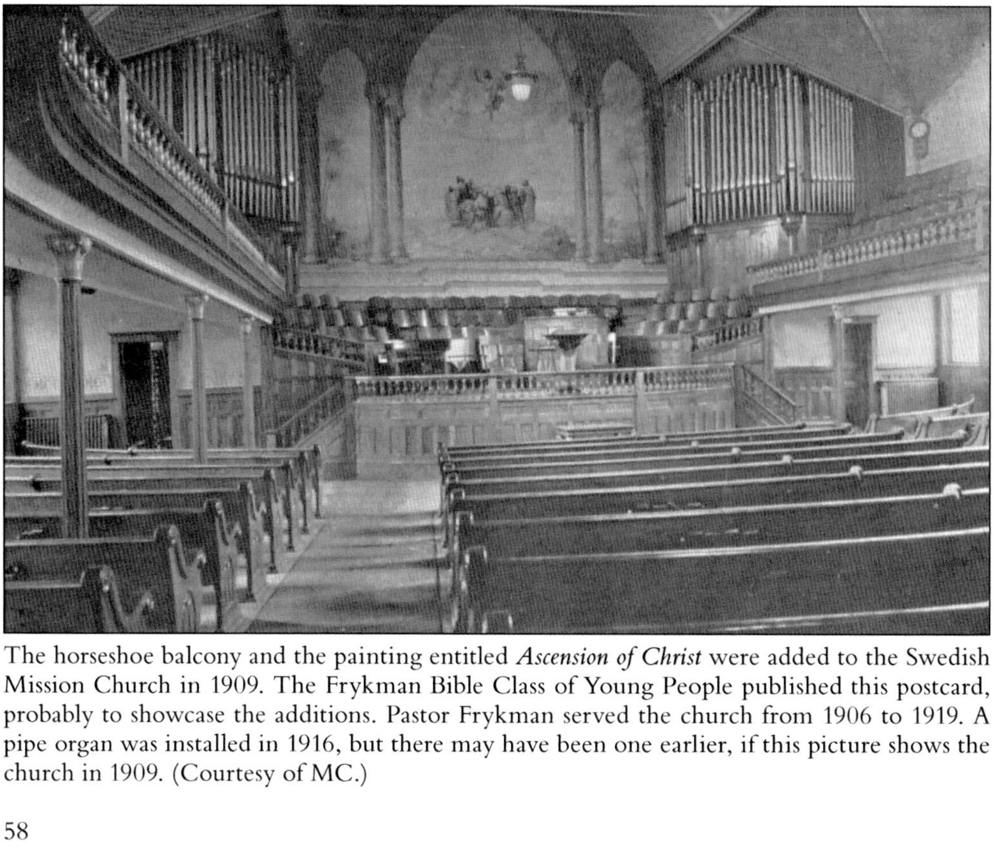

The horseshoe balcony and the painting entitled *Ascension of Christ* were added to the Swedish Mission Church in 1909. The Frykman Bible Class of Young People published this postcard, probably to showcase the additions. Pastor Frykman served the church from 1906 to 1919. A pipe organ was installed in 1916, but there may have been one earlier, if this picture shows the church in 1909. (Courtesy of MC.)

Beginning in 1894 as the Swedish Christian Zion Church, the Zion Mission Church was built in 1897 on College Street near the Swedish churches on Chandler Street. After a few months in 1900, a union with the First Mission Church proved unsuccessful. It continued on College Street until the 1960s, when the purchase of the property by the Jamestown Public Schools forced the move to Fairmount Avenue.

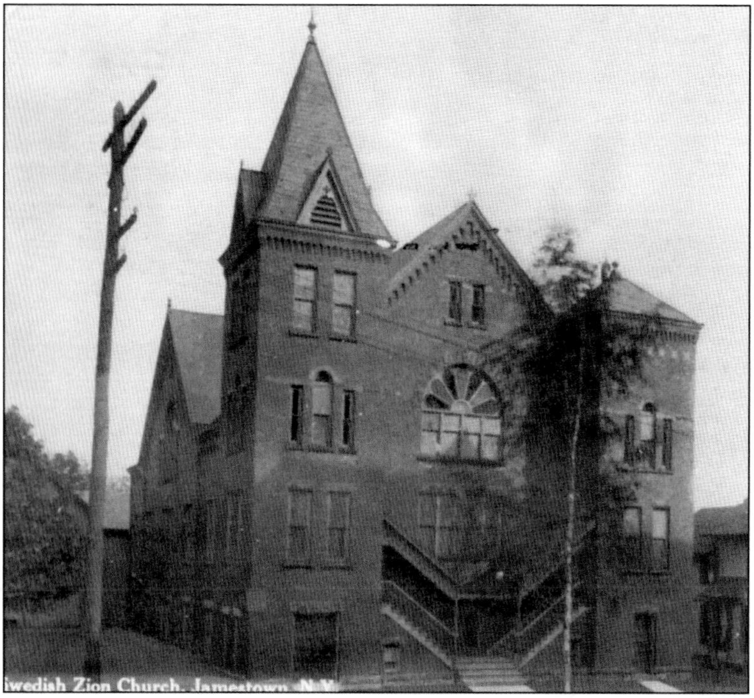

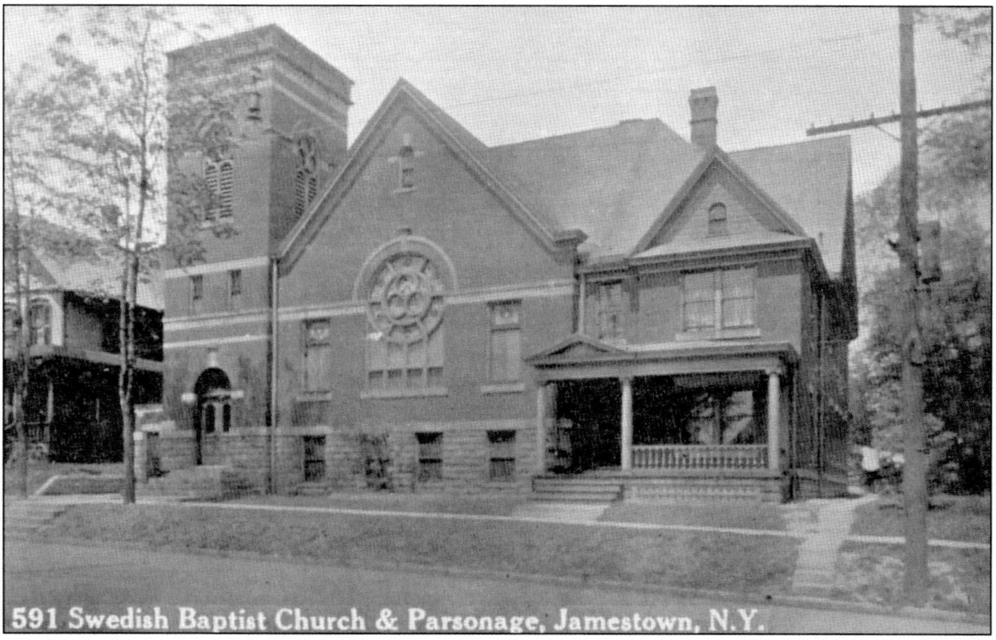

The Swedish Baptist Church began in 1884 with 13 Swedish immigrants. The church and parsonage were built in 1906 at 123 Chandler Street near the other Swedish churches. When the use of English for part of the services started in 1943, the name was changed to Chandler Street Baptist Church. Continued growth instigated the move to Hallock Street in 1971, and the name changed to Hillcrest Baptist. (Courtesy of MC.)

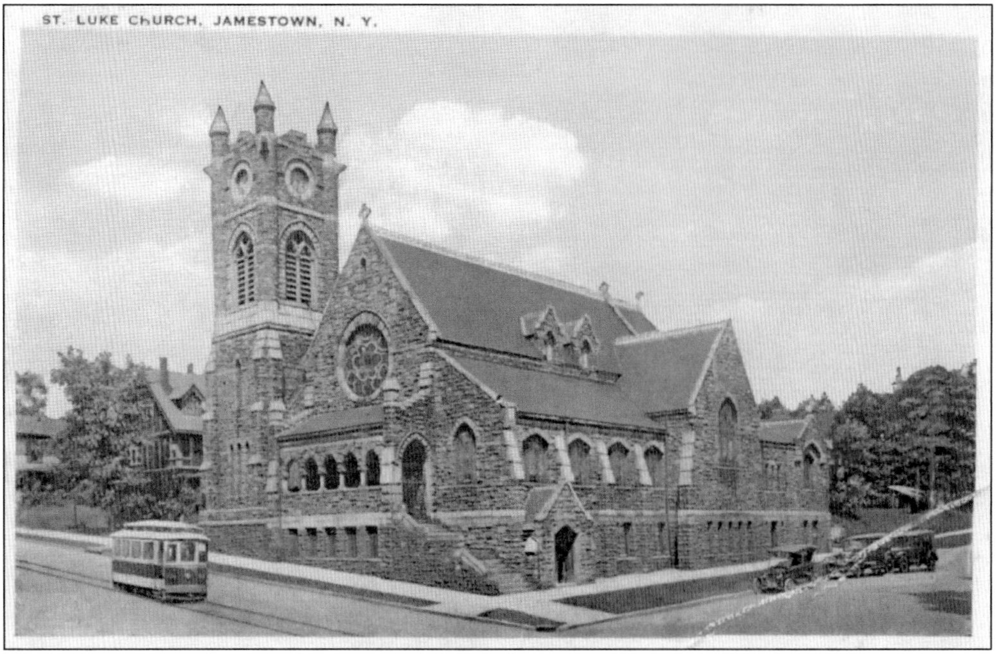

St. Luke's Episcopal Church, organized in 1824, called a rector in 1852 and built a church at the northeast corner of North Main and Fourth Streets in 1856. It was rebuilt after an 1862 fire. In 1890, Mary A. Prendergast left $125,000 to build a new church on the old site in memory of her daughter Catherine. The result is this Gothic Revival, Medina sandstone church and parish house.

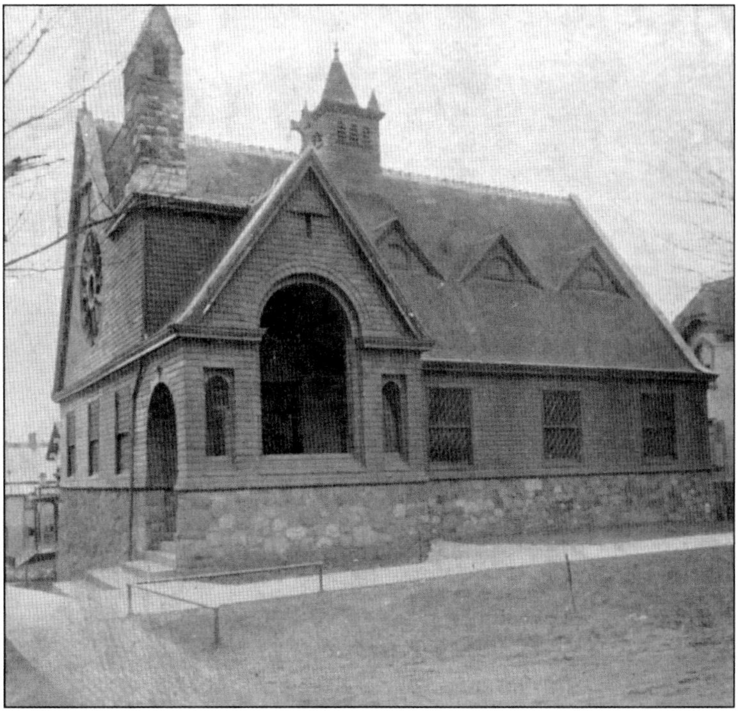

Jamestown's First Church of Christ, Scientist began in 1886, shortly after Mary Baker Eddy founded the Boston church. Rose E. Kent donated land at the southwest corner of Fourth Street and Prendergast Avenue for the church, constructed in 1893. Her son Charles Wetmore, a New York City architect, designed this church, Grand Central Station, and other public buildings. Jamestown's was the fourth Christian Science church built. (Courtesy of FHC.)

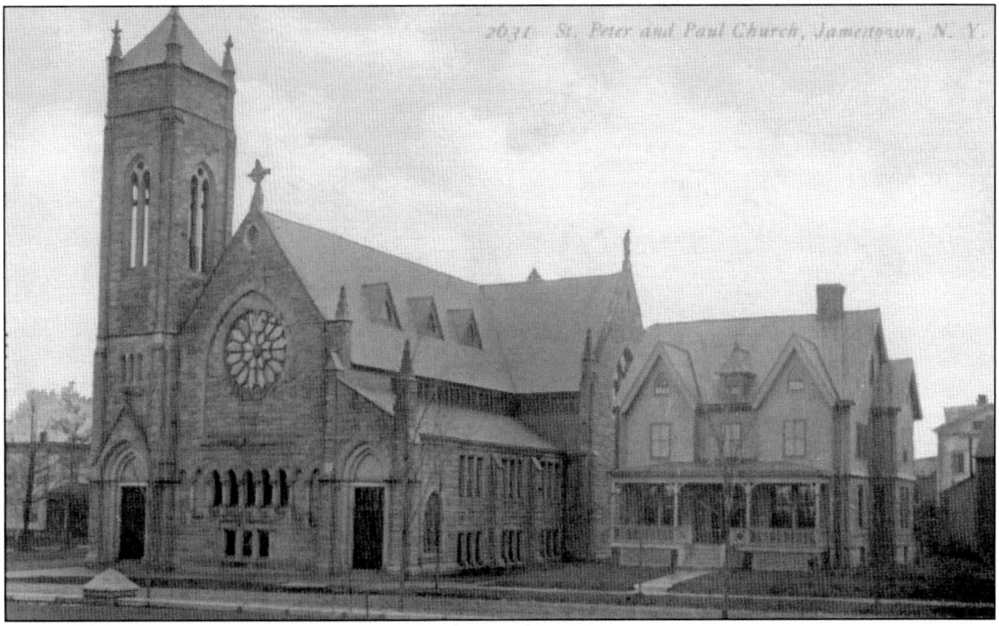

The first church established by Irish immigrants was built in 1853–1854 and burned in 1860. It was the first Roman Catholic church in southern Chautauqua County. Officially incorporated in 1863 as SS. Peter and Paul Roman Catholic Church, the second church was replaced by this Gothic Revival–style edifice and rectory in 1894. From 1875 to 1914, Fr. Richard Coyle shepherded the growth of this parish and the building of this church.

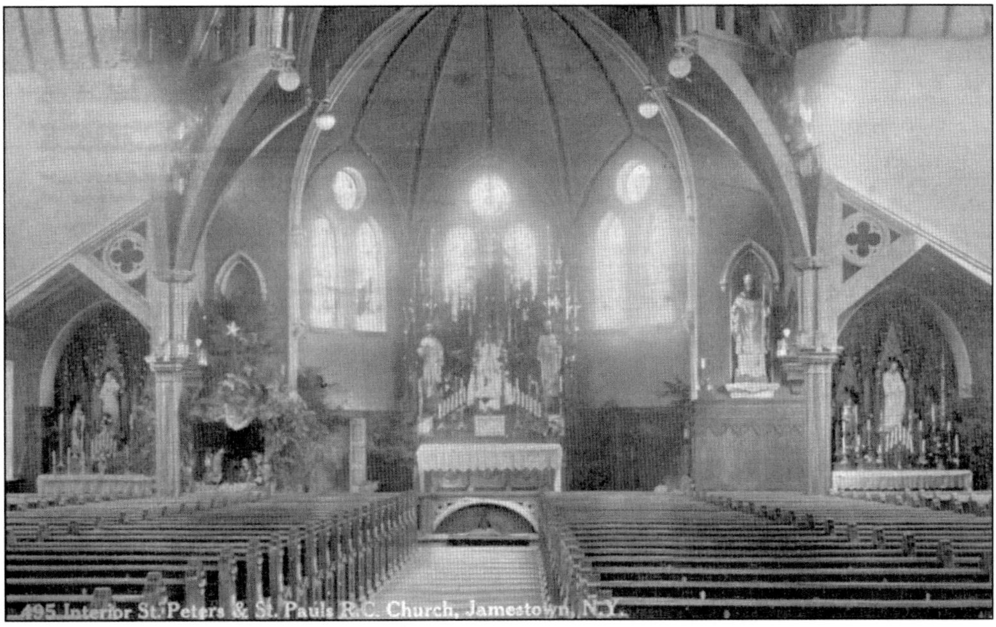

The interior of SS. Peter and Paul Roman Catholic Church, constructed in 1894, continues the Gothic Revival style. Features such as pointed arches, stained-glass windows, a rose window, and an elaborate hammer beam ceiling are evident. The heavy timbers are clad with oak. The trusses have decorative carvings and stenciling. Wood wainscoting continues around the church. Wood paneling continues for the choir and organ loft.

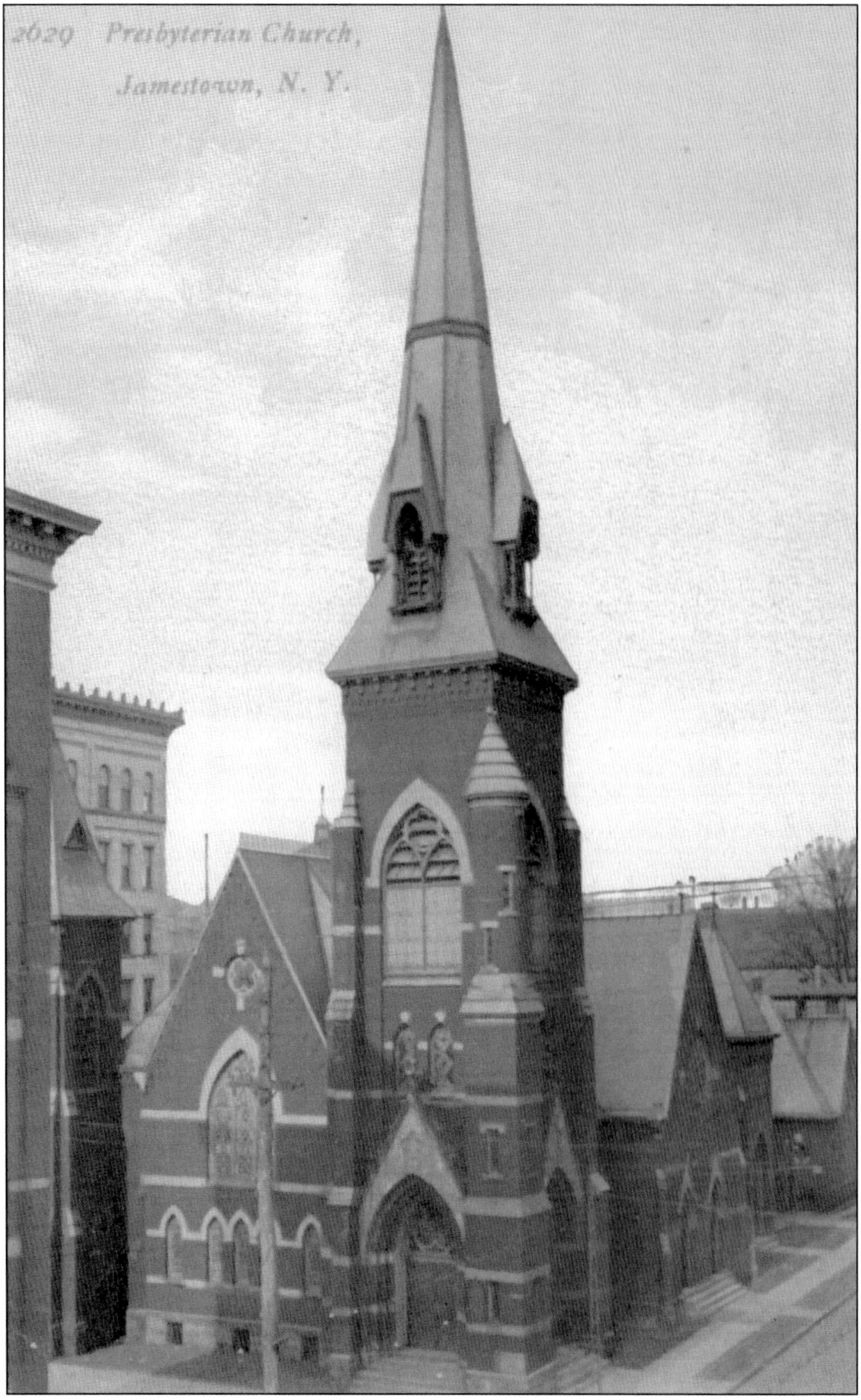

First Presbyterian Church began in 1834, building its first church in 1837 on the northwest corner of Third and Cherry Streets in downtown Jamestown. After the 1877 fire, a large brick church was built on the same site. Razed in 1924, it had been sold to provide a site for the Hotel Jamestown. The new church is on Prendergast Avenue between Fifth and Sixth Streets. (Courtesy of MC.)

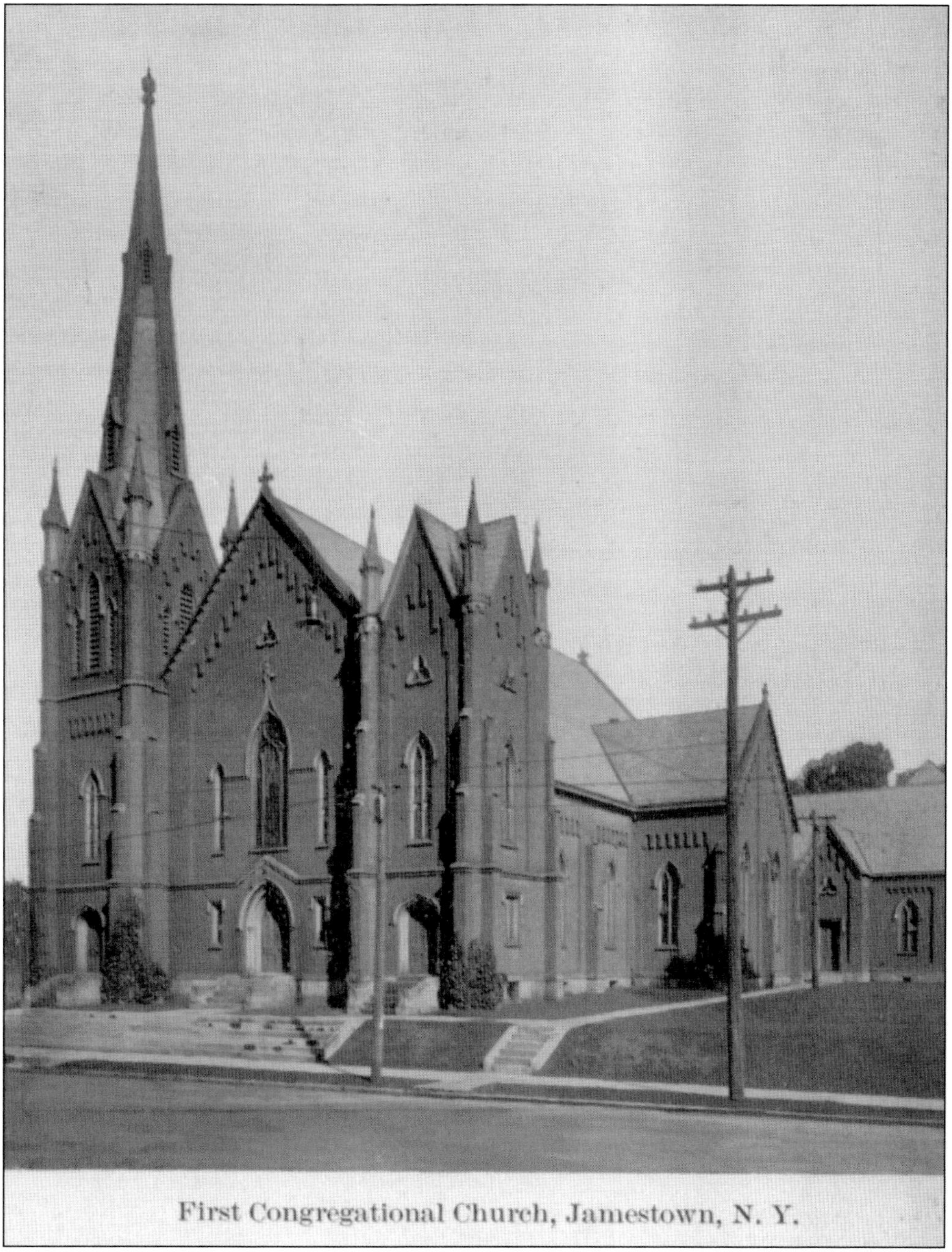

The First Congregational Church, on East Third Street, is Jamestown's oldest public building in continuous use. Local architect Aaron Hall designed this Gothic Revival structure, which was completed in 1869. Besides having the oldest church structure, the church is Jamestown's oldest church, organized in 1816 by circuit rider Rev. John Spencer. This structure has hosted other denominations, including those just beginning and those needing space for worship following a fire. (Courtesy of MC.)

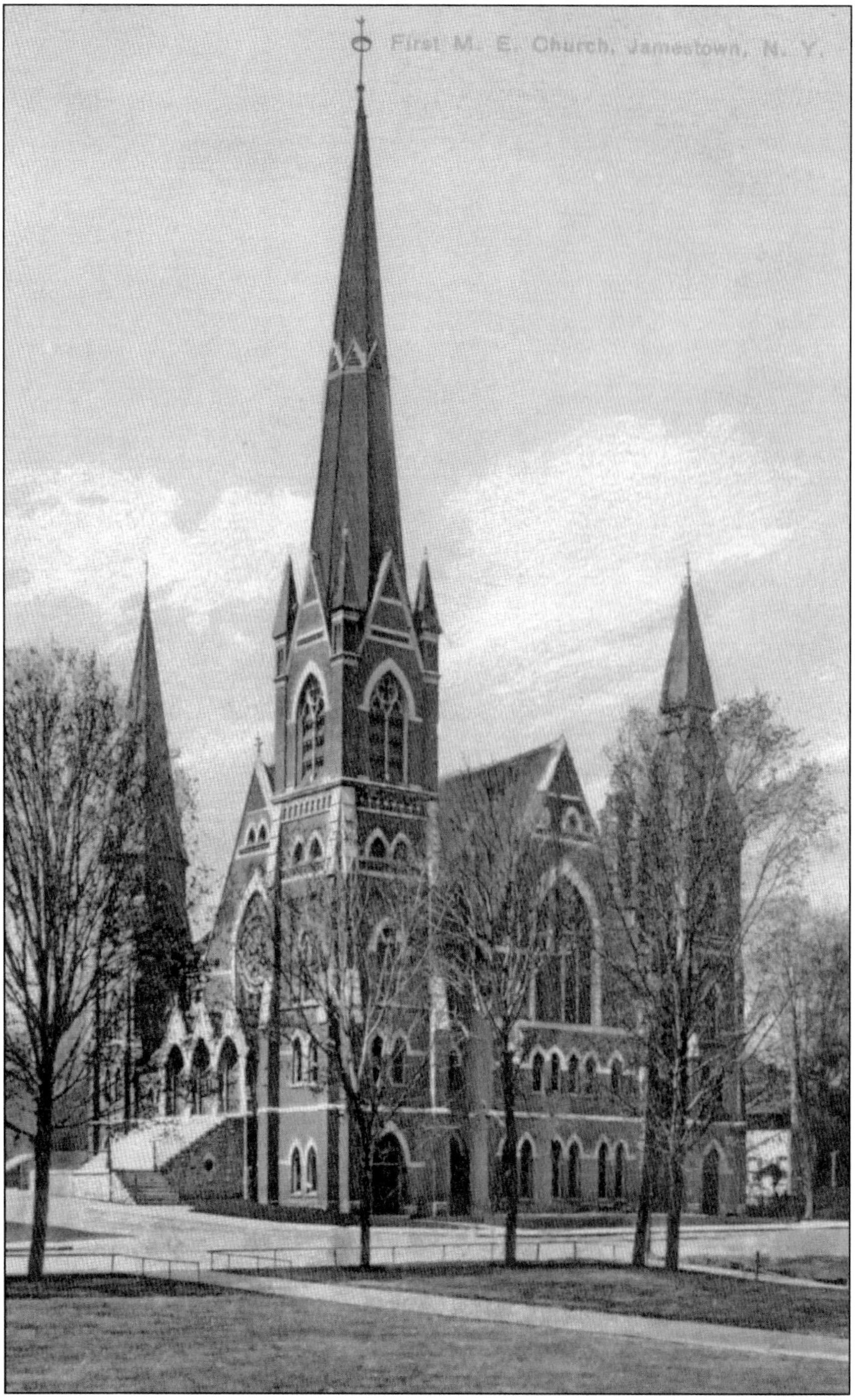

Outgrowing the first church, First Methodist Episcopal Church moved across the street, constructing a large brick edifice at the corner of East Third and East Second Streets. Dedicated in 1886, the church building could seat close to 1,500 people. Facing the length of Third Street, the tall spires and long set of steps leading to the front entrance were impressive. The steps became a favored vantage point for parade spectators.

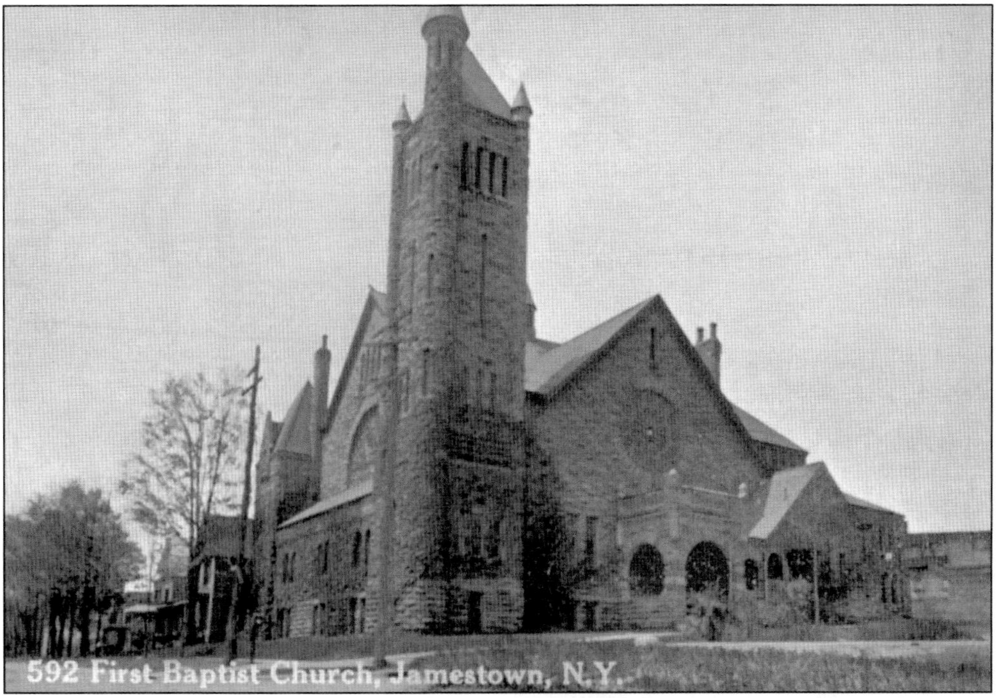

The First Baptist Church, organized in 1832, had a small wooden church before building this church in 1890. Built on the corner of Fourth and Church Streets, it was made of Warsaw bluestone but was damaged by fire in 1914. Repairs changed the steep, slanted roofline to rounded roofs. In 1972, the church burned again, this time almost to the ground. (Courtesy of FHC.)

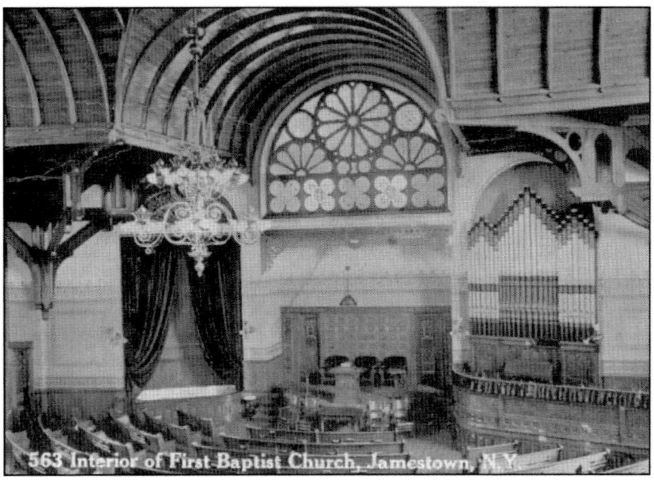

A new pipe organ for the new First Baptist Church was purchased from Johnson Bros. of Westfield, Massachusetts, for $2,500. William J. Maddox, a furniture manufacturer, gave the new carved oak pulpit desk. Mrs. Waffle gave the communion table, and Mrs. Breed gave the oak side stands and vases. Fundraisers, such as socials and concerts, had raised money for the organ, carpets, and curtains.

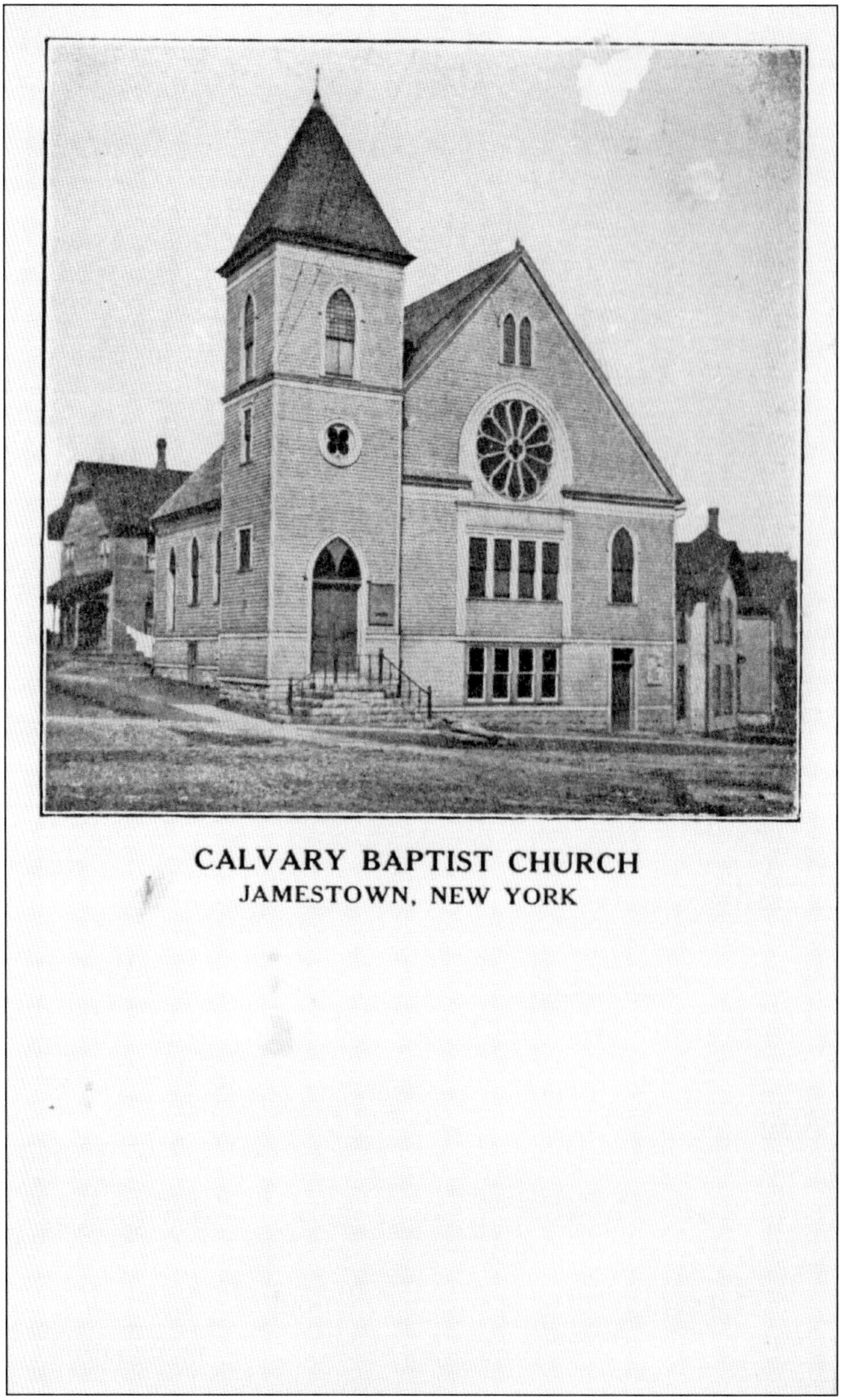

In 1891, members of First Baptist Church started a Sabbath school on the west side. This continued until 1903, when the Calvary Baptist Church was organized there as an independent church. Its church building stands at the intersection of Fairmount Avenue and Seymour Street. Having built and furnished a new church in 1891, First Baptist Church gave its old pulpit desk, pulpit chairs, and organ to the Calvary Baptist Church.

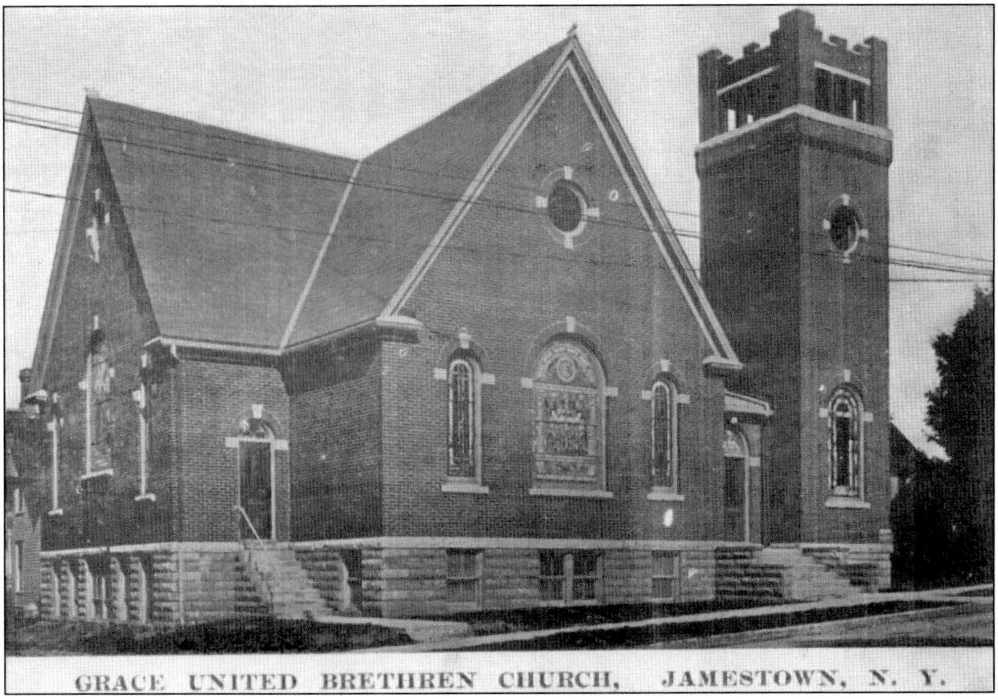

The Church of the United Brethren in Christ established a mission in Jamestown in 1902. The next year, it purchased the Grace Chapel on North Main Street from the First Presbyterian Church. Next, it built a parsonage and continued to make improvements to the church. It became an Evangelical United Brethren church and, in 1968, a United Methodist church.

The Free Methodist church, incorporated in 1874, began with a class in 1871. Its first and only church building was erected in 1884. The church continues today in the original building, located on the corner of Lincoln and Seventh Streets. The house to the left is now gone to make way for an addition to the church and a parking lot.

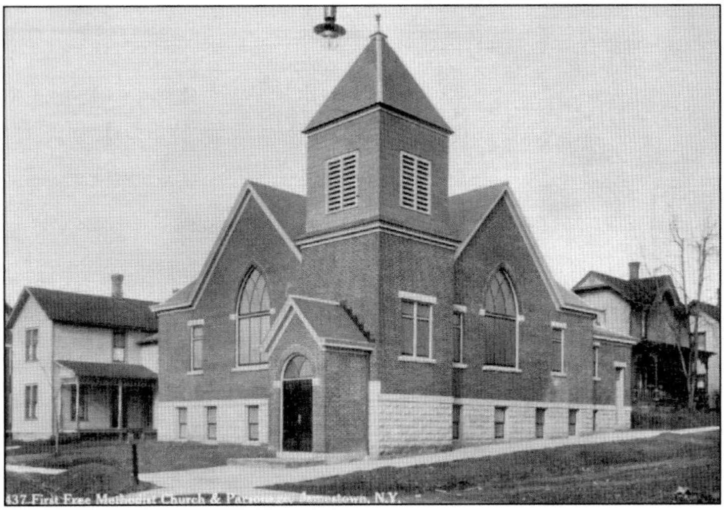

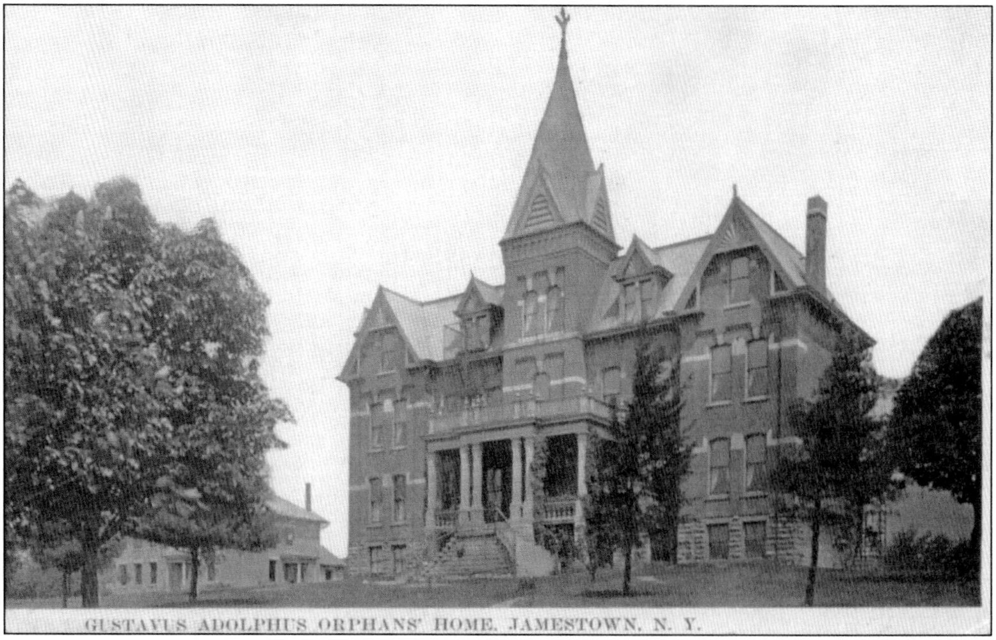

To ensure that orphans of Swedish immigrants would be raised as Lutherans, the Gustavus Adolphus Orphans' Home of the New York Conference of the Scandinavian Evangelical Lutheran Augustana Synod opened in January 1886 in Jamestown, New York. Some of the food, services, and skilled labor were provided by local residents, while the conference provided monetary support. This building was replaced by an expanding modern campus serving youth and the elderly.

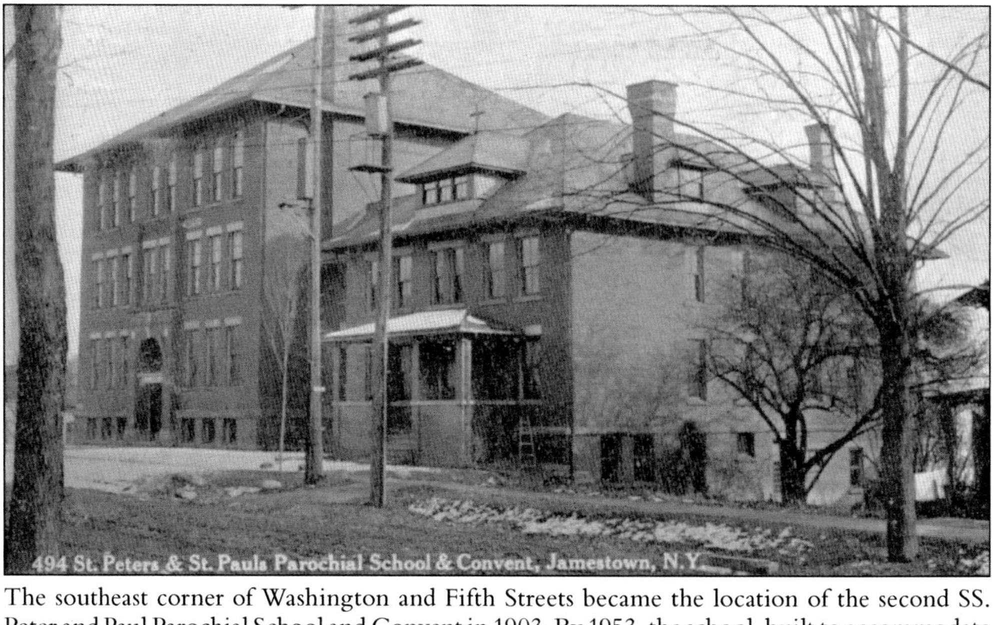

The southeast corner of Washington and Fifth Streets became the location of the second SS. Peter and Paul Parochial School and Convent in 1903. By 1953, the school, built to accommodate only 250 pupils, had 450 pupils attending. Beginning in 1887, the Sisters of Mercy of Buffalo, New York, established their branch house in Jamestown and conducted the school. In 1956, the third and present school opened on North Main Street.

Six

Schools

The education of children and adults was important to Jamestown's founder. Within five years of James and Agnes Prendergast's arrival, James had donated land, erected a building, and hired a teacher for the school. He continued to fund education for 20 years. This first school building served as a town hall and a place of worship. Another early school was the Jamestown Academy, erected on the southeast corner of Fourth and Spring Streets. This served as the intermediate and academic school for the village until the Jamestown Union School and Collegiate Institute was created and a building erected in 1867. The Jamestown Union School and Collegiate Institute is what became Jamestown High School.

There were at least two private educational institutions in Jamestown during the mid-1800s. Beginning in 1833, Mary E. Osborne, a Quaker widow, established a boarding school for young ladies. This school operated for 10 years, educating young ladies from around the country. Teacher Clarissa D. Wheeler opened the Jamestown Female Seminary in 1849. Including subjects thought proper for young ladies, such as penmanship, grammar and spelling, painting, and needlework, the school continued until 1859.

Schools for younger children began to be constructed in neighborhoods. By 1900, there were 12 public schools within the city, including the high school. Soon after 1900, the smaller schools were no longer adequate for some areas, and new schools were built. These are the schools that appear on postcards in the early 20th century. Some of them are still part of Jamestown, but few remain as schools. Some of the "postcard schools" have been replaced, while some have been converted to apartment buildings. Like most experiences encountered during a lifetime, schools can be reminiscent of pleasant days. The authors wish the readers pleasant memories from their school days.

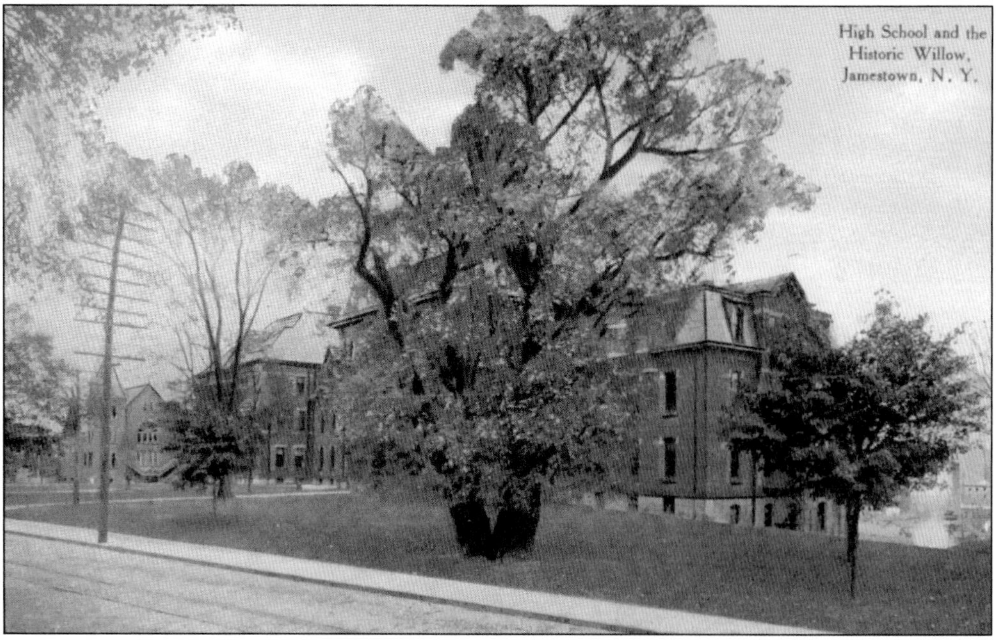

The historic willow tree—located on East Second Street from 1823, when Judge Foote transplanted it to his new home there, until it was taken down in 1918—grew to be a most beloved tree by school students. The school, built on Foote's home site in 1867, spared the tree. The old willow tree has a line in Jamestown High School's alma mater and has been referred to in poetry and student writings.

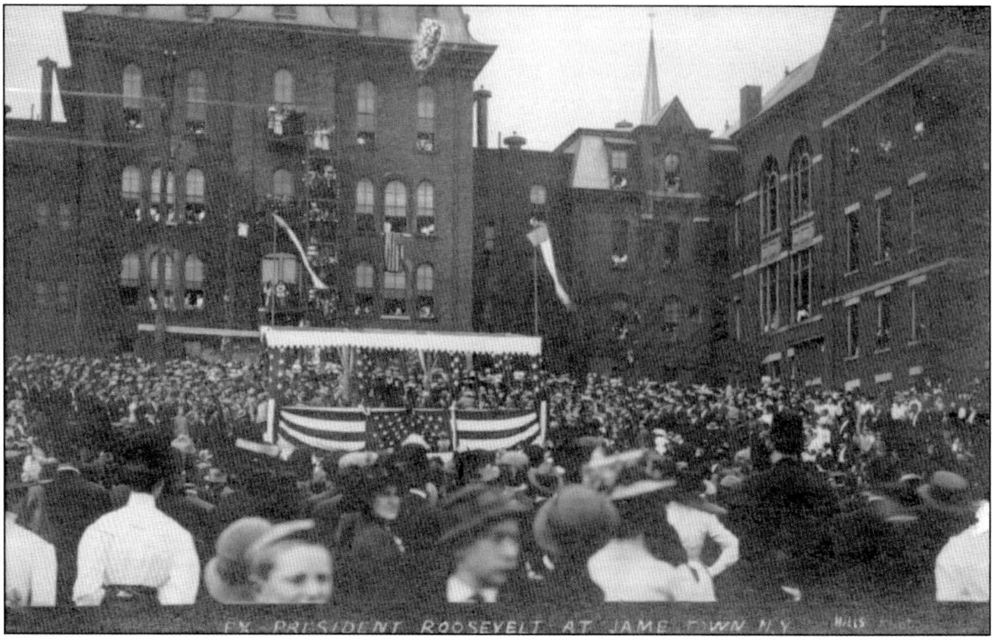

This is former president Theodore Roosevelt in Jamestown in 1910, when he was at Jamestown High School. The Jamestown High School class of 1911 planted a tree on Arbor Day 1908 and called it the Roosevelt Elm in his honor. When coming to Jamestown as the state Republican party chairman, he was prevailed upon to come to the school and to recognize the tree.

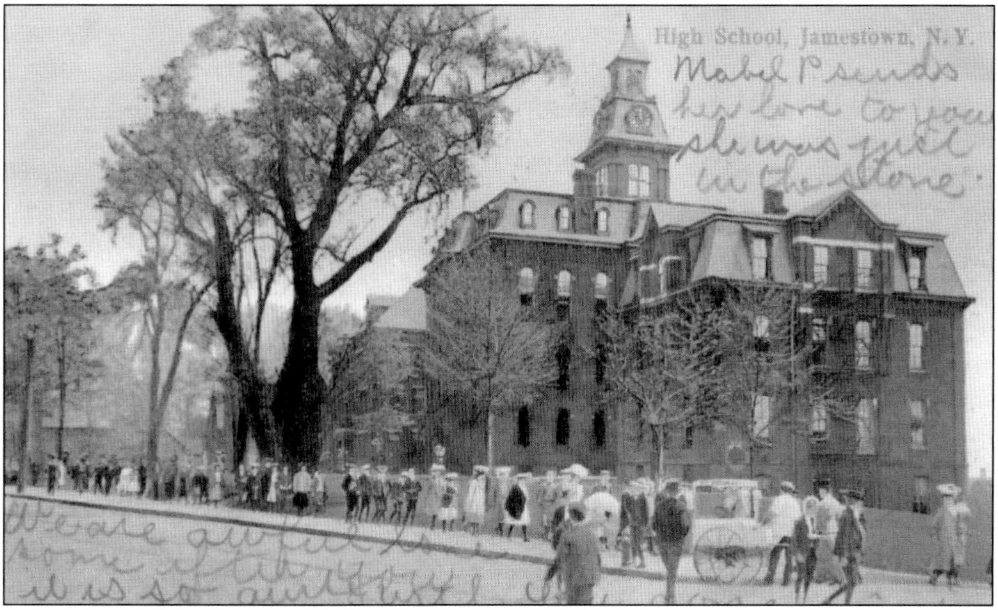

The Jamestown Union School and Collegiate Institute, on East Second Street, graduated its first class in 1868. Pictured is an ice cream vendor waiting for students. The historic willow is still standing guard, and the clock in the tower still counts time. The institute building had additions and became Jamestown High School, but overcrowding forced the construction of a new school on the same site in 1935.

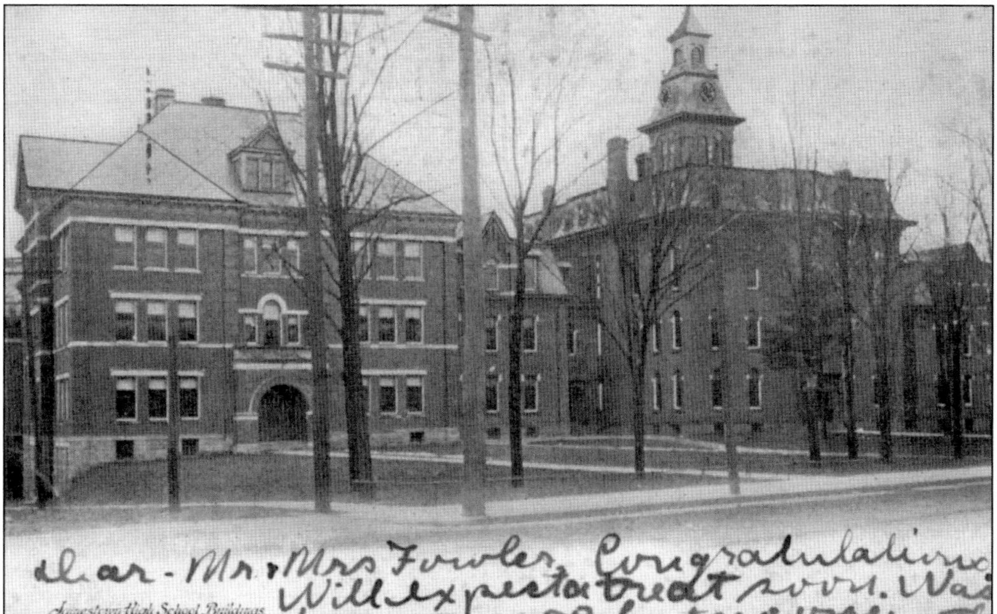

Jamestown High School looked like this before it was torn down and replaced in 1935. The first redbrick building, Institute Hall, was on East Second Street. The grammar school was added on the corner of East Second Street and College Avenue. By the 1930s, temporary wooden buildings surrounded the school on the west. Public Works Administration (PWA) funds were made available for the construction of the new high school.

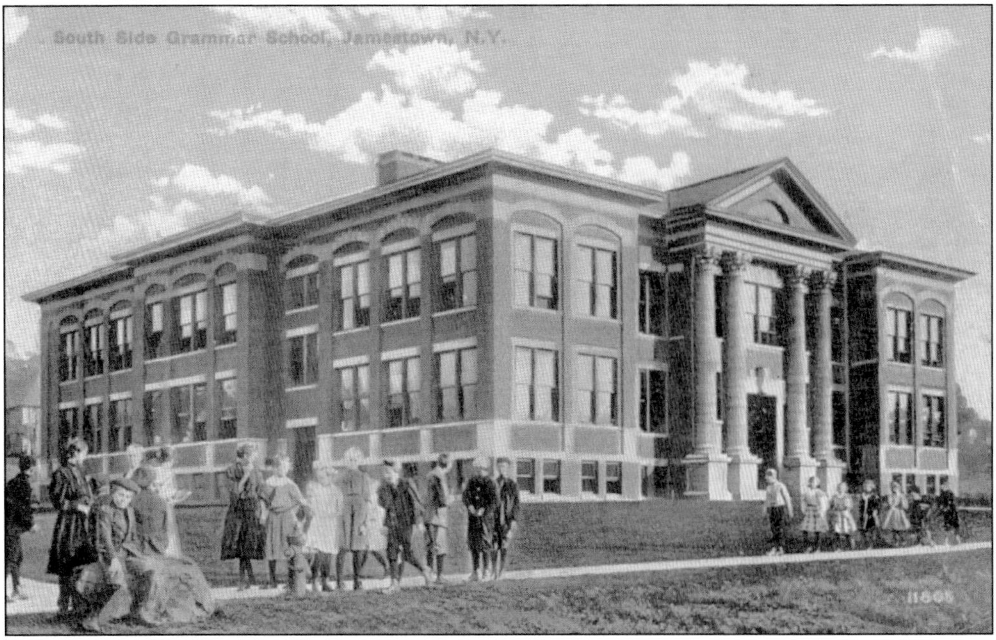

Sherman Street School, once referred to as the Southside School, was located behind what is now WCA Hospital. It was dedicated in October 1907. In 1927, it was renamed the Rovillus R. Rogers School to honor the longtime superintendent. Only the second superintendent since 1868, he served from 1890 to 1918. Today, medical buildings occupy the site. A new Rogers School was built on Hebner Street.

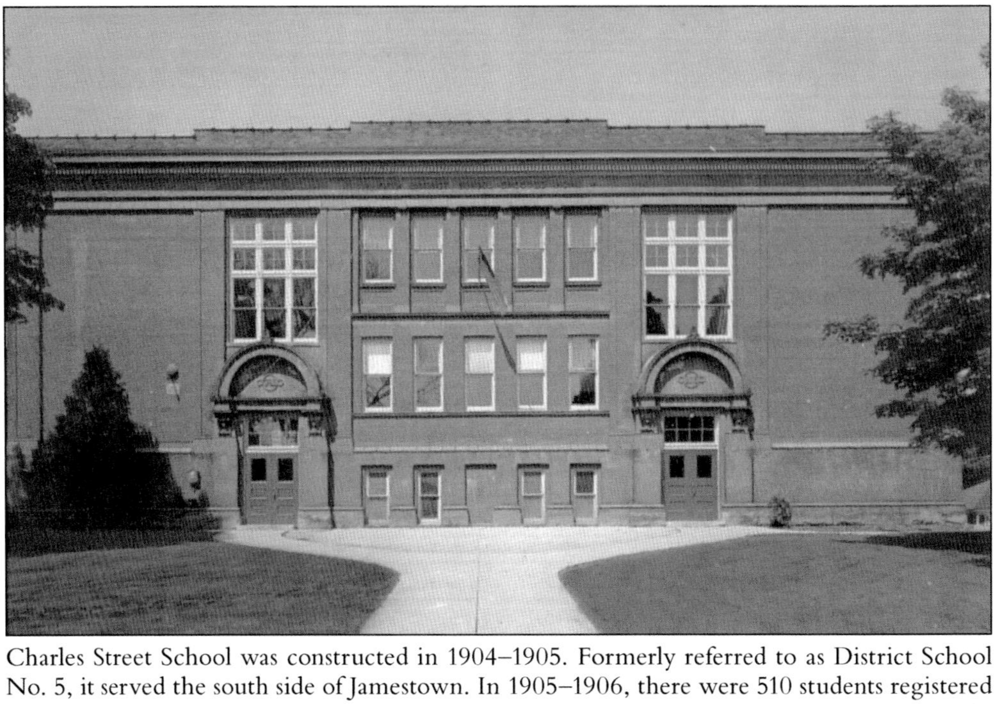

Charles Street School was constructed in 1904–1905. Formerly referred to as District School No. 5, it served the south side of Jamestown. In 1905–1906, there were 510 students registered and 13 teachers. It served as an elementary school until closing in 1971. Mildred Carlson taught there for 46 years, beginning in 1922. She had started kindergarten there as a student in 1908.

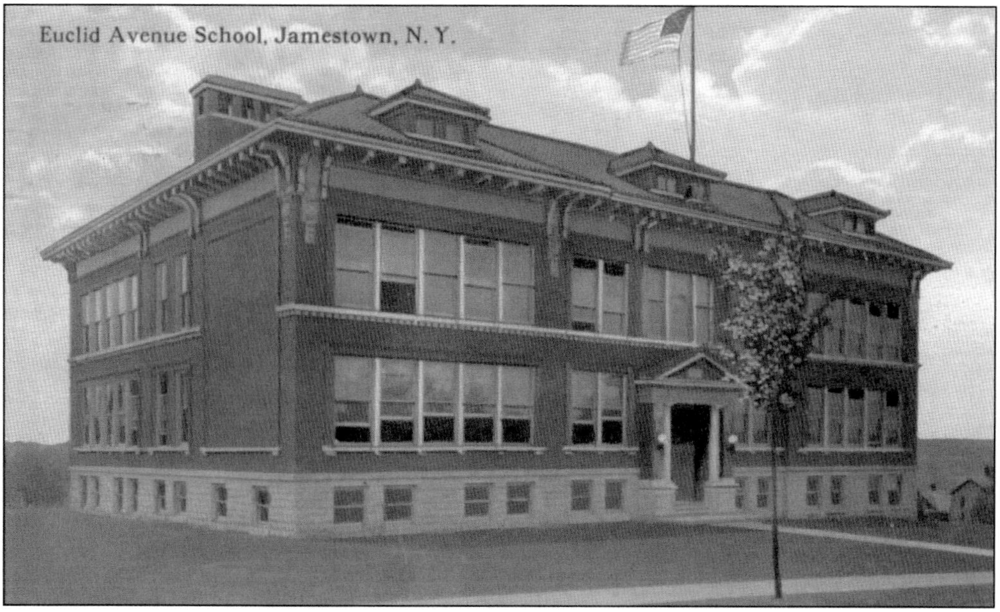

The original building of Euclid Avenue School, built in 1911, was called School No. 6. Designed by local architect C.C. Pedersen in an eclectic style that included Neoclassical-, Spanish Mission–, and Craftsman-style elements, it was built to accommodate the expanding city's growth away from the central business districts. Within 10 years, Pedersen designed an addition to accommodate children moving into the area. Today, it is an apartment building.

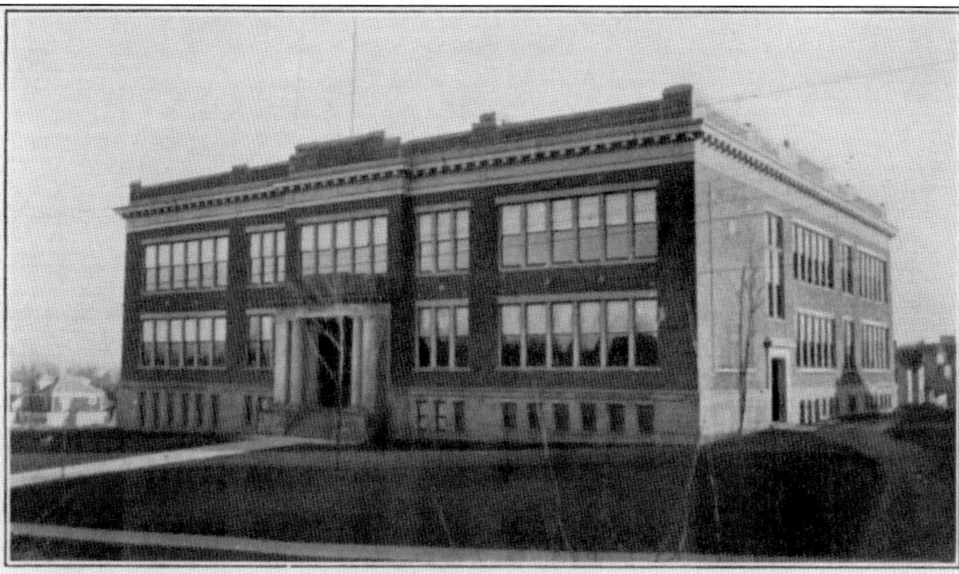

Fairmount School, Jamestown, N. Y.
June 21, 1927

Fairmount Avenue School opened in September 1913 with six teachers and 269 pupils registered from Jamestown's west side. The total cost was $72,373.76, including the beautiful woodwork. A new addition, built in 1926, cost $45,224.54. This added five classrooms accommodating 40 students each. In the 1927–1928 school year, 20 teachers taught 639 students. Charles Haas was the original builder, with Freeburg and Fidler as the architects. Today, it is an apartment building.

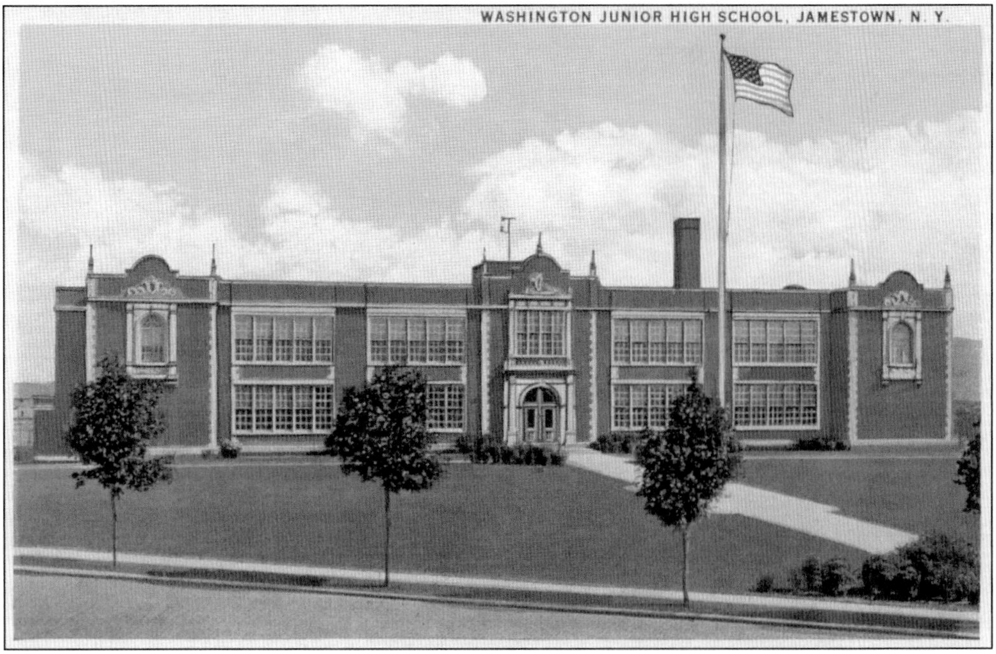

Washington Junior High School was built in 1923–1924 and opened to students on September 3, 1924. The formal opening was held on October 1, 1924. Originally, there were 276 pupils registered and nine teachers. The total cost of the school was $450,000. Besides classrooms, there was a library, a gymnasium, and other special rooms. The 20-acre site allowed for athletic fields and future growth.

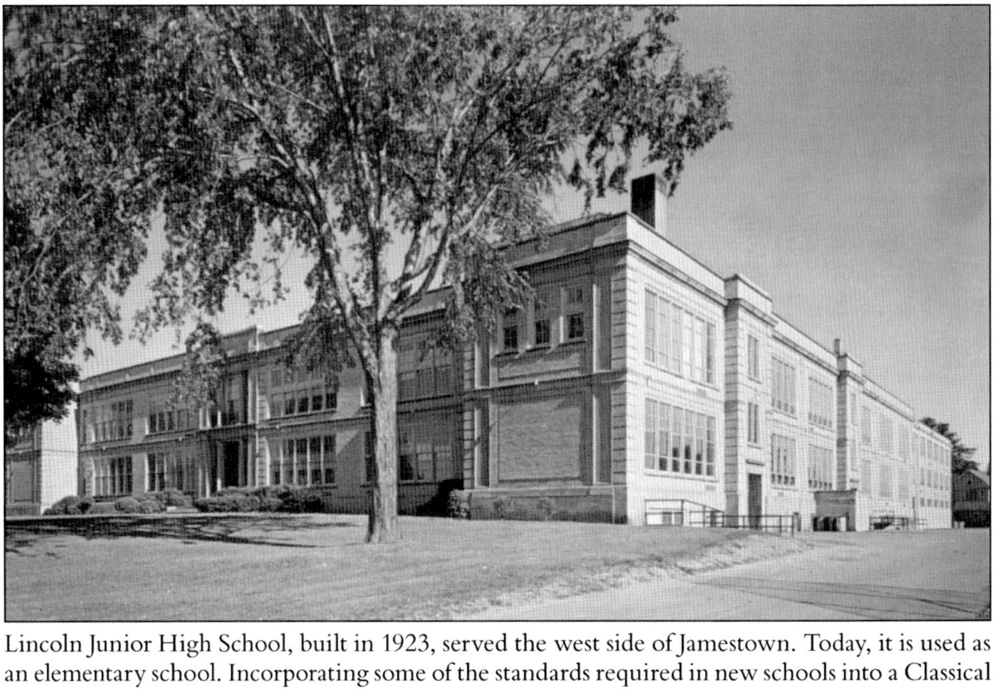

Lincoln Junior High School, built in 1923, served the west side of Jamestown. Today, it is used as an elementary school. Incorporating some of the standards required in new schools into a Classical Revival style, the architect created a school that continues into the 21st century. Large windows allow natural light into the classrooms, and the flat roof was less expensive and more fireproof.

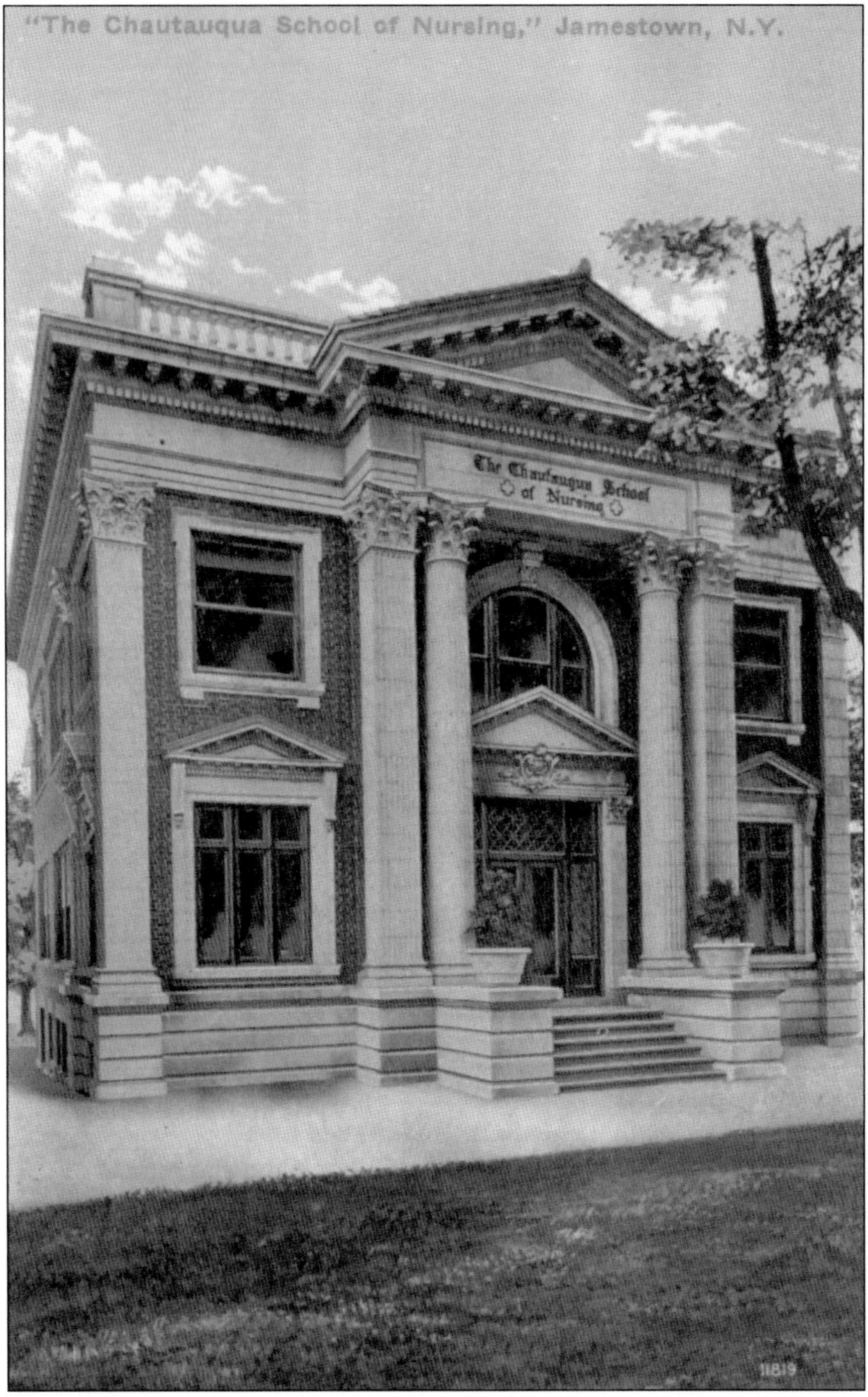

Chautauqua School of Nursing offered a correspondence course to educate women to serve as nurses. Printed lectures were sent to students. Examinations were taken at home and returned to the school. Diplomas were issued to the successful students. Students near and far took advantage of this course. The building on the southeast corner of East Fourth and Pine Streets is a Classical Revival–style structure of brick with stone trim.

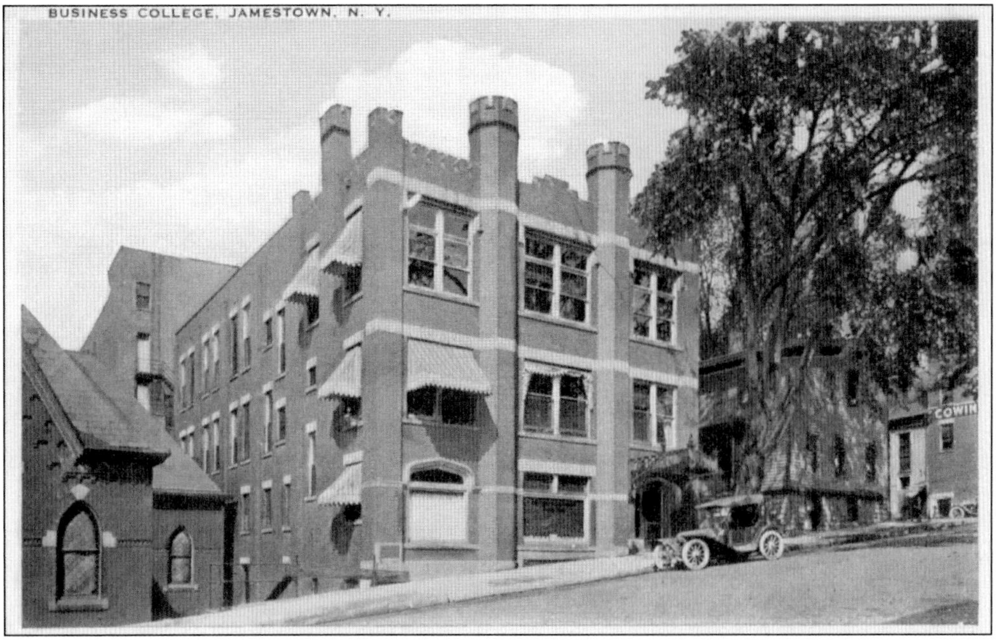

After the Gokey fire in 1910, Jamestown Business College relocated to a new fireproof building on the west side of Cherry Street, opening in April 1911. Started in 1886 and incorporated in 1889, the college prepared students for a career in commercial pursuits. The new building included the latest pattern of Edison business phonographs, Burroughs adding machines, and other modern business devices. The president was H.E.V. Porter.

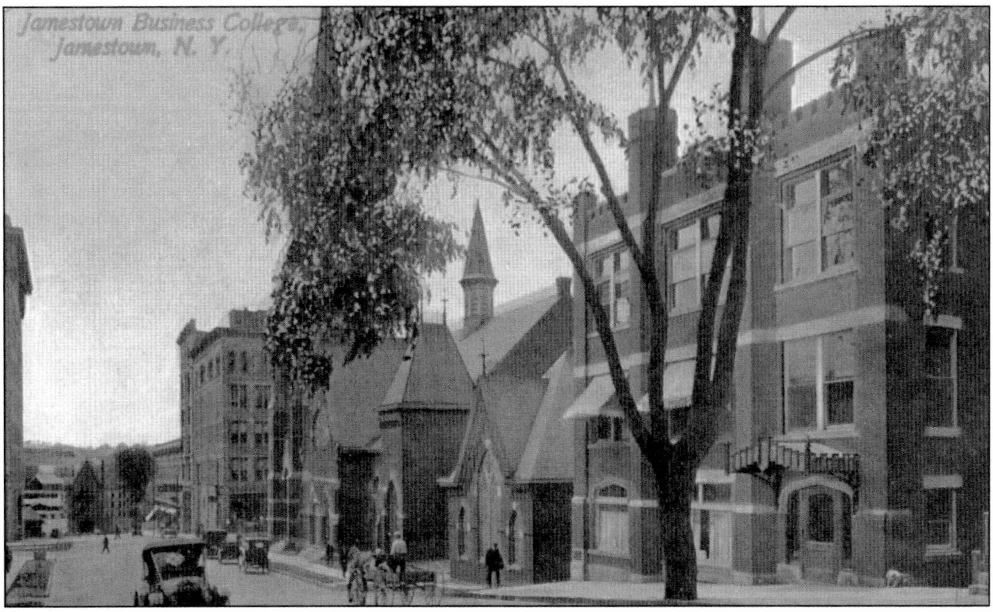

Jamestown Business College is on the right, just north of the First Presbyterian Church, with the Wellman Building next, across West Third Street. Across the end of Cherry Street is the train station. On the left, the side of the Samuels Hotel appears. The postcard was postmarked 1917, a few years after the hotel and the college were built and a few years before the church was razed.

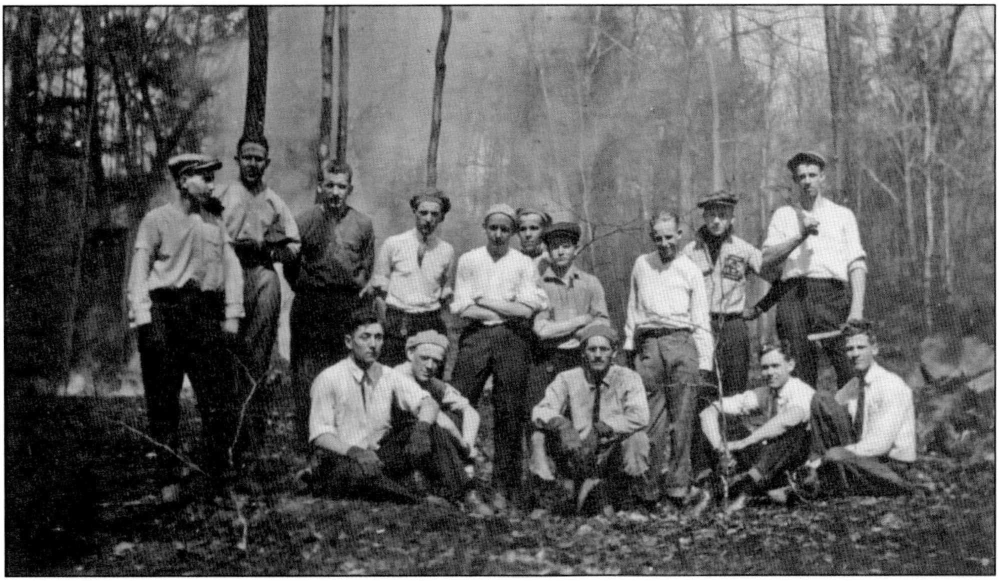

The Hundred Acre Lot on Curtis Street was purchased in 1913–1914 by the School Park Association. To start the campaign to save this native woodland, the 1913 Jamestown High School graduating class gave $100. Community leaders signed a bank note for the purchase money, which halted lumbering. Children brought their pennies, and within two years, 52 acres were turned over to the school board. Senior boys helped during the "Brush Burning Bee." (Courtesy of FHC.)

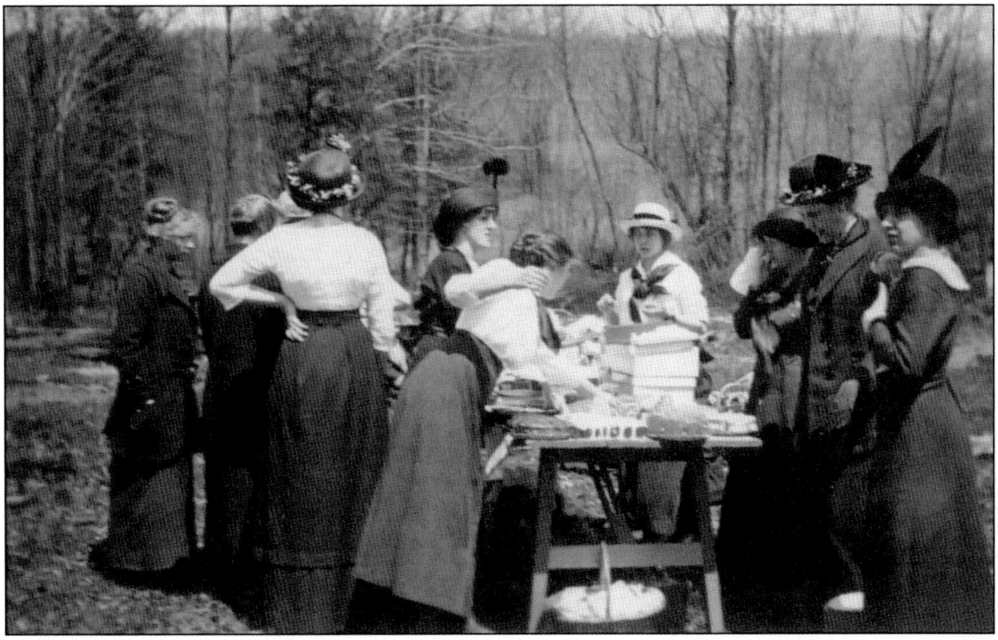

During the Brush Burning Bee, this group of senior high girls is wondering what is keeping the boys from arriving for the lunch the girls and their teachers have prepared. School children of all ages purchased this land, and many generations have enjoyed it. Many school outings and family picnics have taken place here, enabling participants to explore nature near the city. (Courtesy of FHC.)

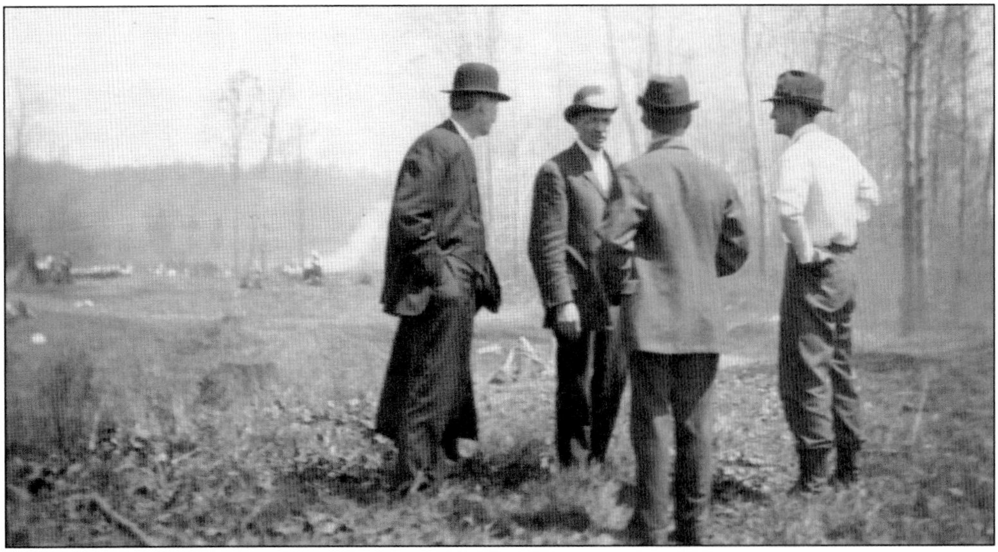

During the Brush Burning Bee, Arthur Amidon, Milton J. Fletcher, George Persell, and an unidentified man are having a meeting. Both Fletcher and Persell were superintendents of Jamestown Public Schools and had schools named for them. The Hundred Acre Lot is now owned and maintained by Jamestown Community College. Officially known as College Park, it is still the Hundred Acre Lot to many. (Courtesy of FHC.)

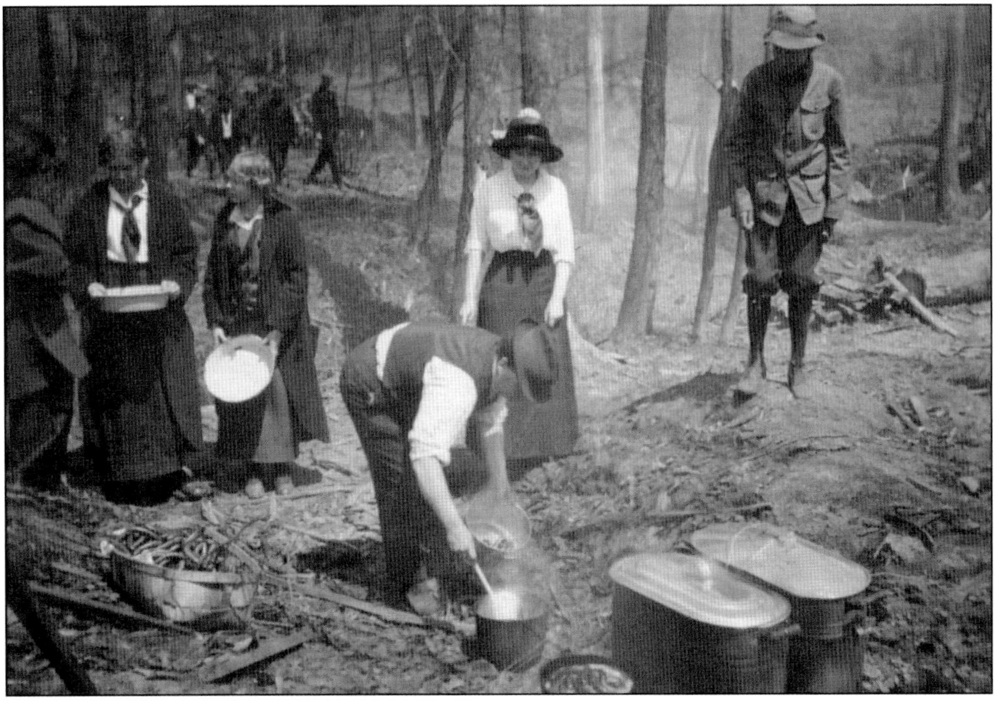

While senior high boys and Boy Scouts worked during the Brush Burning Bee at the Hundred Acre Lot, others were busy preparing lunch. An unidentified man is stirring the pot while being watched by Boy Scout Gerald Bodine. The bee helped ready the Hundred Acre Lot so that school groups and the public could enjoy a clean but wooded area for picnics and nature study. (Courtesy of FHC.)

Seven

Police and Fire

Early Jamestown did not have a police department. The town seldom needed a peace officer or the sheriff's office, which handled policing matters throughout the county. Early Jamestown did have a volunteer fire department. As early as 1827, in the village charter, future fire departments were established. Also, it gave the village trustees power to require "all inhabitants or owners of dwelling houses or businesses . . . to provide themselves . . . with fire buckets, to be ready . . . for the purpose of extinguishing fires." In June 1827, a fire company was formed, and a tax raised money for a fire engine and a firehouse. At the time, men pulled the fire engines to the fire and pumped water from the reservoir of the engine onto the fire by hand. These men—and the men who formed subsequent fire companies—worked very hard responding to fires. The fire companies had dinners, dances, and other fundraisers through the years to support the firehouse and buy equipment. They were all volunteers until the 1890s, when the city paid the drivers of the new horse-drawn fire wagons.

Photographs of fires were popular items and were readily transformed into postcards during the postcard era. There are many postcards of fires and firemen but few postcards of police and police work. Fires can be spectacular to see; police arresting someone may not be as dramatic.

There is only one postcard of the Jamestown police, and the past historian for the police department had not seen it. There are a number of postcards of fires and of the volunteer fire departments' horse-drawn equipment. Photographs were taken of the new equipment and the horses in the late 1890s. At that time, the men no longer had to pull the equipment to the fire, so the horses were of great interest and a source of pride as the fire companies acquired them.

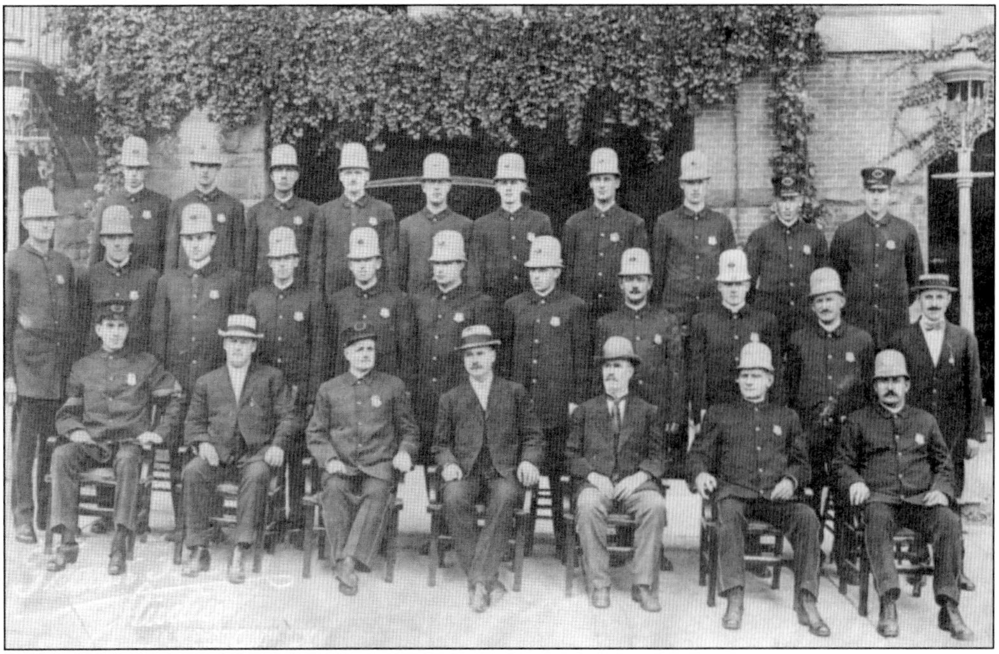

The night watch, which began as early as the 1850s, had the primary duty of watching for fires. When Jamestown was incorporated as a city, a police department with a chief and six men was organized. The English bobby-style hats indicate this photograph was taken before 1914, which is the year the department changed to the Pershing-style hats. (Courtesy of FHC.)

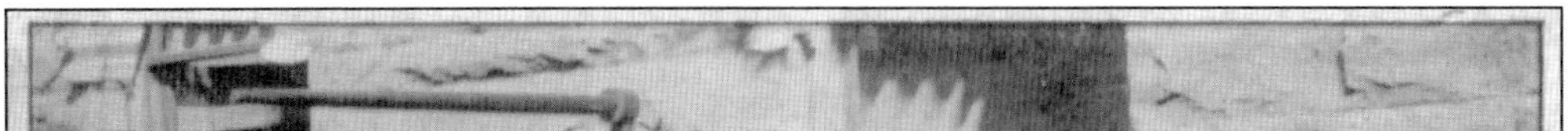

Incorporated in 1827, the village of Jamestown's charter called for fire wardens and all homes and businesses to have fire buckets. A tax raised money to purchase a fire engine and equipment and build an engine house. In August 1829, the fire engine was ordered, and Fire Company No. 1 was formed. The engine was named *Active*. It operated until 1859, when it became a standby unit. (Courtesy of FHC.)

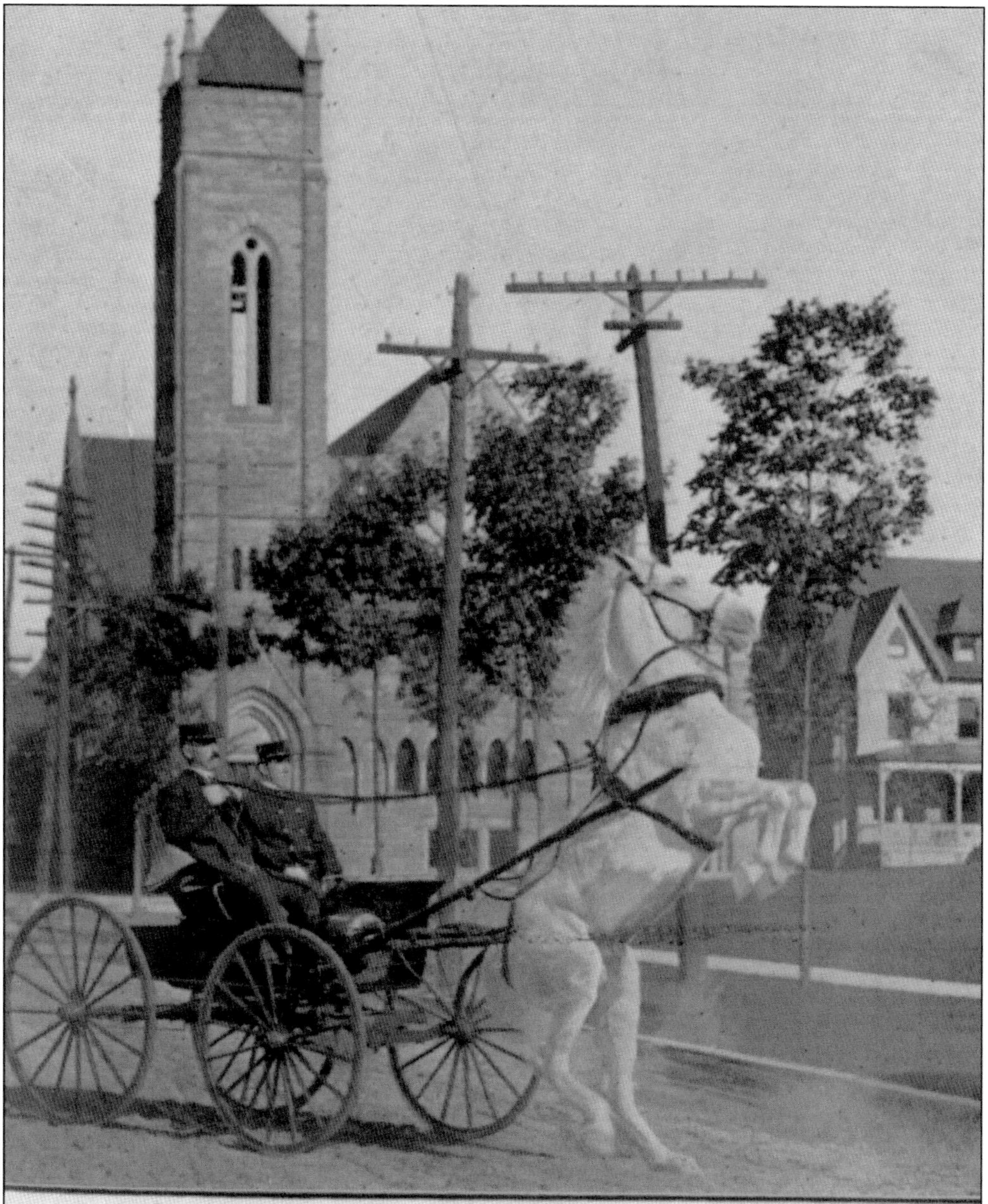

"Don" in Action—Jamestown Fire Department.

Fred Wilson was chief of the fire department from 1898 to 1915. He led the department from a volunteer status to a paid, professional department. By 1898, it was changing to horse-drawn equipment, and it would become motorized while he was chief. Here, he is seen with his horse Don on Sixth Street with SS. Peter and Paul Church and Rectory in the background.

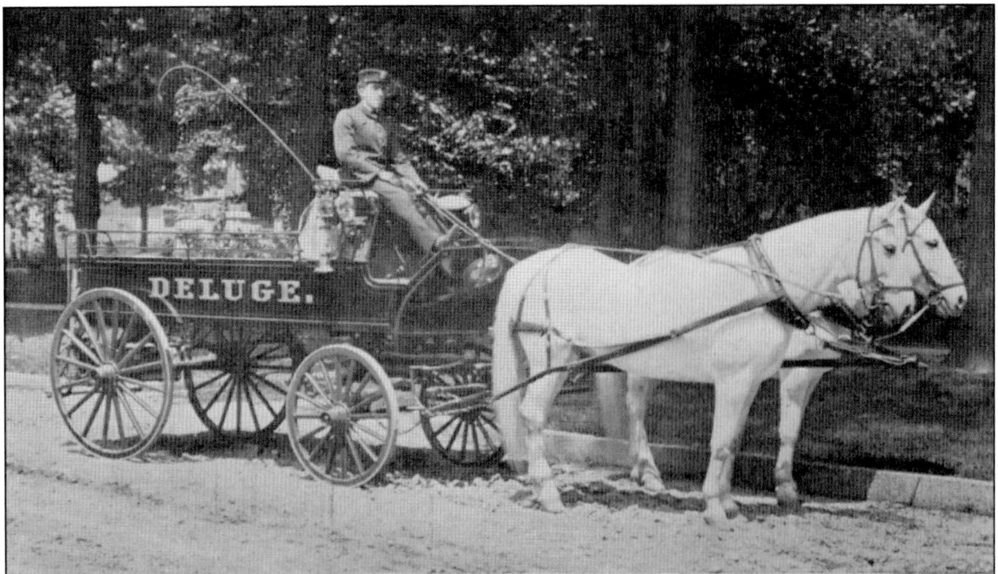

Deluge Engine Company, No. 1, Jamestown, N. Y.

Engine Company No. 1, which was formed in 1829, became the Deluge Engine Company No. 1, named for its 1859 engine. Its first horse-drawn fire wagon, locally made by John Herby Wagon Works, was also used by police to pick up those who were intoxicated and as an ambulance. The first paid driver, James Lynch, started in October 1896. In 1910, first assistant foreman Alfred E. Shoesmith became the first member of the department to die in service.

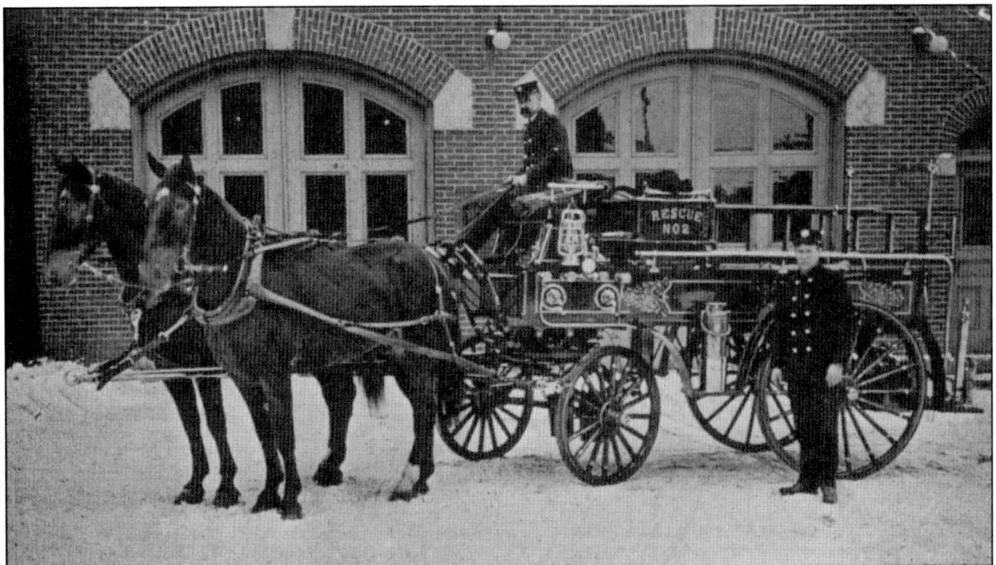

Rescue Engine Company, No. 2, Jamestown, N. Y.

Activated in 1843 as Engine Company No. 2, this company took the name Rescue from the engine it received in 1859. In 1893, it purchased a team of horses and its first hose wagon, made in Jamestown by John Herby. Frank A. Anderson was hired as the driver. This postcard shows the 1908 Holloway chemical-hose wagon. Rescue Engine Company No. 2 was located in three different firehouses during its 52 years of service.

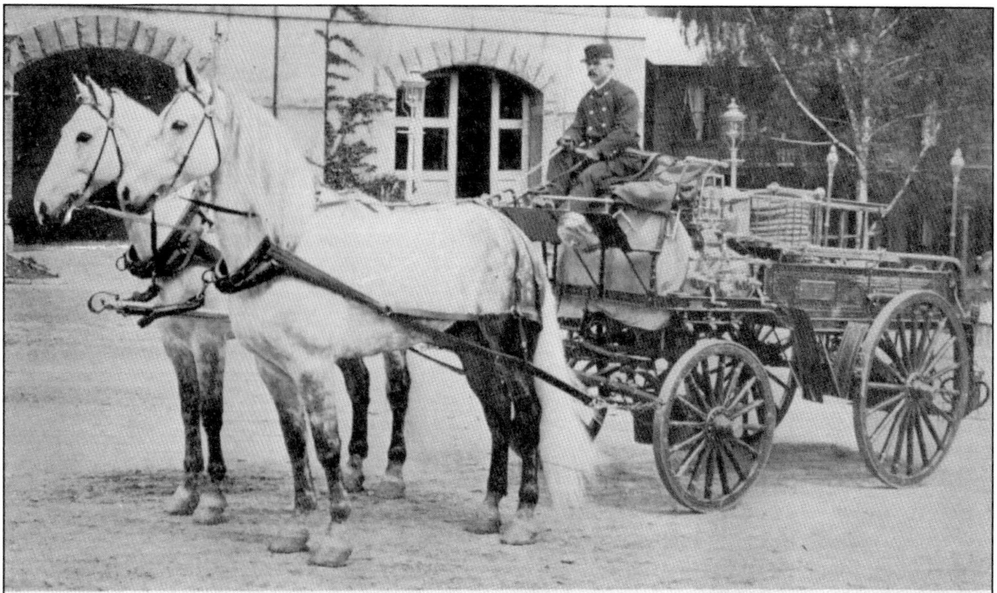

Prendergast Hose Company, No. 1, Jamestown, N. Y.

Beginning in 1873 as City Hose Company No. 1, by 1874, this company became the Prendergast Hose Company No. 1. Its first horse-drawn fire wagon was introduced in 1896. Walter Saxton was the driver. Just two years later, the company received the city's first chemical-hose wagon, seen in this postcard. This was the last horse-drawn equipment used by the paid department, which is answering a fire alarm on July 6, 1927.

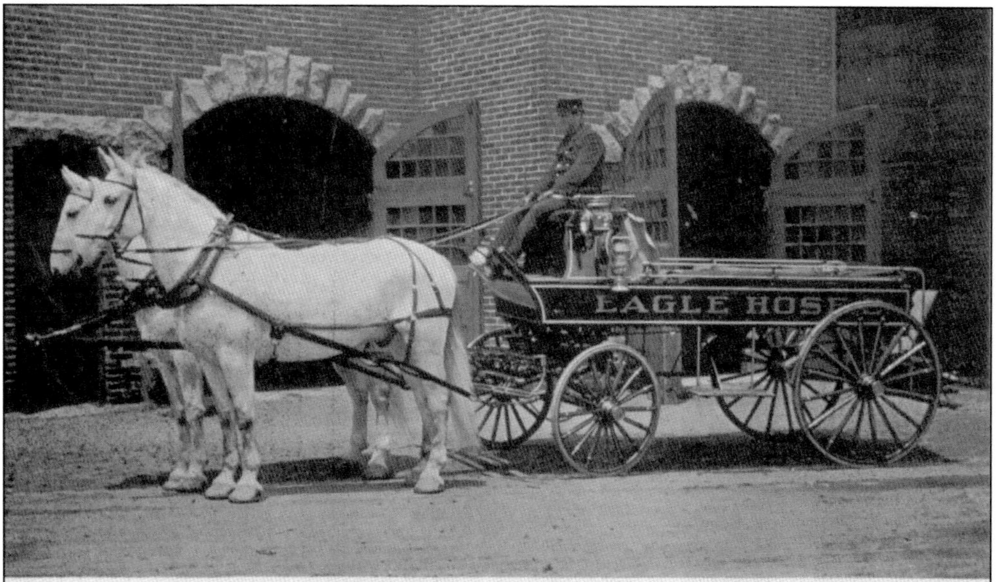

Eagle Hose Company, No. 2, Jamestown, N. Y.

Eagle Hose Company No. 2, located near Brooklyn Square, began in 1873. It received its horse-drawn Herby hose wagon 22 years later. Augustus Olson was its first paid driver. In 1899, the company received the first steamer in the city and continued to use the Herby wagon. The three-story firehouse, the largest of the volunteer firehouses, included a three-story fireman's sliding pole.

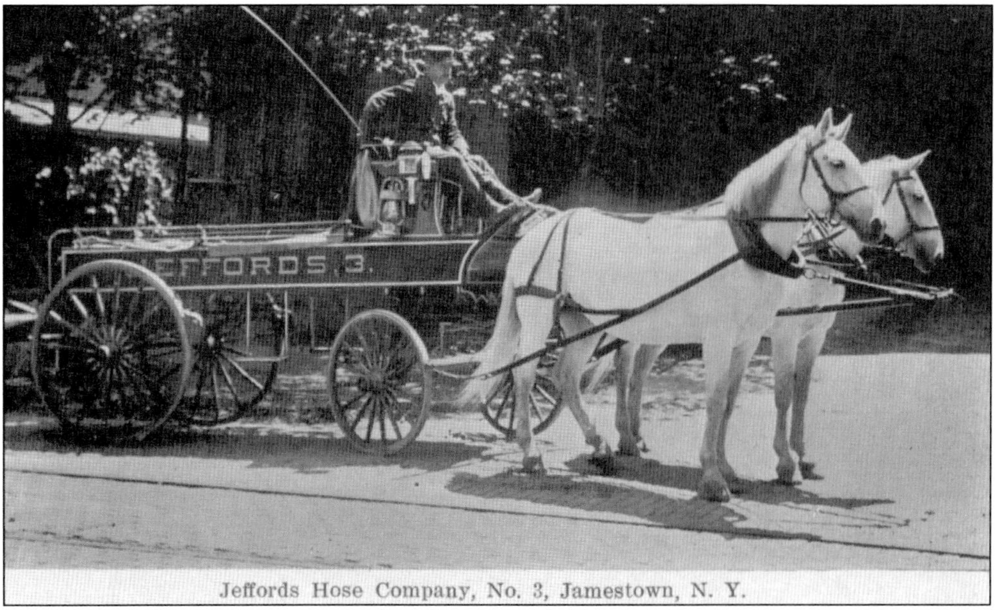

Jeffords Hose Company No. 3, located in East Jamestown, was accepted by the city in 1883. It was given an old hose reel and some other equipment. In 1896, the company received its first horse-drawn Herby hose wagon. Its paid driver was Ullman S. Ayers. Like some other firehouses, Jeffords firehouse, on East Second Street, had a large ballroom where dances and banquets were held.

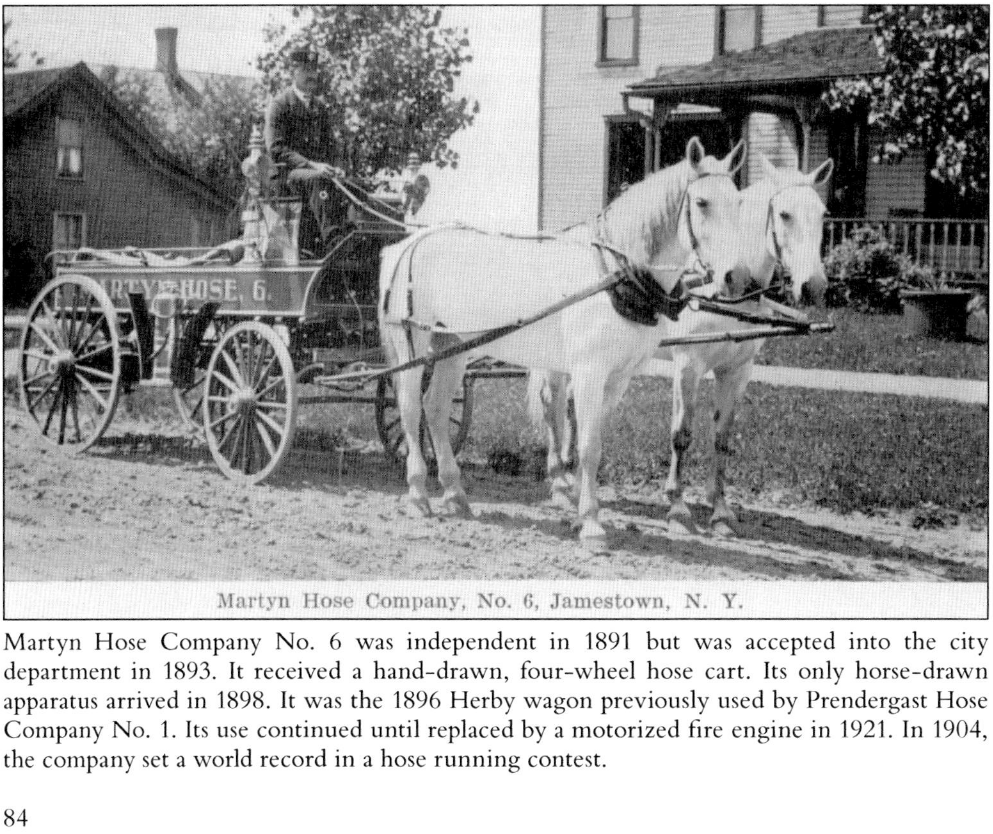

Martyn Hose Company No. 6 was independent in 1891 but was accepted into the city department in 1893. It received a hand-drawn, four-wheel hose cart. Its only horse-drawn apparatus arrived in 1898. It was the 1896 Herby wagon previously used by Prendergast Hose Company No. 1. Its use continued until replaced by a motorized fire engine in 1921. In 1904, the company set a world record in a hose running contest.

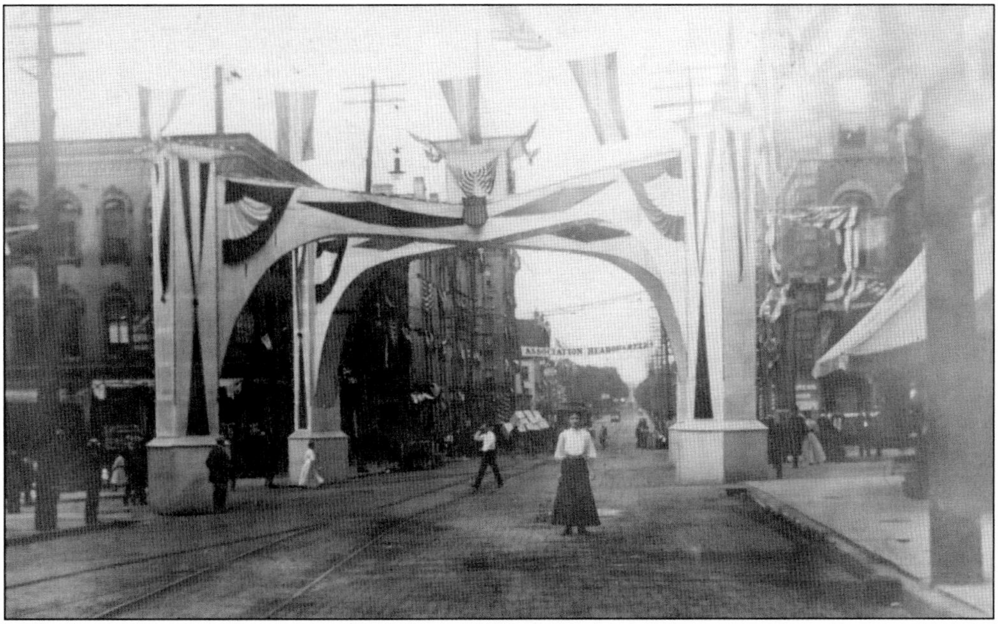

During the late 19th century and the early 20th century, arches were popular for many events, celebrations, or parades. This arch is at the intersection of Third and North Main Streets. It is for the August 1906 New York State Firemen's Association Convention. Many buildings were decorated with flags and bunting. A banner across Third Street identifies the association's headquarters, which was probably the New Sherman House. (Courtesy of FHC.)

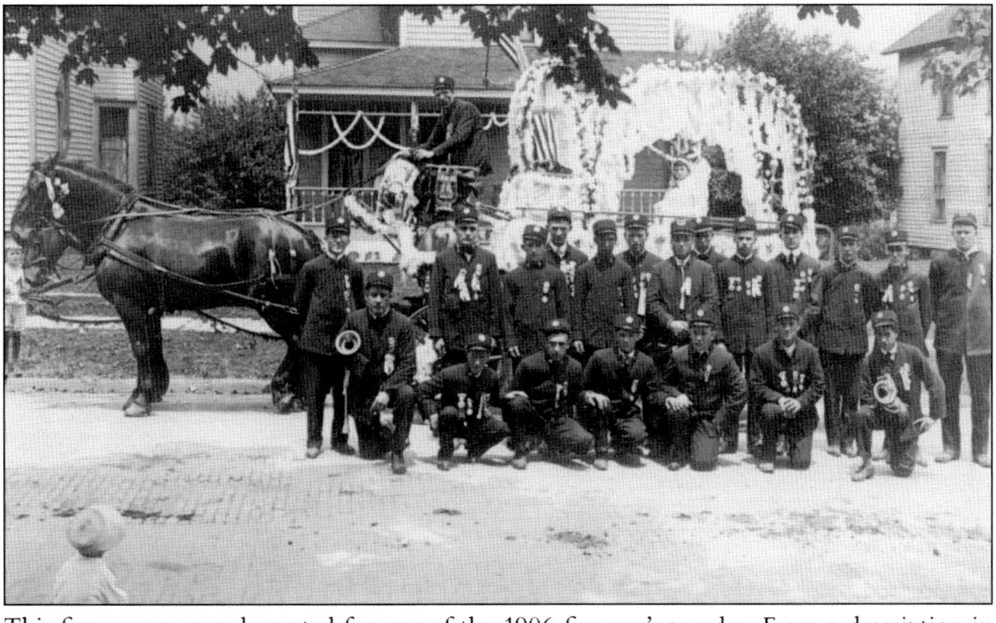

This fire wagon was decorated for one of the 1906 fireman's parades. From a description in an article about the convention, this is probably a visiting fire company from Fredonia. The description was of a decorated fire wagon with a little girl riding in it. Of the assembled firemen, two appear to be holding fire trumpets, which were used at a fire to call out orders. (Courtesy of FHC.)

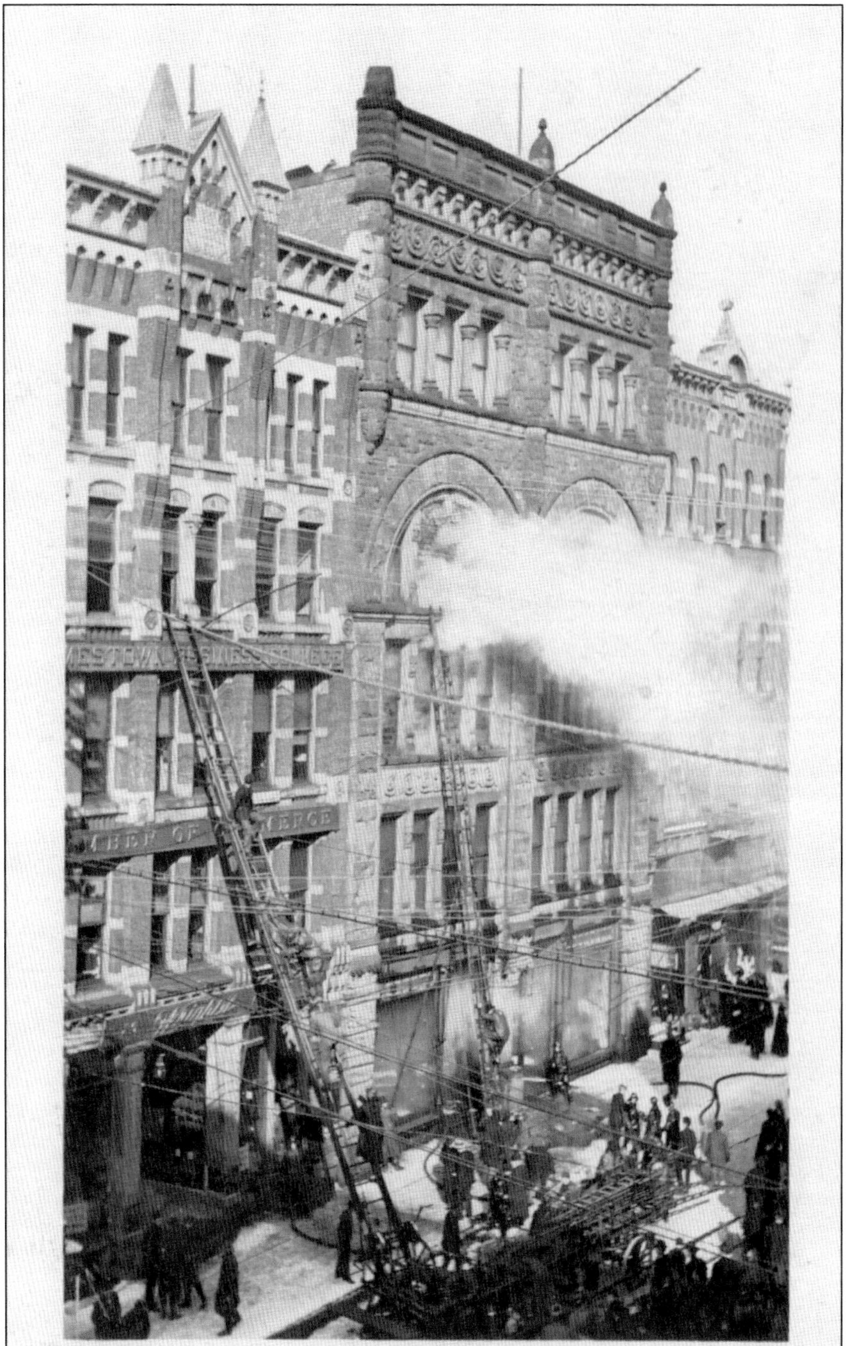

On the afternoon of February 17, 1909, a lighted match head flew into a quantity of cotton batting in the basement of the Gokey Block on West Third Street. The smoke from the fire drove all occupants of the building out, most by fire escape and ladder. Some found their way over iron bridges to neighboring buildings. The Duffee store in the center, where the fire started, was the most heavily damaged.

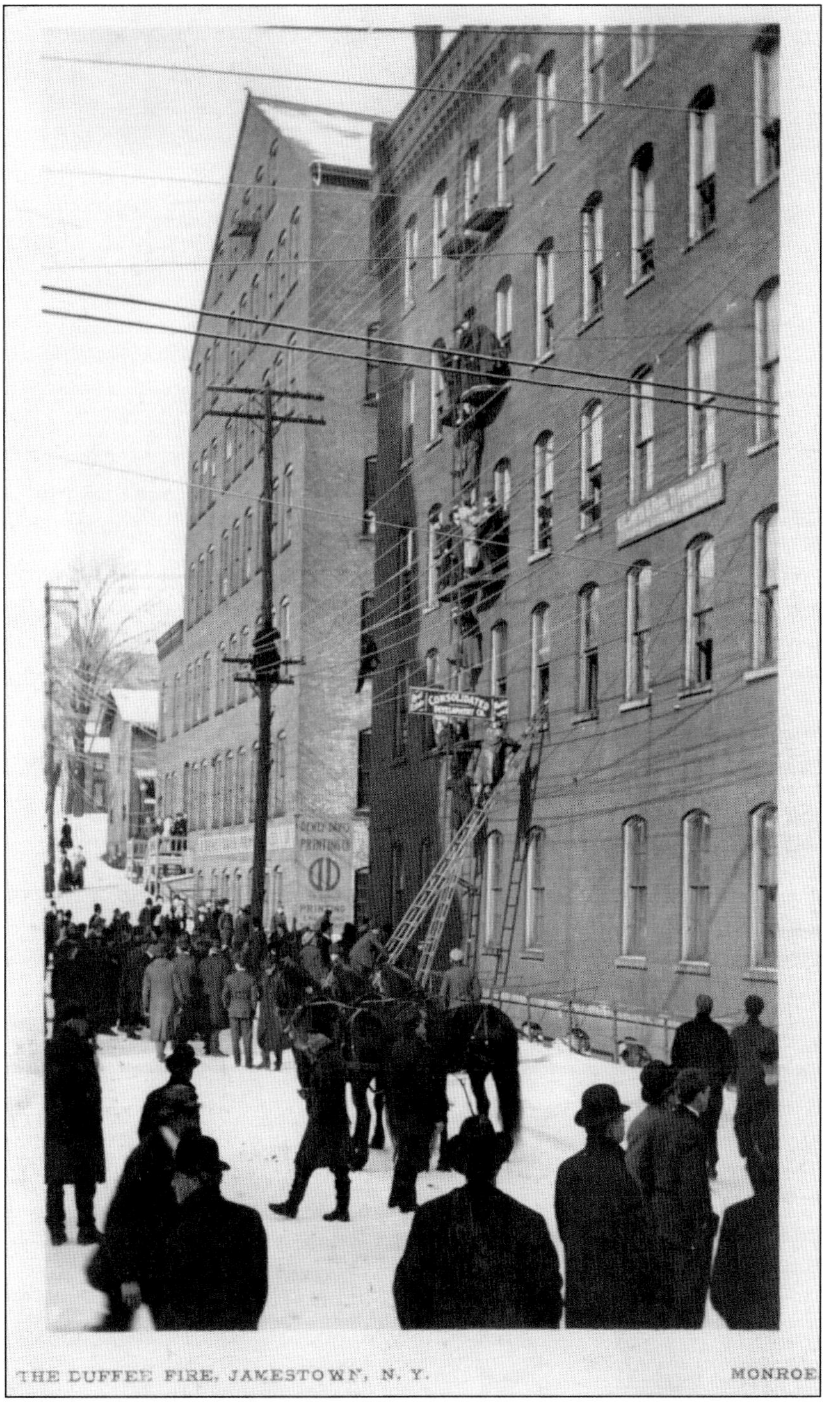

On the Cherry Street side of the Gokey Block, the 125 students of Jamestown Business College and some other occupants climbed down the fire escapes and the firemen's ladders to escape the smoke-filled stairways. The other large building in the background was the Gokey Shoe Factory, which rented space to many other businesses and industries. The afternoon event attracted many observers to the downtown area. (Courtesy of FHC.)

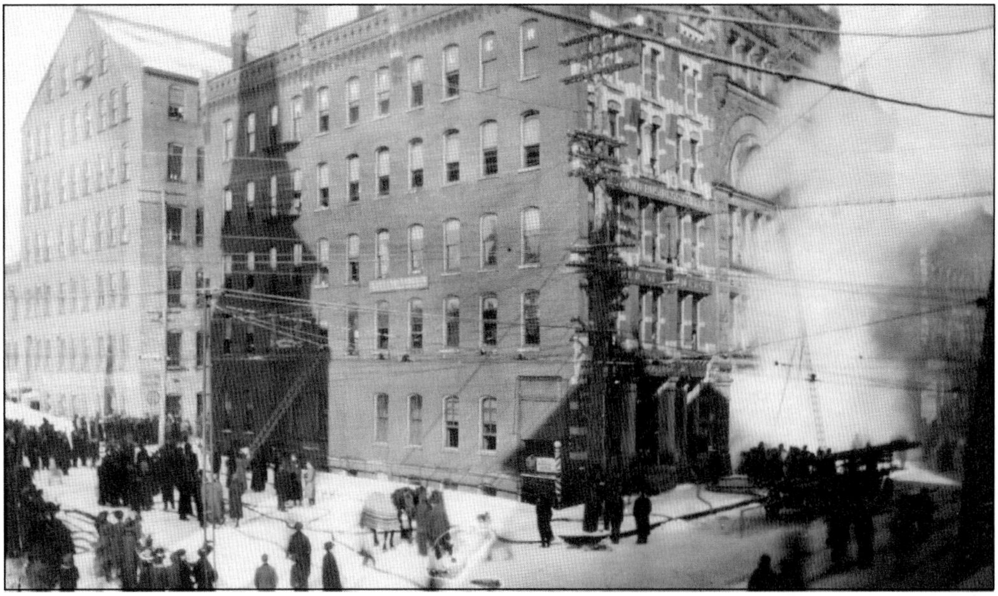

This view shows the two Gokey buildings as smoke continues to pour from the Third Street side. The snow was not deep enough to hinder the rescue efforts. The shadow cast on the building is that of the First Presbyterian Church steeple. This view is taken later than the previous picture of the escape, denoted by the shadow that has moved as the sun advances westward. (Courtesy of FHC.)

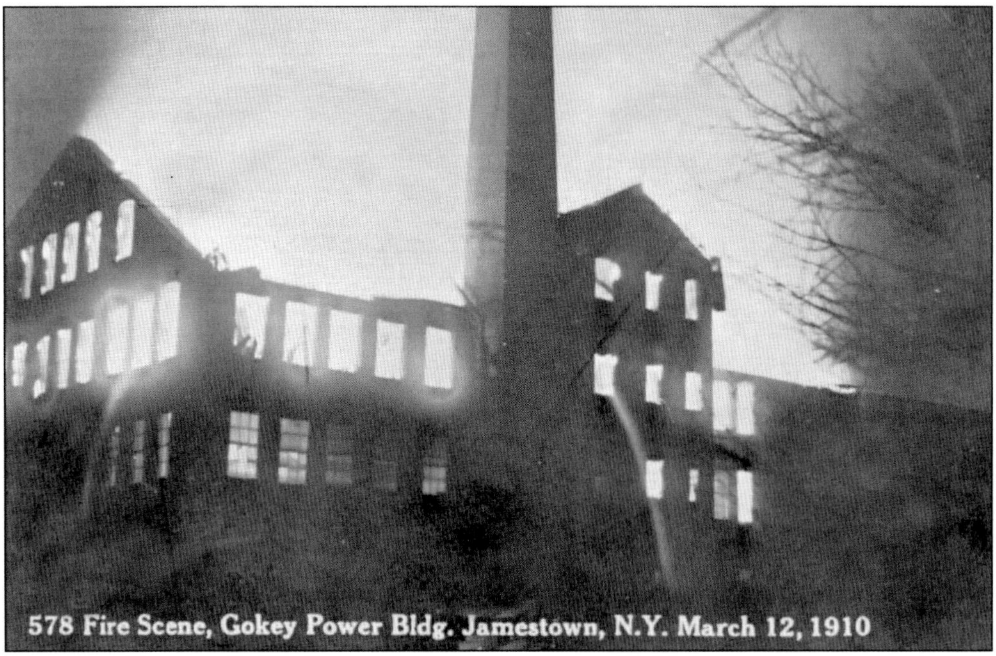

Just 13 months after the Duffee fire, volunteer firemen responded to flames that were showing in the top southeast corner of the Gokey Shoe Factory. The seven-story building burned through the night, but other buildings were spared. Fireman Alfred Shoesmith died after falling through a hole in the fifth floor that had been made by the water tank that fell through to the third floor from the roof.

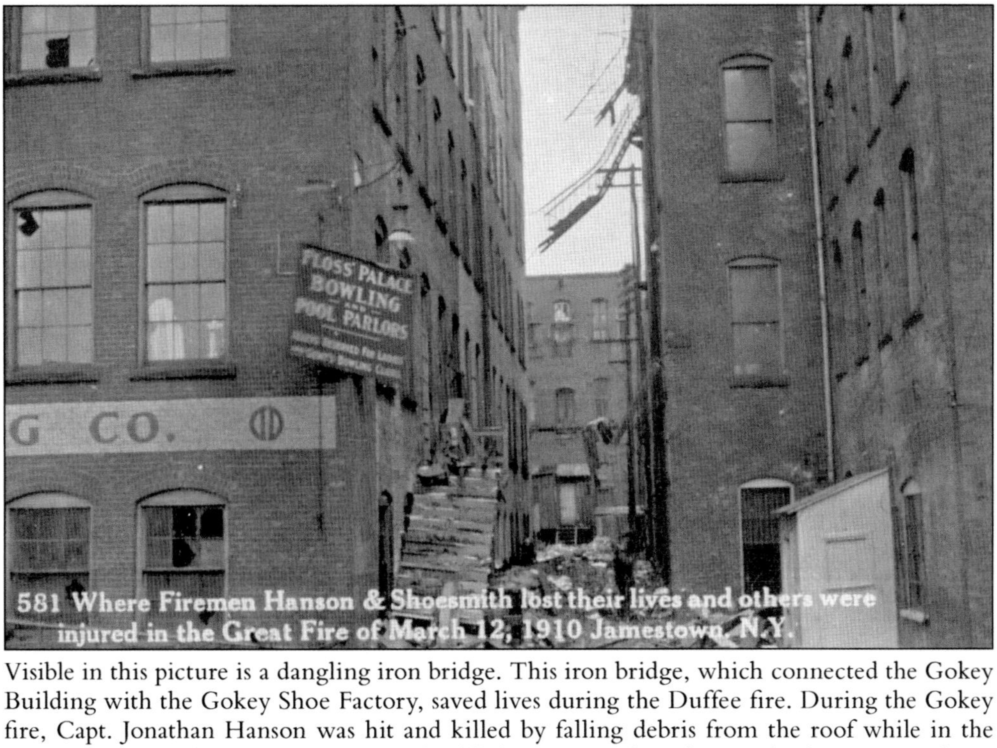

581 Where Firemen Hanson & Shoesmith lost their lives and others were injured in the Great Fire of March 12, 1910 Jamestown, N.Y.

Visible in this picture is a dangling iron bridge. This iron bridge, which connected the Gokey Building with the Gokey Shoe Factory, saved lives during the Duffee fire. During the Gokey fire, Capt. Jonathan Hanson was hit and killed by falling debris from the roof while in the alley. Fireman Joel Oberg was injured; he fell five stories when the iron bridge was torn loose by falling debris.

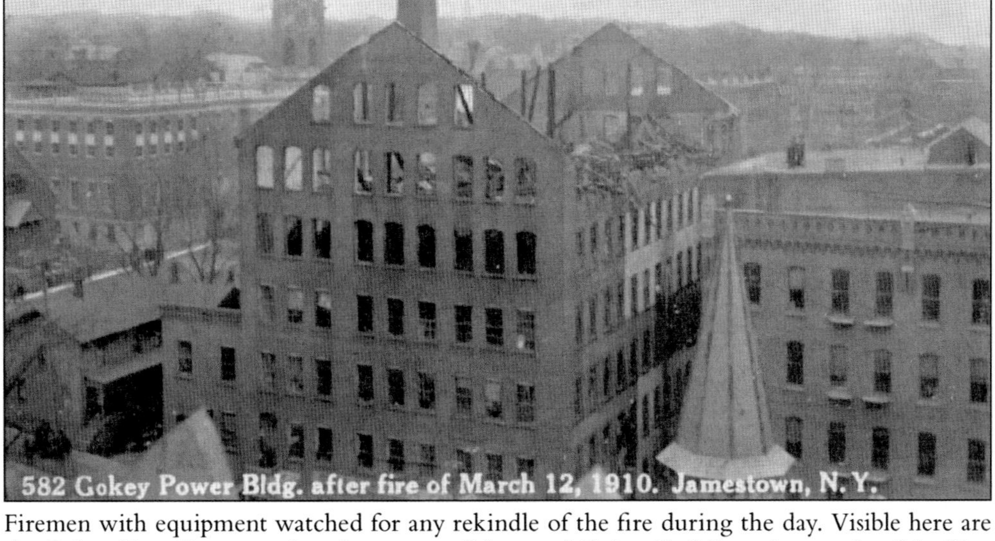

582 Gokey Power Bldg. after fire of March 12, 1910. Jamestown, N.Y.

Firemen with equipment watched for any rekindle of the fire during the day. Visible here are the Gokey Shoe Factory ruins, the corner of the saved Gokey Building, the steeple of the First Presbyterian Church, and the city beyond. Besides the Gokey shoe and boot business, the fire displaced and destroyed equipment of Dahlstrom Metallic Door, Gurney Ball Bearing, two textile-manufacturing companies, and a few other businesses.

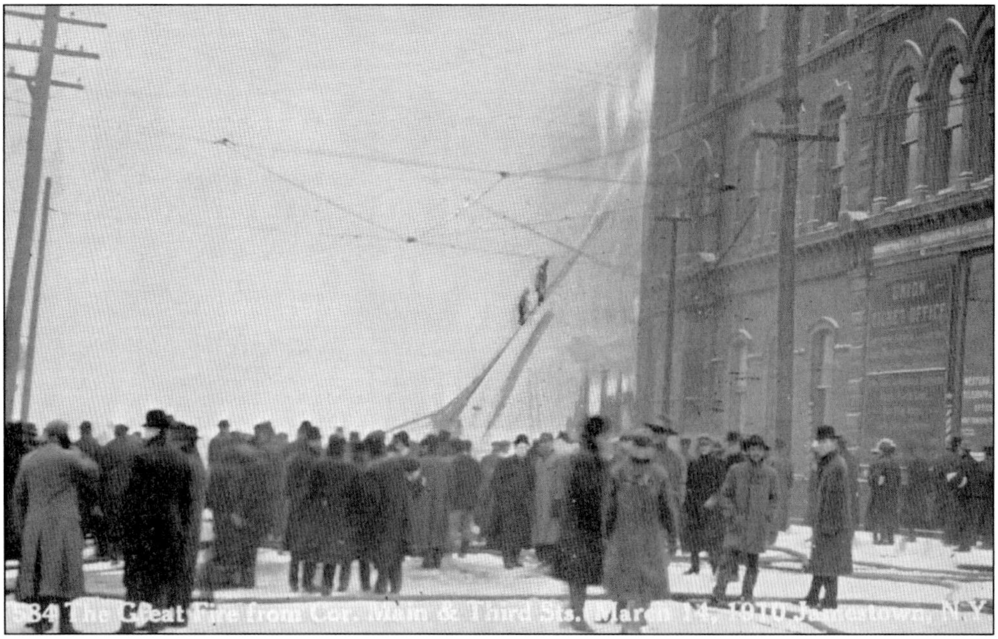

Ladders were hoisted, but not to rescue people from a burning building. This time, firemen used the ladders to bring hoses closer to the fires. Despite precautions, hot spots flared up, fanned by shifting winds. The flames, spotted by policemen on the beat, erupted before firemen arrived. Crowds gathered for a second night as the fire consumed the Gokey Block, crossed West Third Street, and leveled the New Sherman House.

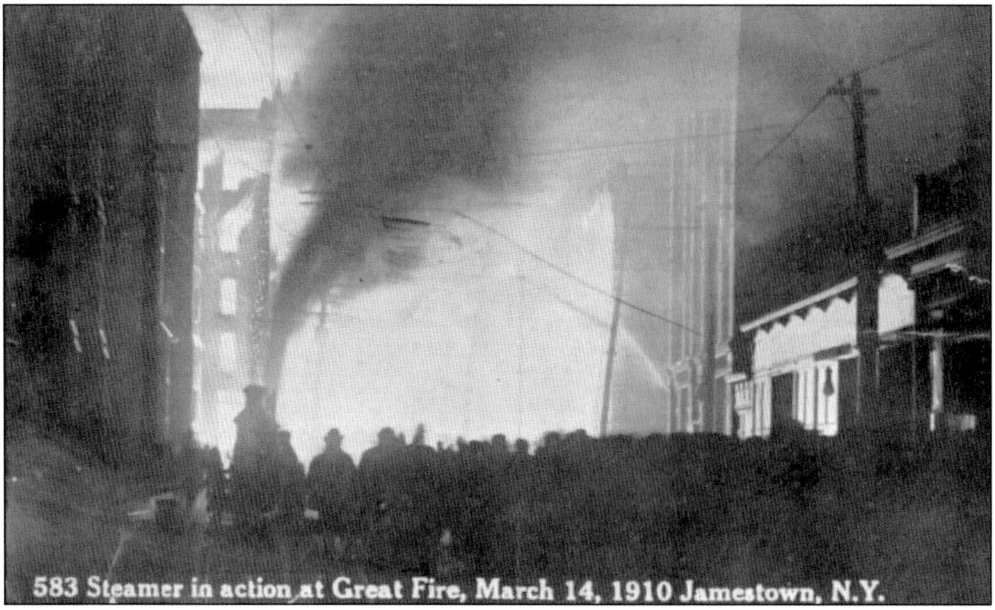

The steam-powered pumper acquired in 1899 by the Eagle Hose Company No. 2 was stationed in Brooklyn Square. Proving itself during the 1910 fire, a second steamer was added to the paid department in 1911. The Gokey fire was the impetus for Jamestown to switch from volunteers to a paid fire department in 1911. Neighboring fire departments sent help, and even Buffalo was preparing to send men and equipment.

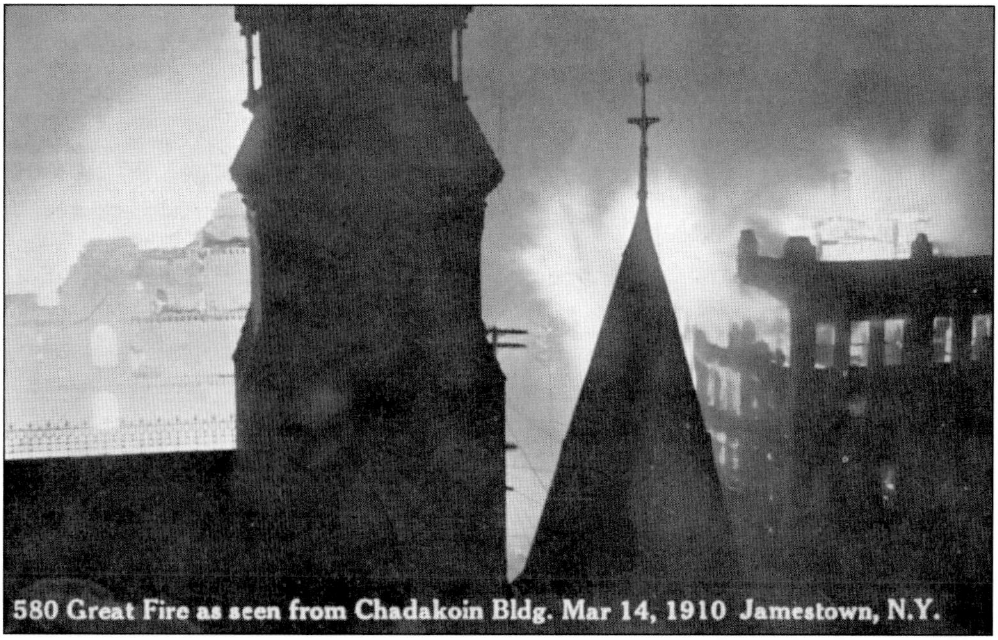

580 Great Fire as seen from Chadakoin Bldg. Mar 14, 1910 Jamestown, N.Y.

When the fire rekindled, winds took it south through the Gokey Building, across the street, and into the New Sherman House. Flames coming out of the top-floor windows of the New Sherman House were caught by the photographer while a safe distance away. Taken from the Chadakoin Building, the silhouettes of the steeple and tower of the First Presbyterian Church block the view of some of the fire.

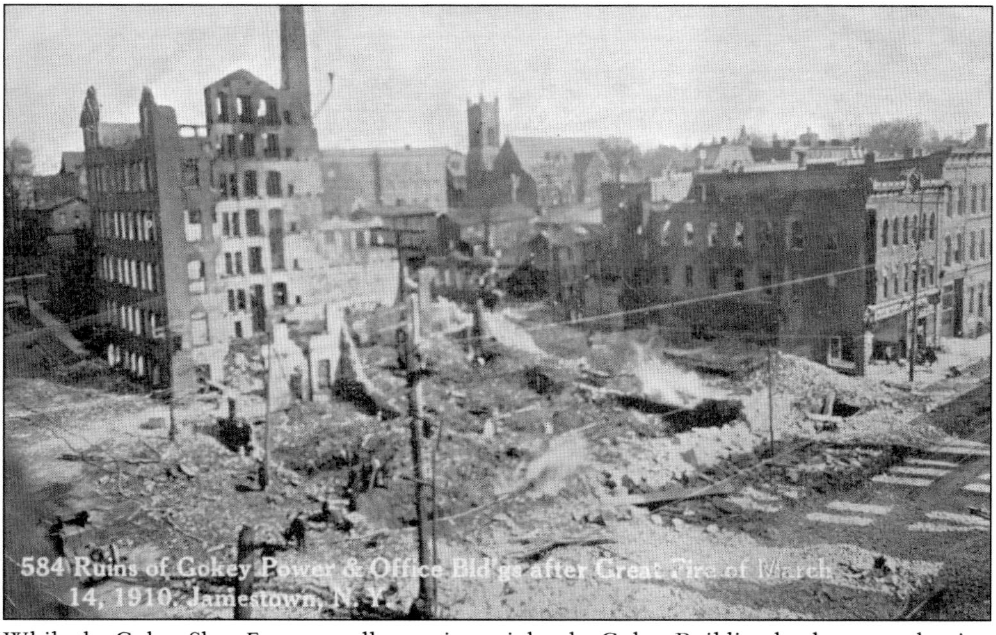

584 Ruins of Gokey Power & Office Bld'gs after Great Fire of March 14, 1910. Jamestown, N.Y.

While the Gokey Shoe Factory walls remain upright, the Gokey Building has been razed, using dynamite to take some of it down. The photograph may have been taken on March 15, 1910, as told by the shadow across West Third Street cast by the burned-out New Sherman House. The razing of the remaining walls of the New Sherman House began the next morning.

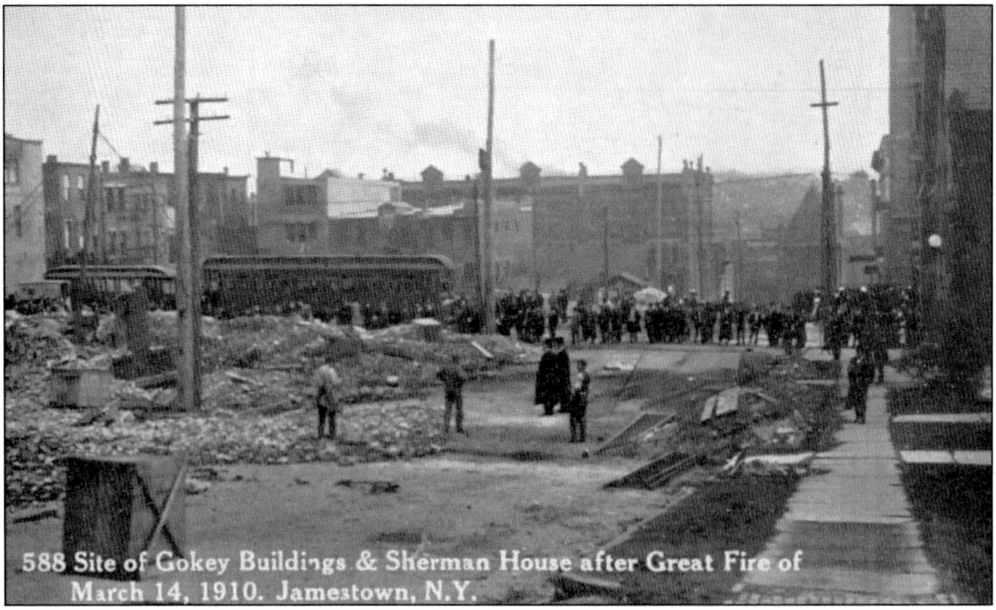

The site of the great Gokey fire was a magnet for many who came to look. This is after the fire-gutted structures had been razed and the trolley line restored to service through the area. The early estimate was more than a half-million dollars in losses. Adjacent buildings suffered smoke and water damage, adding to the total loss. (Courtesy of FHC.)

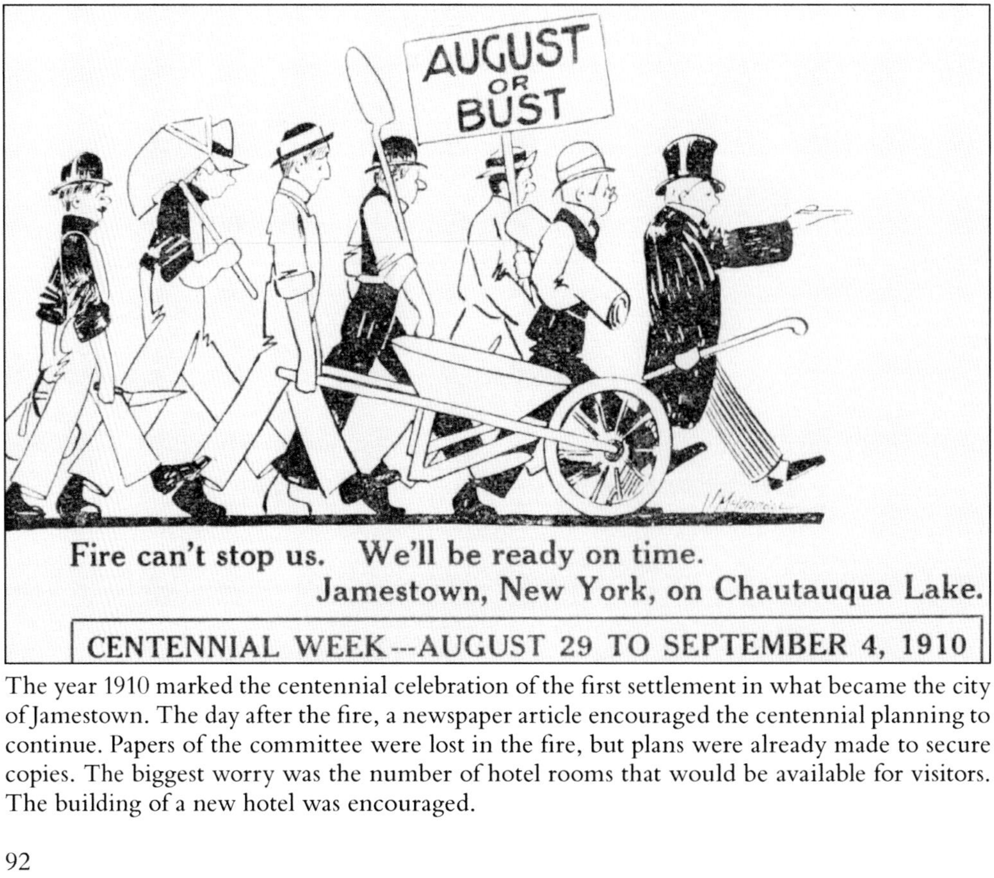

The year 1910 marked the centennial celebration of the first settlement in what became the city of Jamestown. The day after the fire, a newspaper article encouraged the centennial planning to continue. Papers of the committee were lost in the fire, but plans were already made to secure copies. The biggest worry was the number of hotel rooms that would be available for visitors. The building of a new hotel was encouraged.

Eight

Business and Industry

Jamestown began with lumbering. Wood was a readily available commodity in addition to farm land. Even before much farming could take place, trees had to be cut down to prepare the land for farming. The sawmill was the early industry, transforming logs into lumber to build houses, barns, and whatever settlers may need. Waterpower ran the sawmill and then the gristmill to grind the grain for farmers. Early settlers had the skills a frontier community needed, such as the blacksmith, the potter, and the merchant to keep a store. The abundance of wood helped to establish an early furniture industry, especially the production of chairs.

When the train arrived in Jamestown in 1860, the ability to ship products faster gave a boost to the economy and increased production. Entrepreneurship was alive and well in Jamestown. With the help of successful businessmen and local banks, many small companies were started.

By the late 1800s, many wood furniture factories were in operation. The textile industry was in full swing, with a number of mills producing worsted fabric and other auxiliary industries producing yarn and towels. Metal furniture was produced by the Fenton Metallic Manufacturing Company by 1890. They also produced bicycles for a few years and were closely allied with the new industry that produced the mechanical-lever voting machine. Fenton Metallic Manufacturing became Art Metal Company, which produced metal office furniture but also outfitted more than 300 ships before and during World War I and shipped products around the world. Crescent Tool Company produced the world-famous Crescent wrench and other tools. Blackstone made washing machines, Alhstrom's made pianos, and Dahlstrom made fireproof doors and other building components.

Besides the industry, businesses—from stores to restaurants to hotels—supported the community. For all the factories and different businesses, not many appeared on postcards. Normally, postcard images were of the places people visited, and factories were not the views preferred by visitors. Businesses did use postcards for advertising, and some of the postcards here are examples of such.

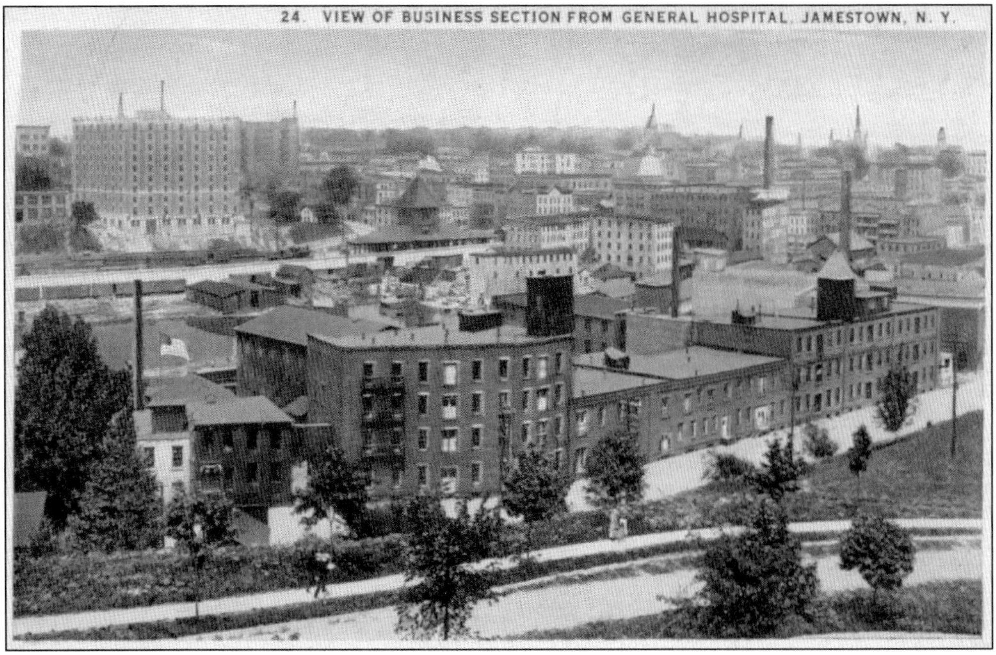

Overlooking Jamestown from Jones Hill, the buildings in the foreground are on Steele Street. At one time, those buildings housed the Jamestown Wood Seat Chair Company and the Jamestown Bedstead Company. Later, Tillottson Furniture Company was located there. In the back, near the left, is the Furniture Exposition Building, built in 1917. Left of center, with the pointed-roof tower, is the train station at the foot of Cherry Street.

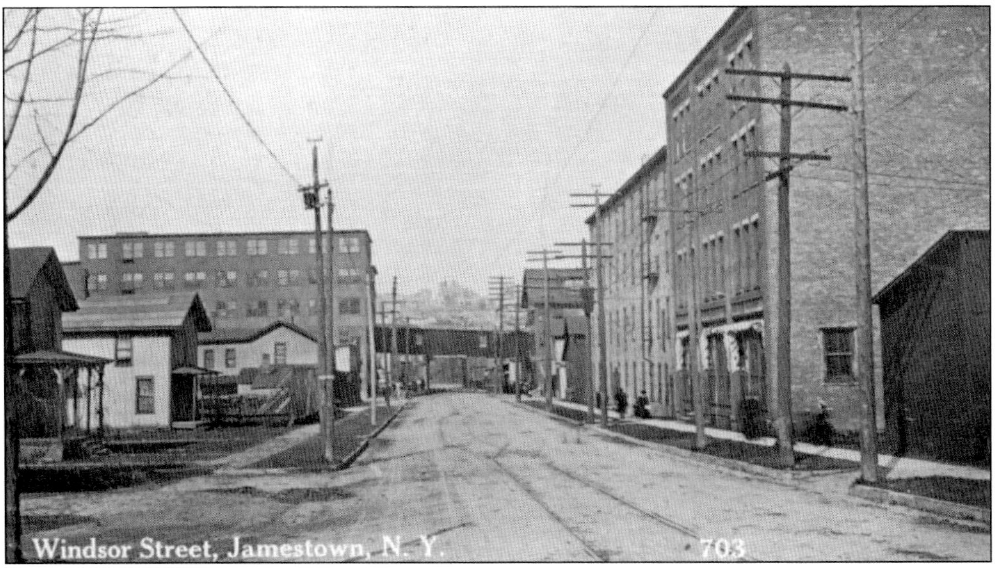

Looking from the corner of Water and Windsor Streets, the large building on the left is the Bailey Furniture Company. The iron bridge spanning Windsor Street connected to another Bailey Furniture Company building at the corner of Windsor and Harrison Streets. The company changed names as owners changed. In 1891, Maddox and Bailey moved to this location, and it was called Maddox, Bailey & Company. In 1898, it became Bailey, Jones Company, then Bailey Table Company by 1912.

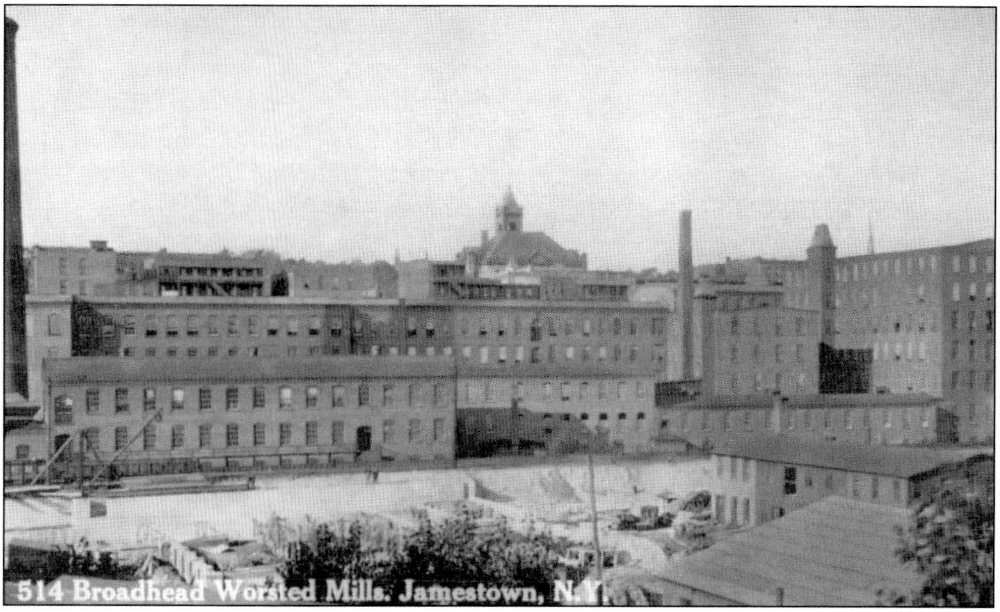

William Broadhead, visiting his boyhood home in England, saw the successful textile industry in 1872. Back in Jamestown, he established a textile mill, importing equipment and labor from England. In 1875, he established Broadhead Worsted Mills on First Street; it grew to include 12 buildings and employ 1,200 workers by 1900. Some buildings still stand, including the 175-feet-high brick chimney, seen on the extreme left.

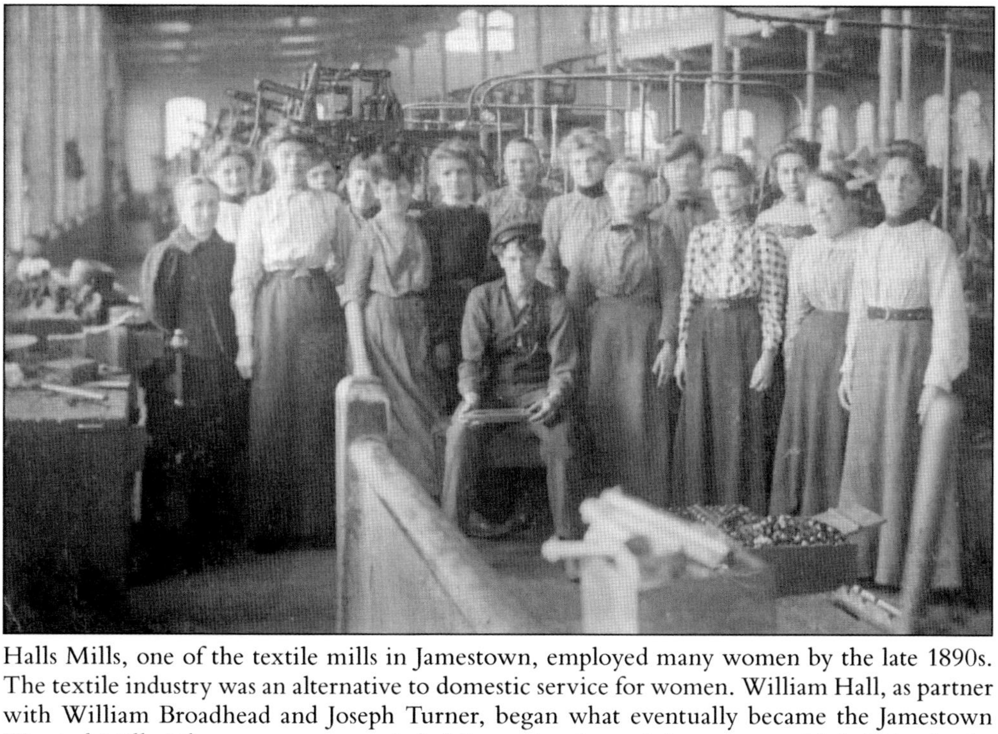

Halls Mills, one of the textile mills in Jamestown, employed many women by the late 1890s. The textile industry was an alternative to domestic service for women. William Hall, as partner with William Broadhead and Joseph Turner, began what eventually became the Jamestown Worsted Mills. The one young man is holding a shuttle, and the women with bobbins in the foreground may be of the spinning department. (Courtesy of FHC.)

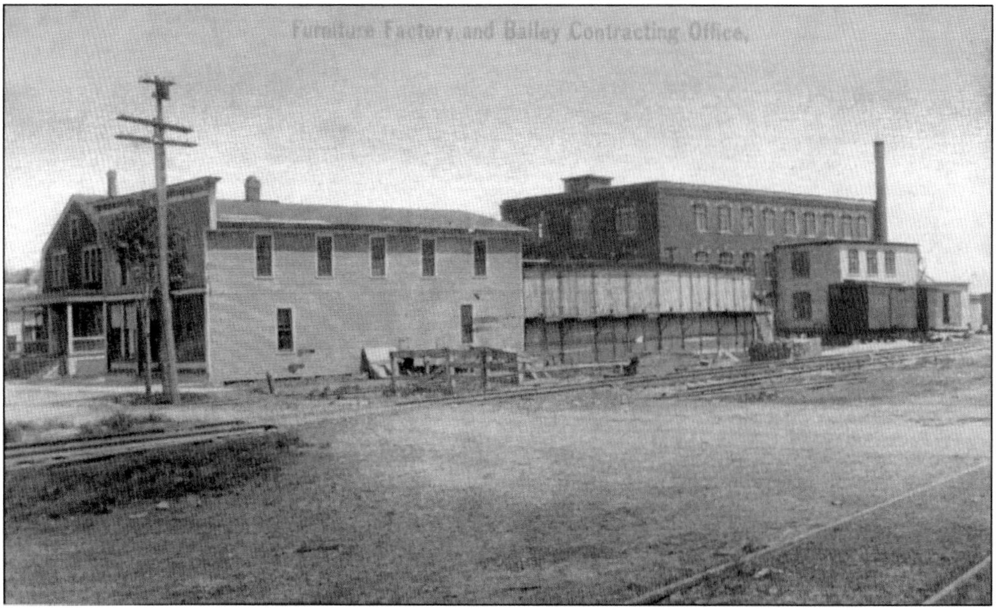

Maddox, Bailey & Company was located at 560 East Second Street until the shop burned. In March 1891, it relocated to Windsor Street in the old Breed Company buildings. Within two years, it was employing almost 200 men at an average wage of $1.75 per day. In 1898, the company changed names to the Bailey, Jones Company. In about 1912, it became known as the Bailey Table Company.

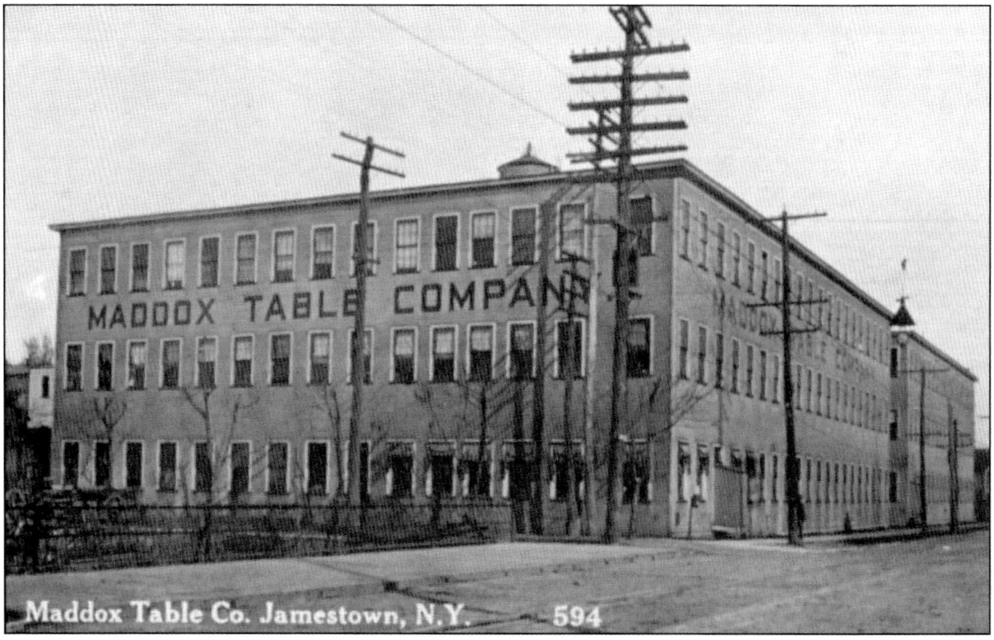

The Maddox Table Company, founded in 1898, continued for more than 85 years at its first location at 101-125 Harrison Street. This large, wooden building was not far from Brooklyn Square and only lost part of its top floor to a tornado in 1945. William Maddox invented a machine that could produce a top-quality tabletop without the labor-intensive hand rubbing. This contributed to the long success of the company. (Courtesy of FHC.)

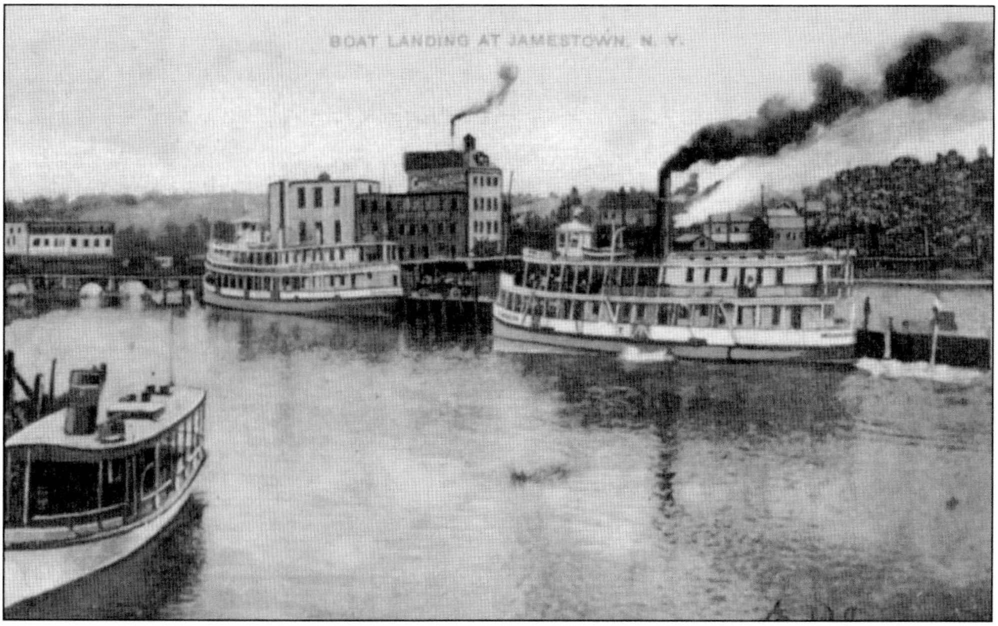

The boat landing area included some industries as well as the usual docks and ticket offices. In the background is the Jamestown Brewery. The steamboats transported passengers and some freight but were used in the early season to pull rafts of logs to the sawmills in Jamestown to supply numerous furniture factories. Lumber was sometimes hauled back up the lake for building projects.

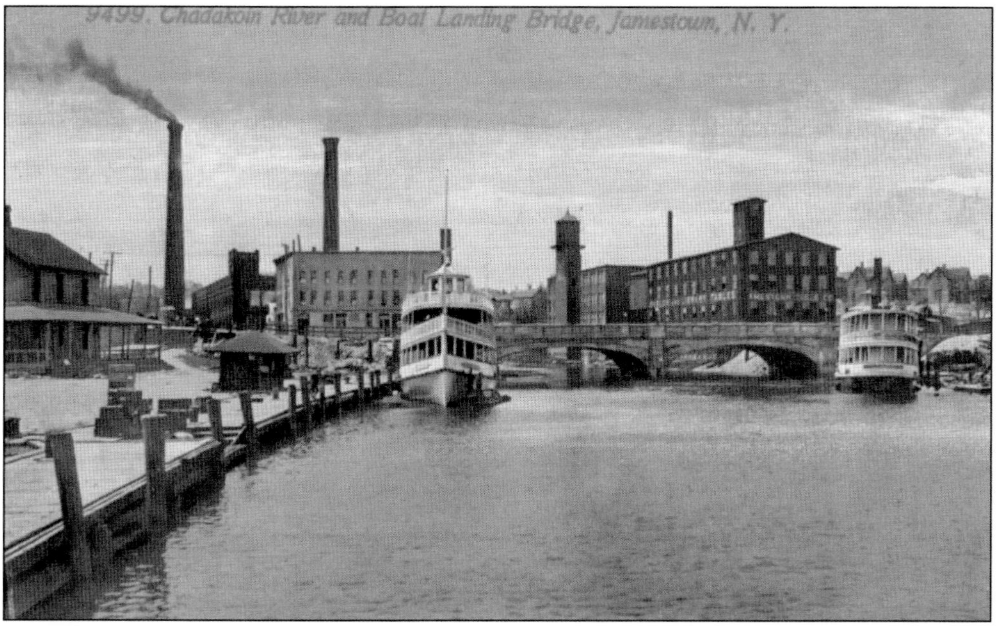

Looking downriver at the boat landing, one large furniture factory is evident. This is the Jamestown Table Company, which occupies what was the Morgan Manufacturing Company. The old iron bridge was replaced with a concrete bridge in 1911. Smokestacks from other factories are behind the Riverside Hotel on the left. Various items of freight are on the dock, waiting to be loaded on a boat.

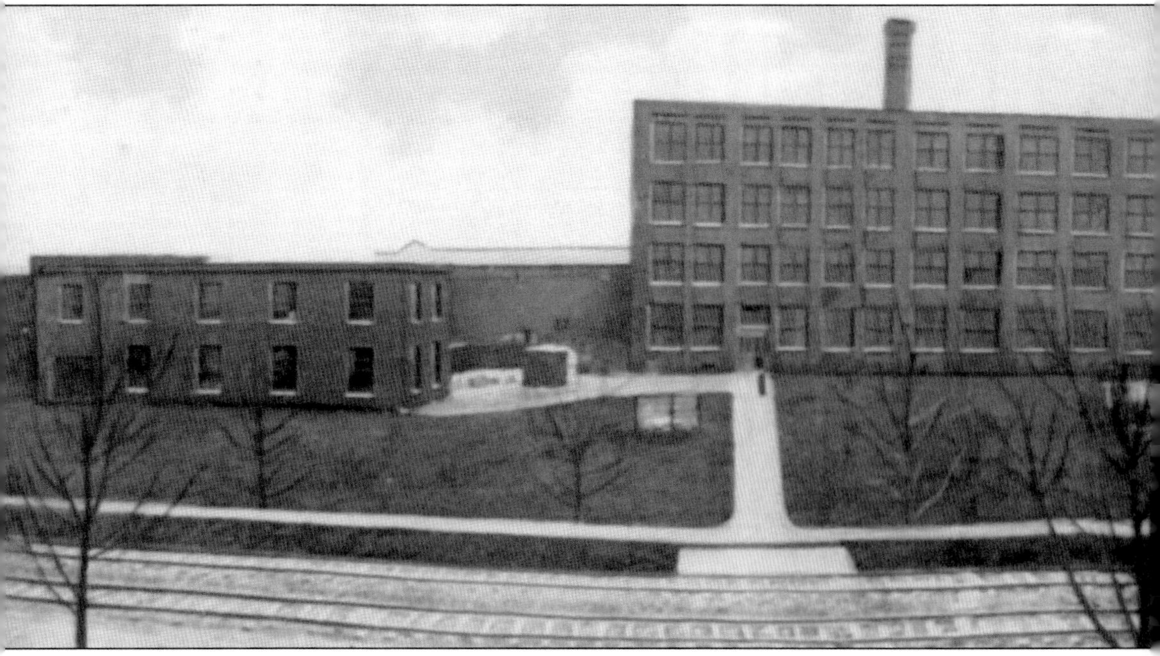

The Art Metal Construction Company began in 1888 as the Fenton Metallic Manufacturing Company. Its plant at Jones and Gifford Avenue employed 450 men in 1900. Within a decade, the workforce grew to 1,000, and an added plant on Taylor Street employed 300 more men. The company's metal office furniture became recognized for its quality and functionality. Besides equipping libraries, courthouses, banks, and office buildings, steel furniture for hundreds

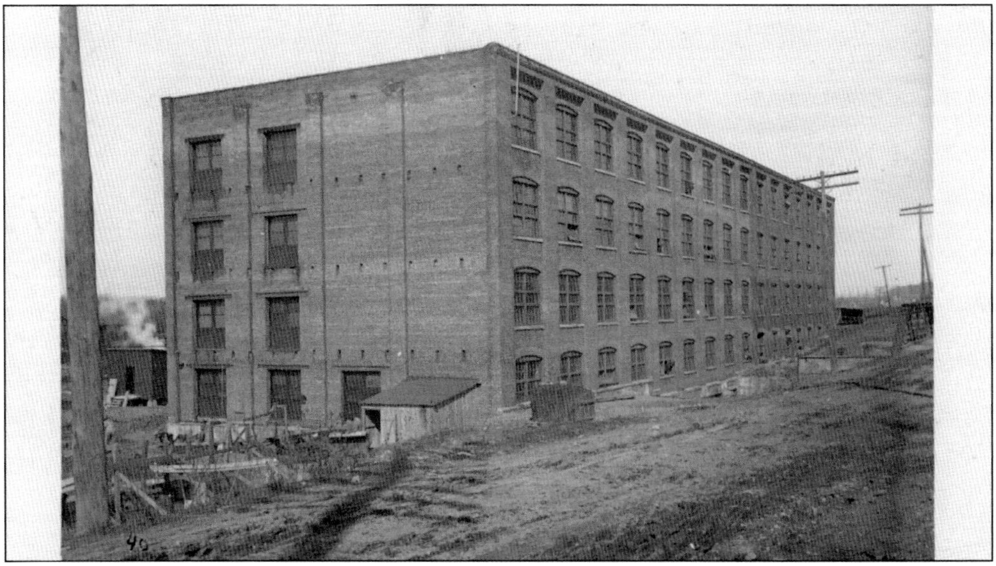

Dahlstrom Metallic Door Company was founded in 1904 by Charles P. Dahlstrom, a Swedish immigrant. After patenting a fireproof door in 1903, he started his own manufacturing company. When substituted for wood in an otherwise fireproof construction, Dahlstrom's fireproof doors, window casings, partitions, and trim completed the fireproofing of the structure. This building on Buffalo Street was the original 1904 factory with the later addition that spanned the Chadakoin River. (Courtesy of FHC.)

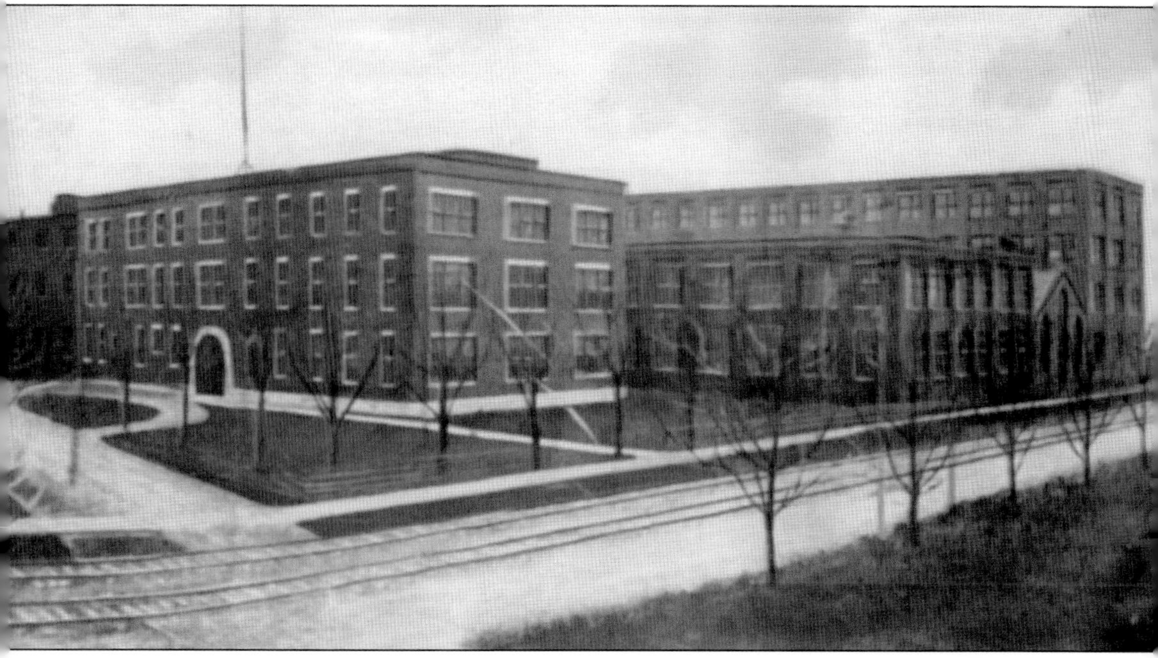

naval ships was supplied before and during World War I. Products for the modern office were added. It shipped products across the United States and expanded its market around the world, especially South America. Besides producing metal office furniture, the company emphasized efficient office practices, using its own furniture. Like other Jamestown companies, Art Metal sponsored an annual picnic for employees and their families. (Courtesy of MC.)

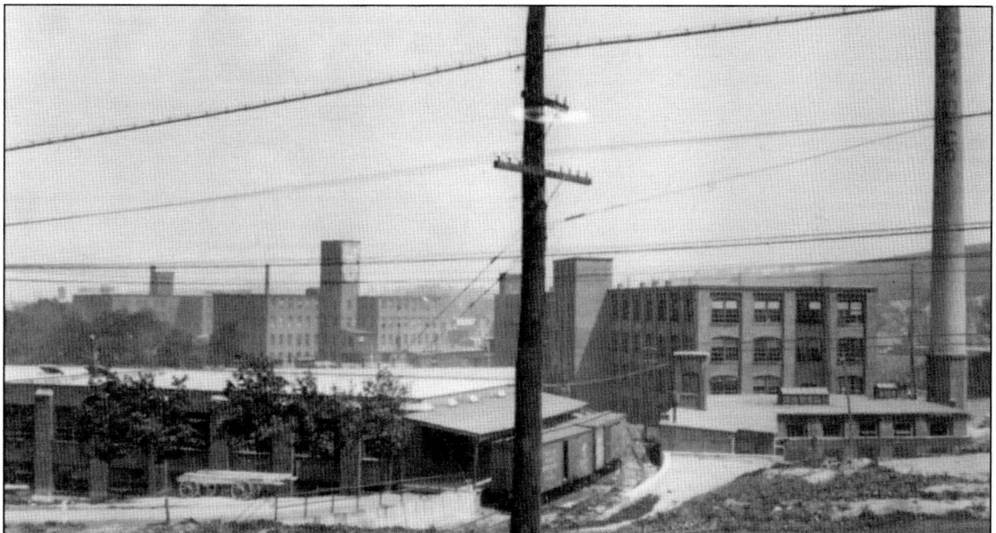

This is the later Dahlstrom Manufacturing Company's complex, which grew to answer the demand for the fireproof doors and other products. Elevator doors were soon added to the line. All of these fireproof building components enabled the building industry to erect taller and taller buildings. Known for craftsmanship, quality, and reliability, Dahlstrom products made their way into many buildings, including the Empire State Building. (Courtesy of FHC.)

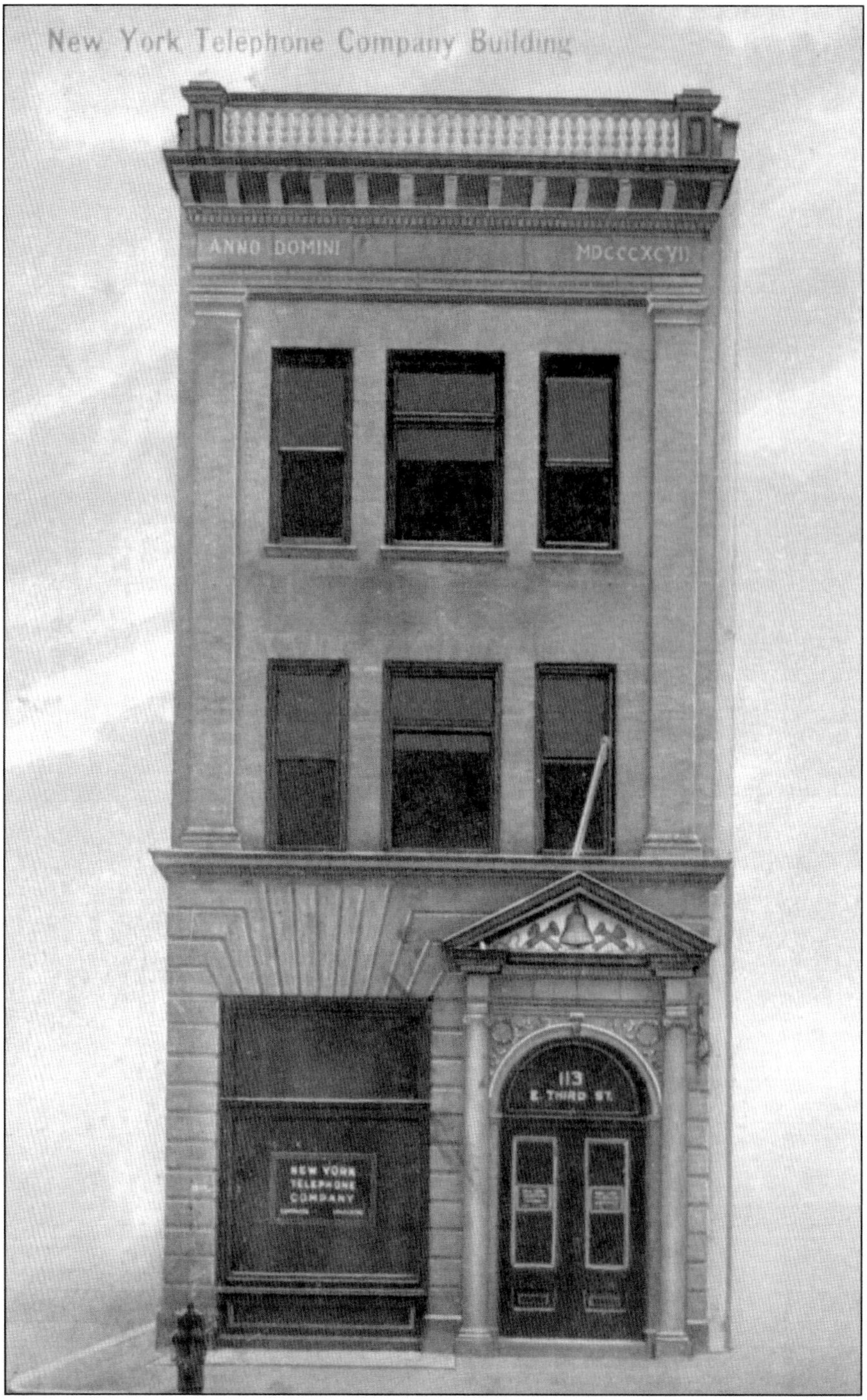

The New York Telephone Company, part of the Bell System, had a large exchange in Jamestown at 113 East Third Street. It used the same type of modern telephone apparatus used in New York City, and its rates were as low as 5¢ a day. In 1919, the local, smaller competitor Home Telephone Company bought the New York Telephone Company. The switchboard continued at the Third Street location.

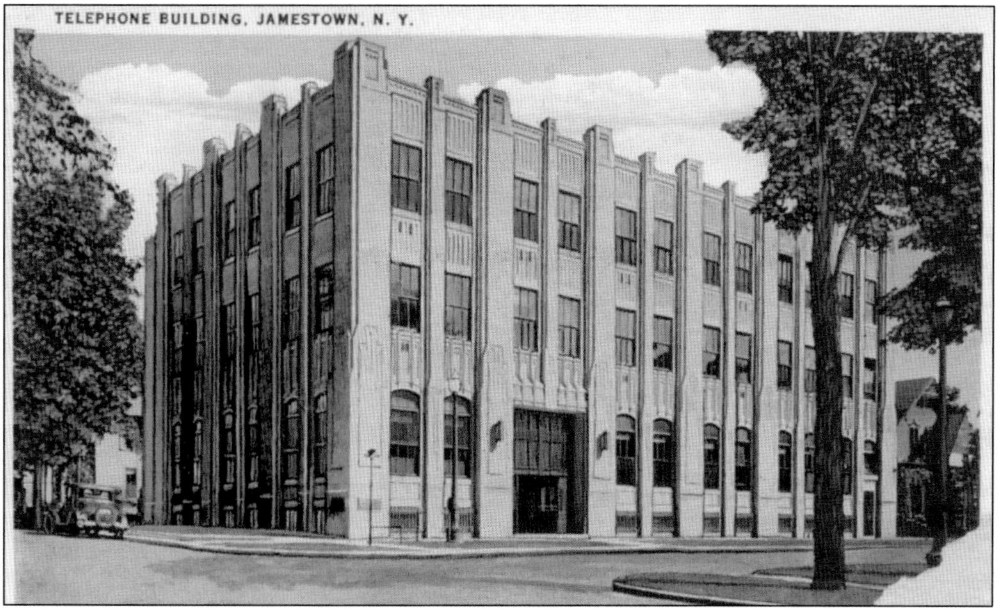

After purchasing the New York Telephone Company and expanding its business, Home Telephone Company became the Jamestown Telephone Company in 1919. Despite using the Third Street location and the original office at 210 Pine Street, the new company needed larger quarters as it expanded. In 1929, this need forced the construction of its new building at the corner of East Fourth and Spring Streets on the site of the former Preston Mansion.

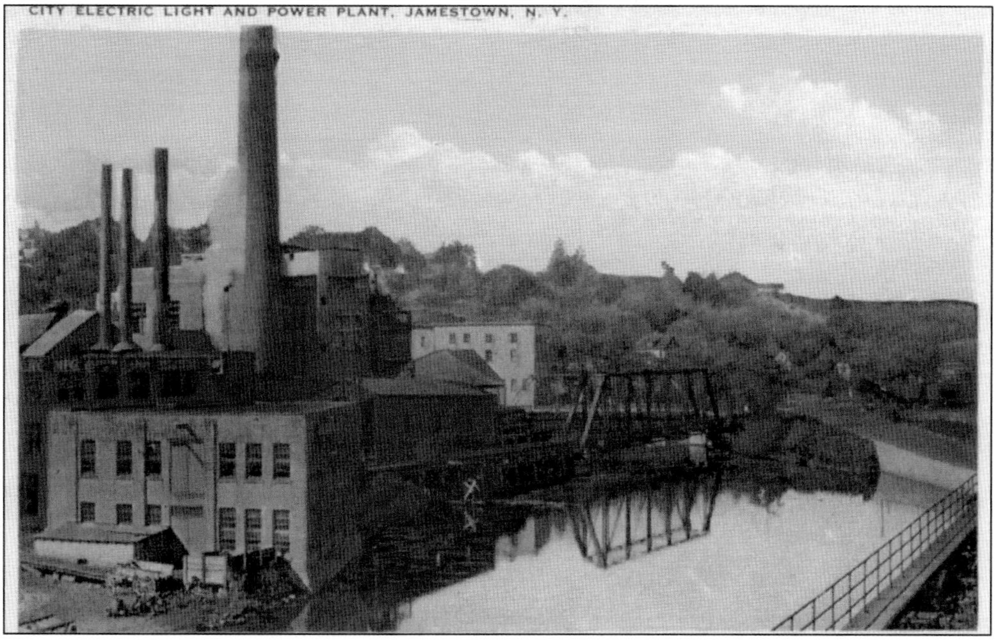

Electric power was produced for industry by their own power plants. The Jamestown Street Railway electrified its streetcars in 1891. Street lighting changed to electric in the 1870s, and the first retail store to use electric lights was Proudfit's in 1881. Eventually, the city purchased the electric company, and it continues to operate its own generating facility, which keeps rates low for residential and business customers in the area.

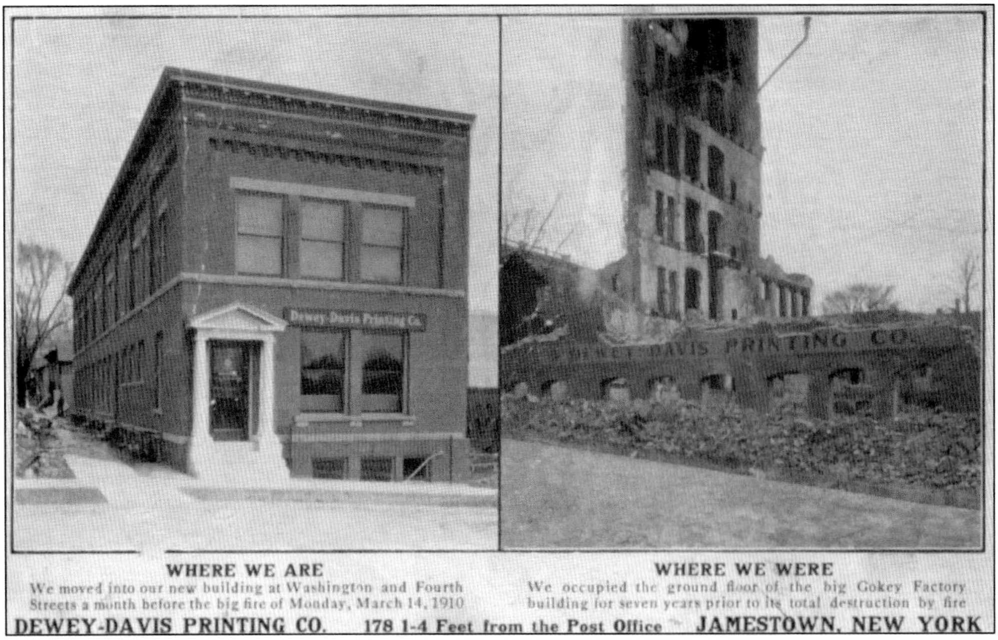

Dewey-Davis Printing Company was located in the Gokey Shoe Factory building for seven years. It moved in February 1910 after building its own plant one block away, on Washington Street below West Fourth Street. The next month, the Gokey Shoe Factory was destroyed by fire. Dewey-Davis Printing supplied commercial printing of stationery, business cards, and all manners of business publications. Engraved wedding invitations, calling cards, and stationery were available.

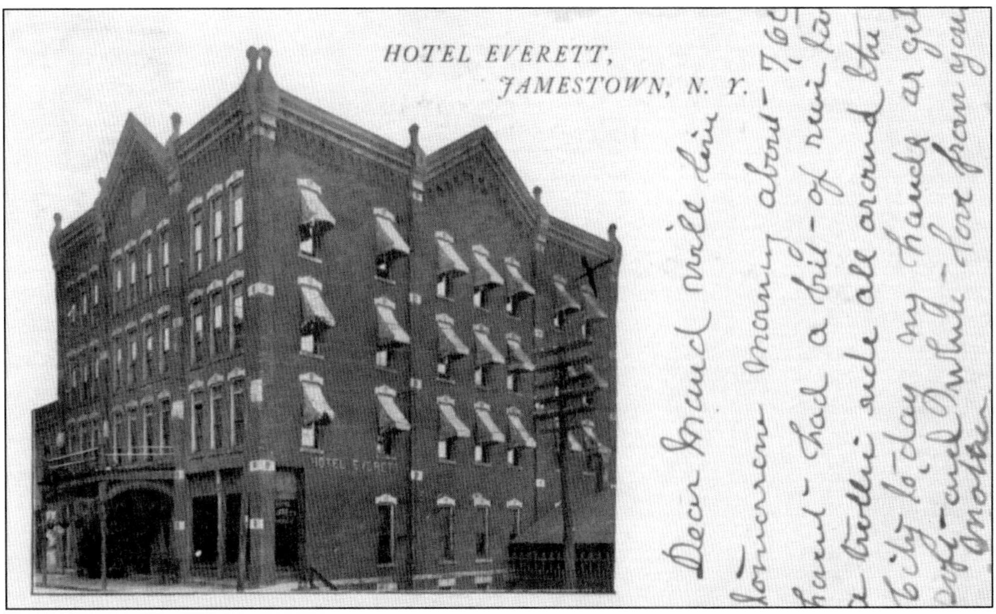

The Hotel Everett was located at West First and Cherry Streets, near the train station and convenient to the business district. The four-story brick structure had 75 rooms, a spacious dining room on the same level as the office, and a lounging room with a well-stocked bar on the basement level. In 1900, the rate was $2 a day. The hotel served transients as well as resident guests.

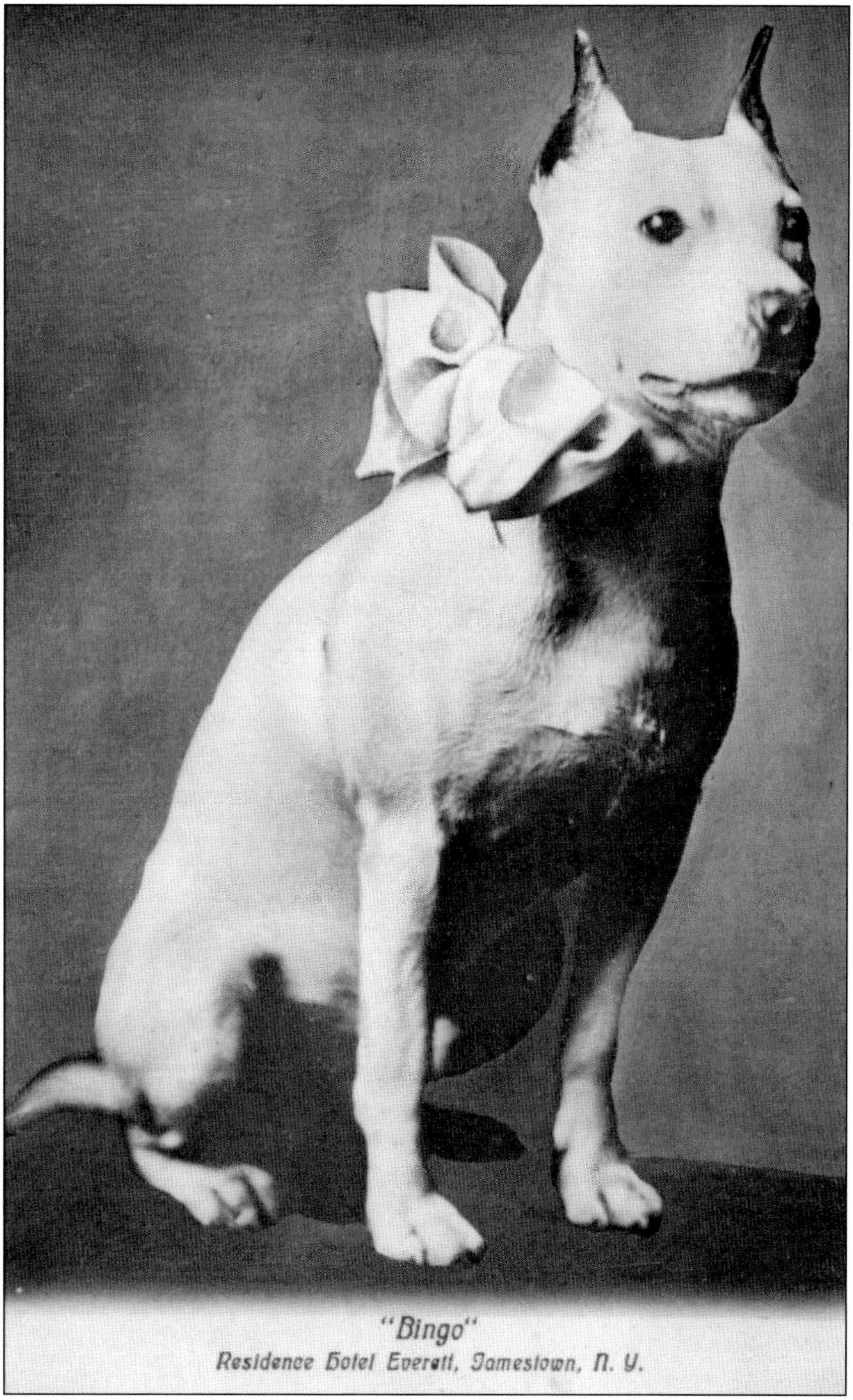

When John E. Penfold became the proprietor of the Hotel Everett in 1910, he had these postcards printed with advertisements on the back. He advertised the hotel's special features—including Sunday dinners and private parties—adding that the place had been newly refitted and furnished. The cards were probably available to guests to send. Someone sent this card, adding the handwritten note, "Same old dog, same old place."

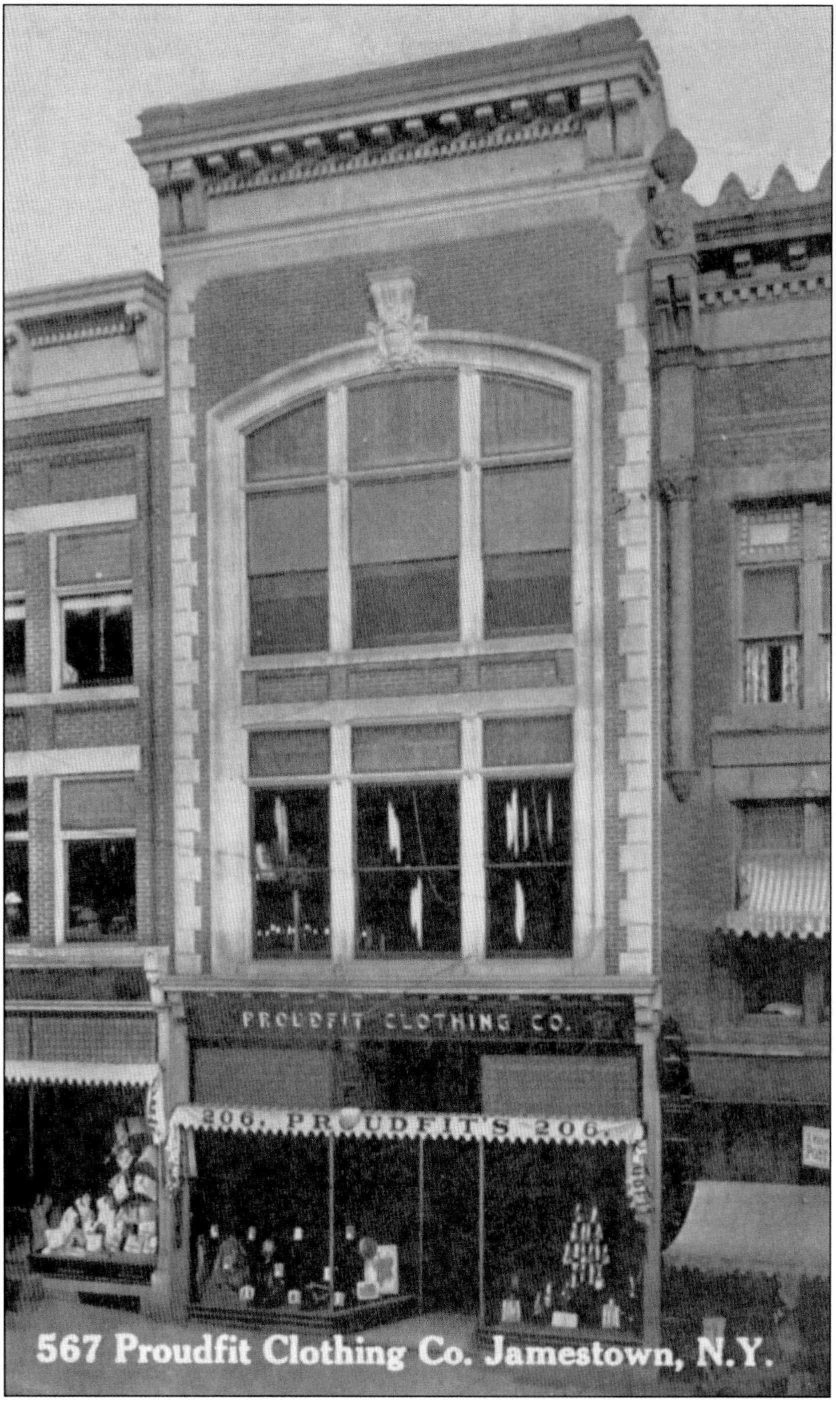

Opening their men's clothing store at 33 Main Street, William H. Proudfit and Richard A. Osmer were partners in the Proudfit Clothing Company, beginning in 1866. When the city renumbered buildings on North Main Street, Proudfit's continued to use 33 as a trademark for advertising purposes. With the number *33* painted on rocks, trees, and other immovable objects along roadsides, people were constantly reminded of the store. The store closed in 1932.

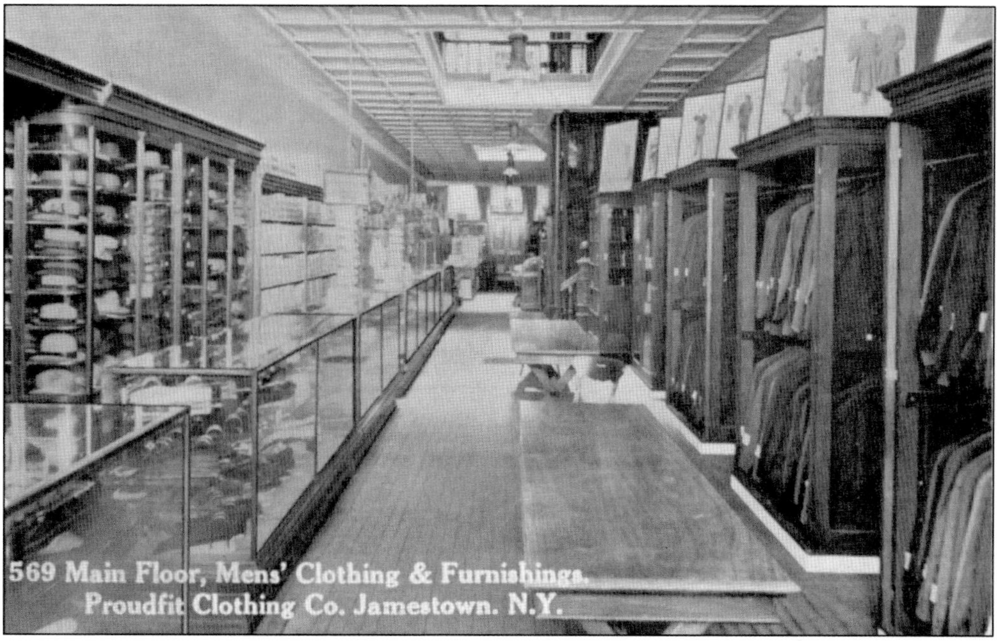

When Proudfit's was first in business, even the ready-made clothing was cut in the store and locally sewn. Custom-made tailoring was done in the store also. In 1895, it employed six salesmen, two cutters, and a bookkeeper. This postcard from 1910 advertises that Proudfit's carries Hart, Shaftner, and Marx and Adler-Rochester clothes. It also carried Knox hats and Hawes hats, which may be the hats in the cabinets on the left. (Courtesy of FHC.)

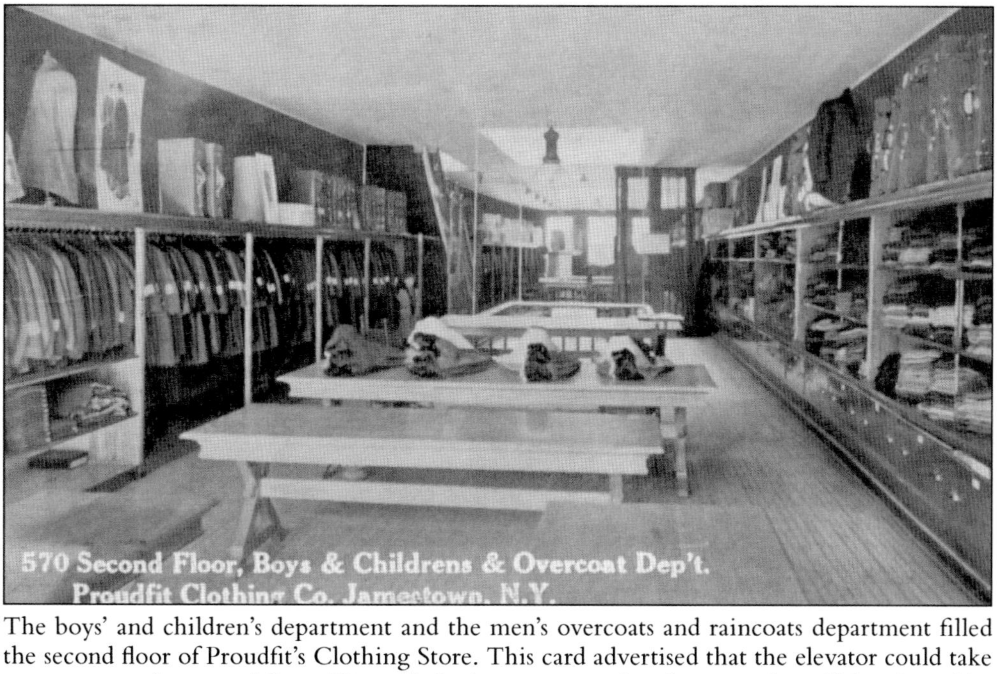

The boys' and children's department and the men's overcoats and raincoats department filled the second floor of Proudfit's Clothing Store. This card advertised that the elevator could take customers to the second floor. The added advantage was that the apparel could be viewed by daylight, of which there was plenty. Proudfit's was the first retail store in Jamestown to have electric lights beginning in 1881. (Courtesy of FHC.)

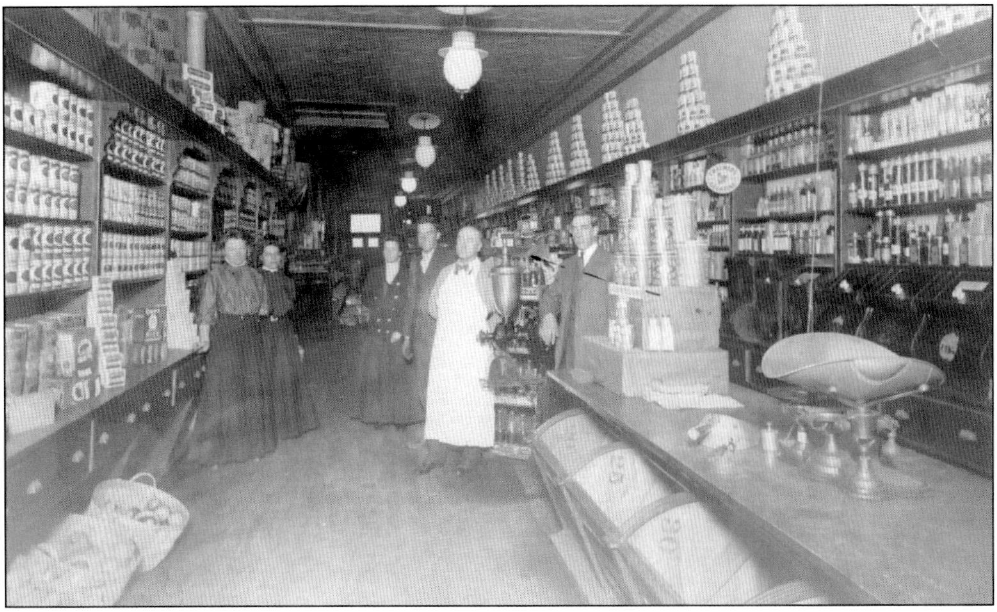

Located at 30-32 North Main Street about 1909, this grocery was operated by the Lally family of Dunkirk. Cook and Treat operated a grocery here before the Lallys. This address puts the store in the Arcade Building. Edna, who sent this postcard, stated that this was where she worked at Lallys. That statement, the postmark of June 1909, and city directories helped to identify this picture. (Courtesy of FHC.)

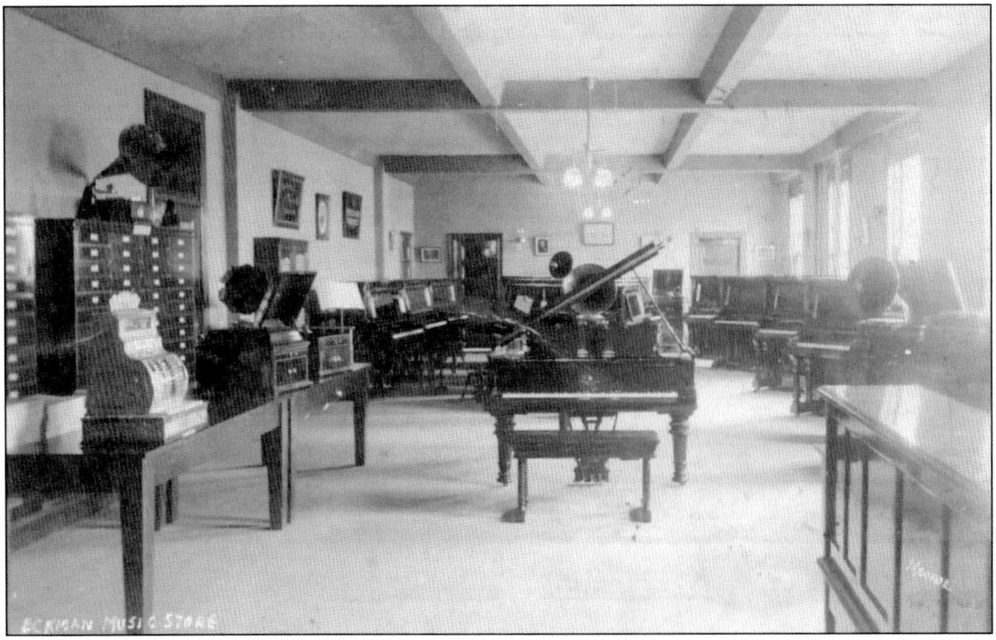

In May 1911, after 10 years on Main Street, Eckman's Music store held its formal opening on the fifth floor of the Wellman Building. It carried a complete line of musical instruments, the famous Victor Talking Machines and Victrolas, and a complete assortment of musical compositions. In April 1911, owner Charles Eckman called five men to meet at the store. The Norden Club was organized at that meeting.

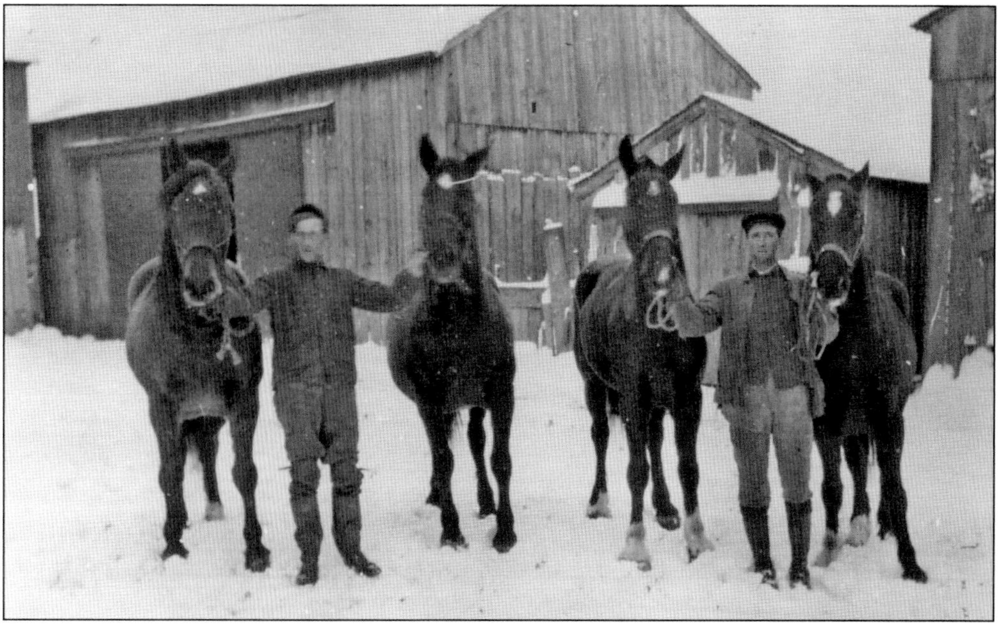

Even into the 20th century, the horse was the mode of transportation for many. By the late 1890s, the fire departments had horse-drawn fire wagons. Livery stables dotted the downtown area, often near hotels. In 1910, after a century of settlement, Jamestown's city directory listed nine livery stables. Horse-drawn snowplows cleared sidewalks of snow into the 1960s. The owners of the barn in the background and the horses are unidentified.

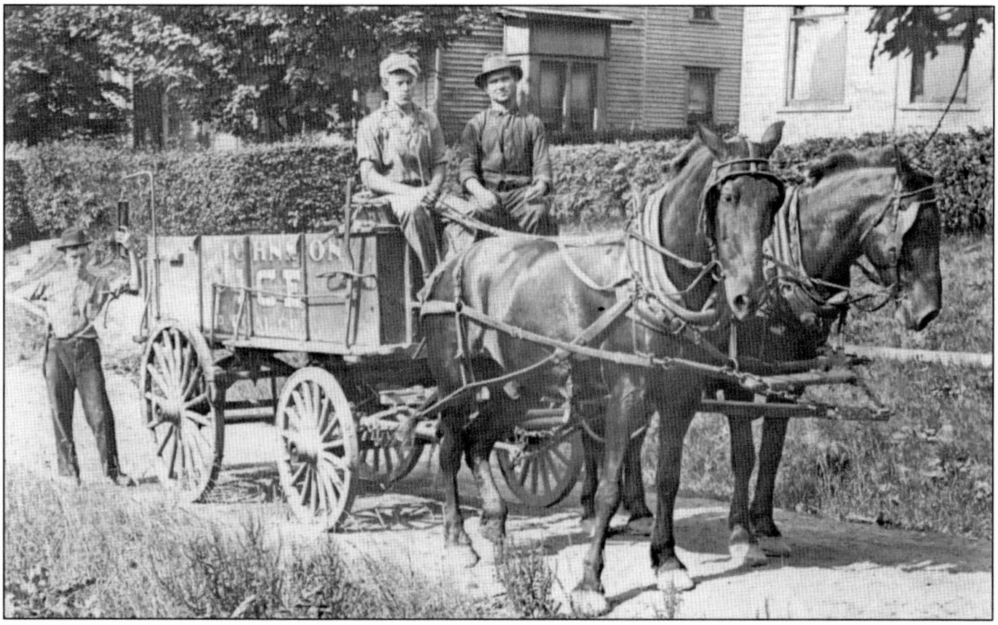

Johnson Ice Company, established in 1881 and formerly the Jamestown Ice Company, had a Jamestown office at 10 West Third Street. The icehouses at the boat landing, Fluvanna, and Clifton could hold 15,000 tons of ice harvested from Chautauqua Lake. In 1900, there were 15 employees with eight wagons to supply ice year round to customers in the Jamestown area. More workers were needed to harvest the ice each winter.

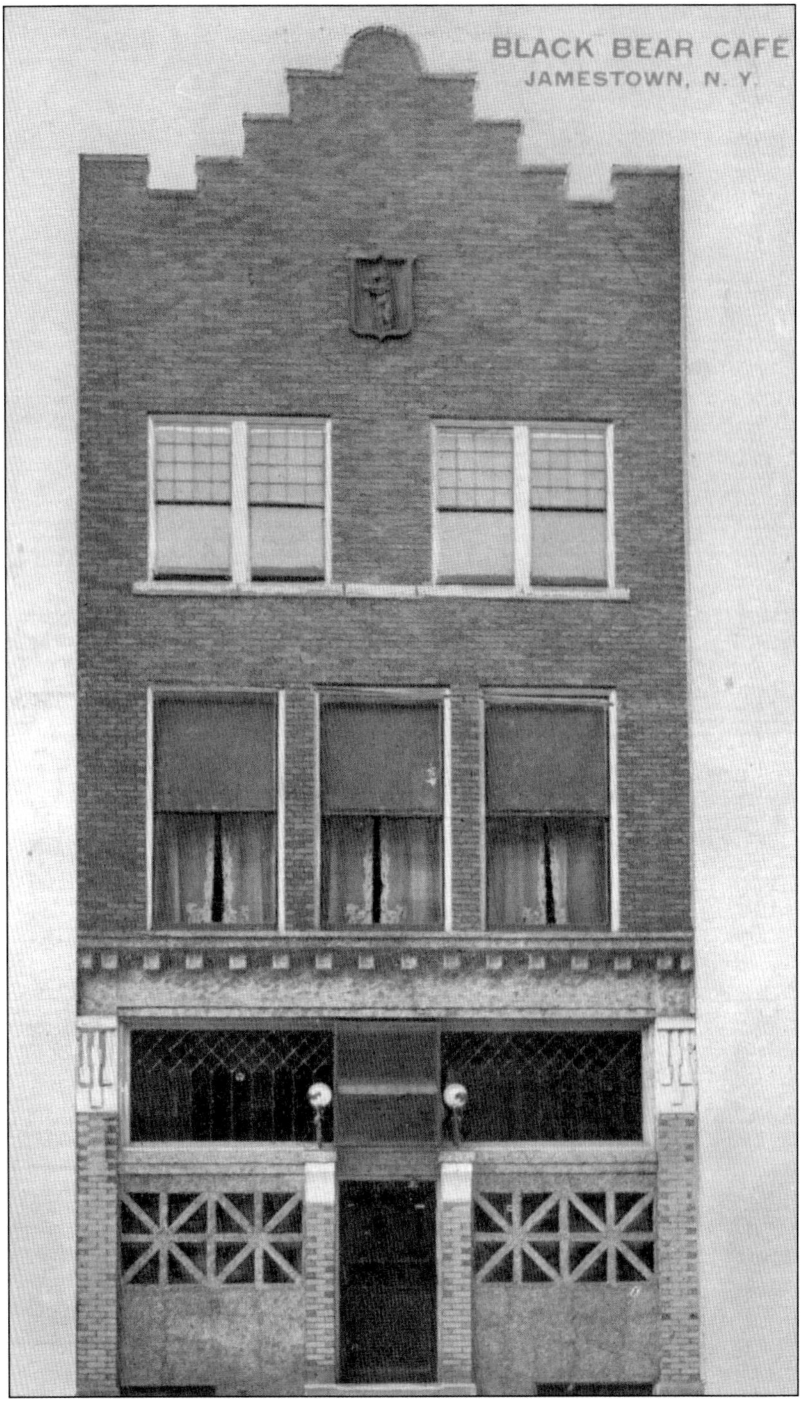

The first listing of the Black Bear Café, at 22 East Third Street, is in the 1895 city directory. As early as 1886, Harry Chamberlain or Fred Bauer had a restaurant, a saloon, and for a short time, a hotel at that address. In 1915, Henry Bauer had the Black Bear Café, and his family lived upstairs. Through the 1920s, various proprietors ran the restaurant. By 1934, the Cake Shop was the occupant.

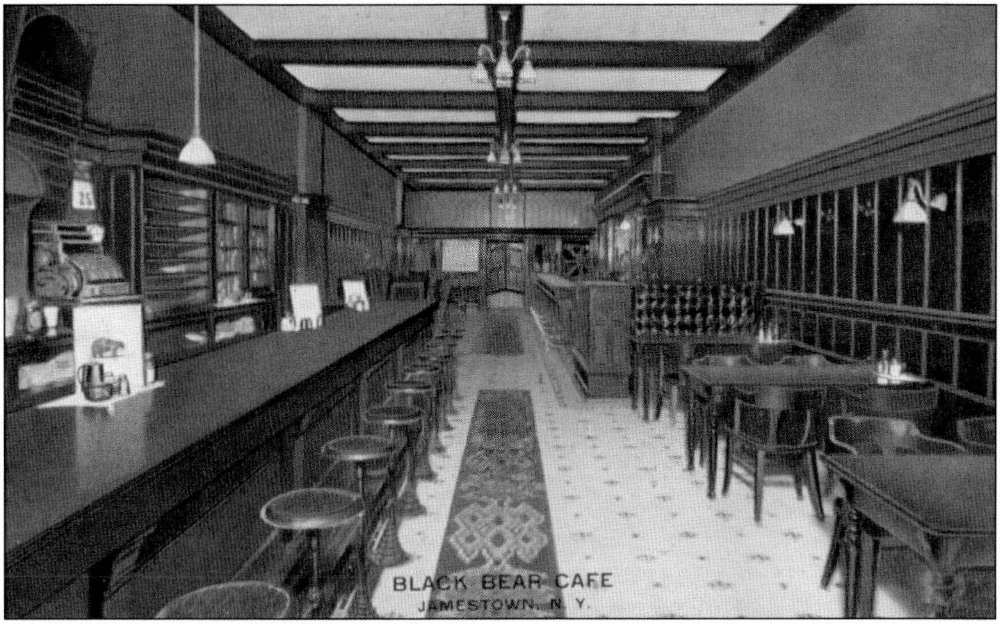

For at least 44 years, this establishment was a restaurant, saloon, or both, and for 35 years, it was the Black Bear Café. There is a bar complete with a brass rail at the rear and a lunch counter with tables in the front. The menus on the lunch counter have a picture of a black bear on the back. (Courtesy of MC.)

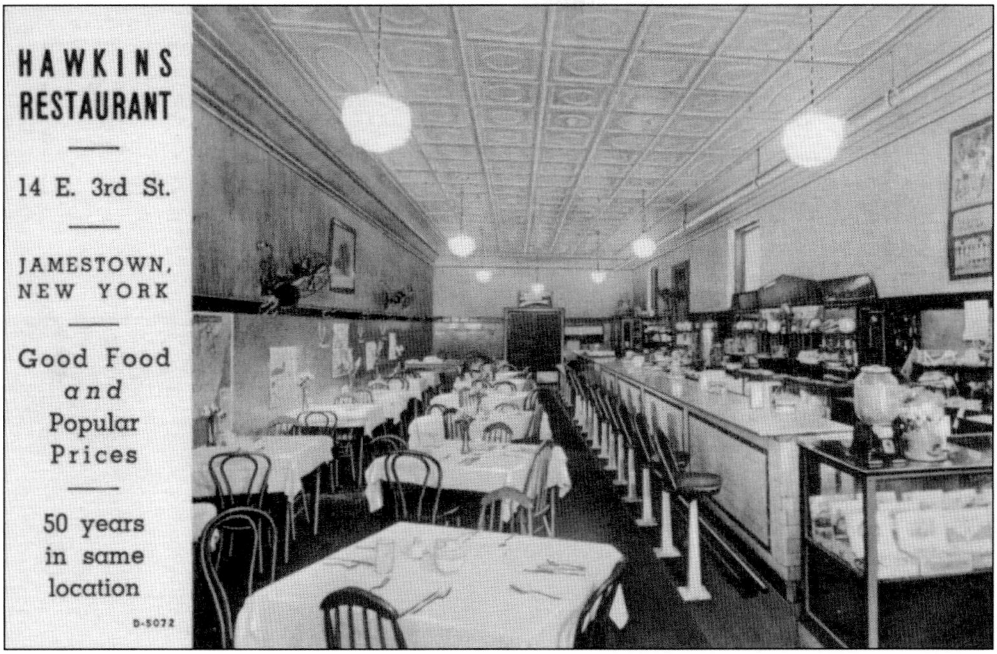

The 1898 city directory has the first entry for Hawkins Restaurant, at 14 East Third Street—Abner J. Hawkins, proprietor. He was still there in 1909 as the Hawkins Restaurant and Oyster House. Proprietors changed over the next few years. The long, narrow space, typical of Third Street establishments, made the lunch counter necessary, providing food preparation space and seating space.

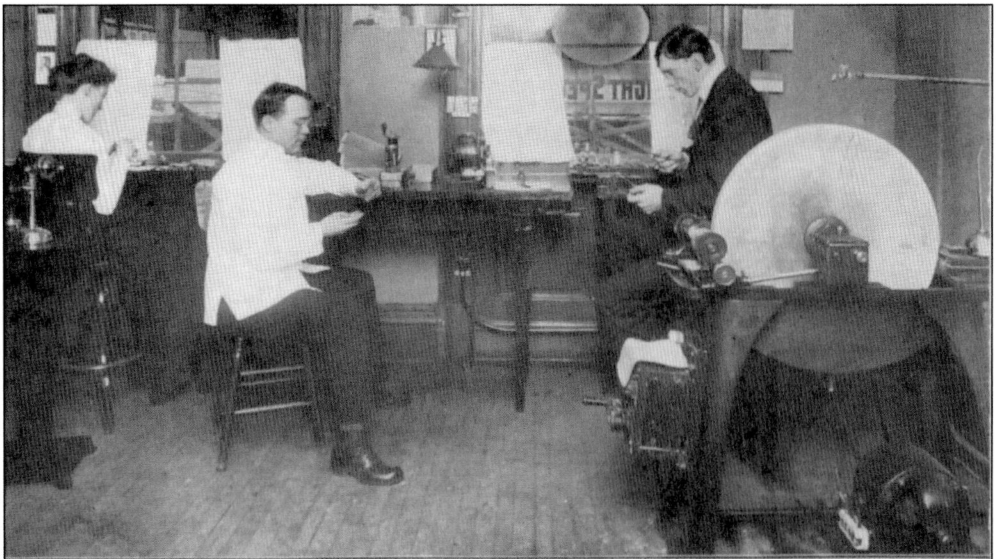

PRESCRIPTION DEPARTMENT—where Lenses are made within one hour—DR. HANVEY, Second Floor Wellman Building, Jamestown, N. Y.

Beginning in 1907, Dr. Hanvey was an eyesight specialist in Jamestown. By 1911, he moved his office to the Wellman Building. The Wellman Building was arranged into three-room suites with a lavatory and toilet room. Dr. Hanvey had this prescription room, the examination room, and a waiting room. Lenses could be made within the hour. From the postcard, there is no way to tell for sure if Dr. Hanvey is wearing the suit or the white coat. (Courtesy of FHC.)

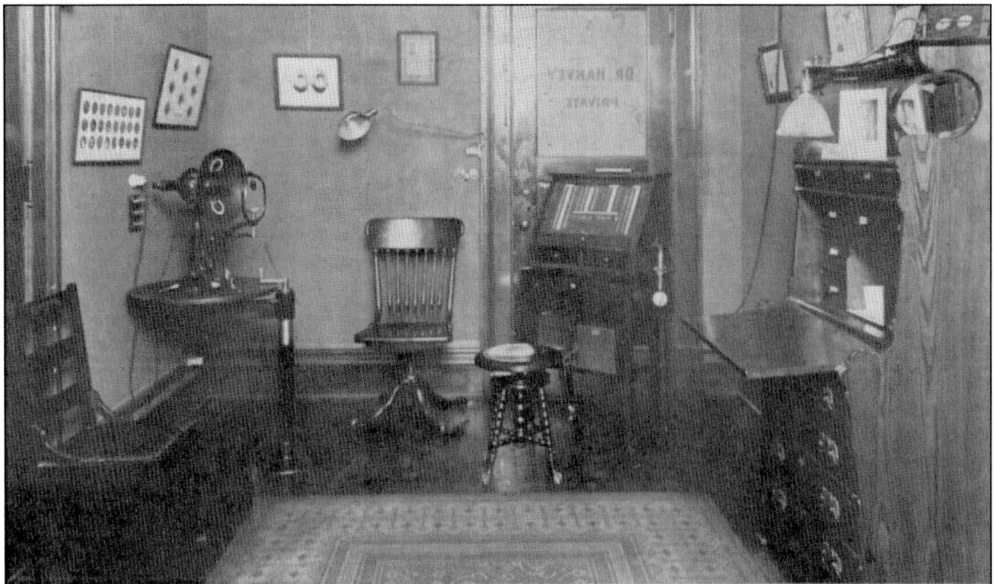

EXAMINATION ROOM—where Modern Methods are used in Examining the Eyes—DR. HANVEY, Second Floor Wellman Building, Jamestown, N. Y.

Dr. Hanvey's examination room on the second floor of the Wellman Building had machines for use with eye examinations. He was first listed in the city directory as an eyesight specialist, later as an optometrist. From 1911 to 1955, he had his office in the Wellman Building. For a few years, it was in his home in Lakewood. He examined eyes for more than 50 years. (Courtesy of FHC.)

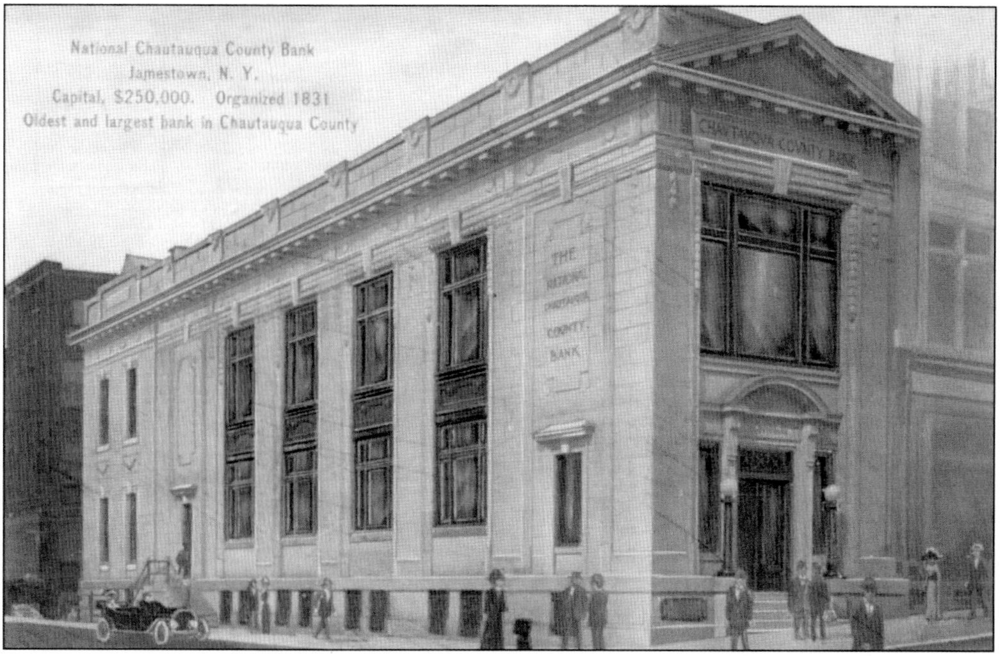

The National Chautauqua County Bank, on the northwest corner of West Second and North Main Streets, is the first and oldest bank chartered in Chautauqua County. The original building on this site was replaced by a larger building that burned in the great fire of 1861. In 1910, this stone building was constructed in the Greek Renaissance style to replace a brick building. In 1924, it was expanded and remodeled. (Courtesy of FHC.)

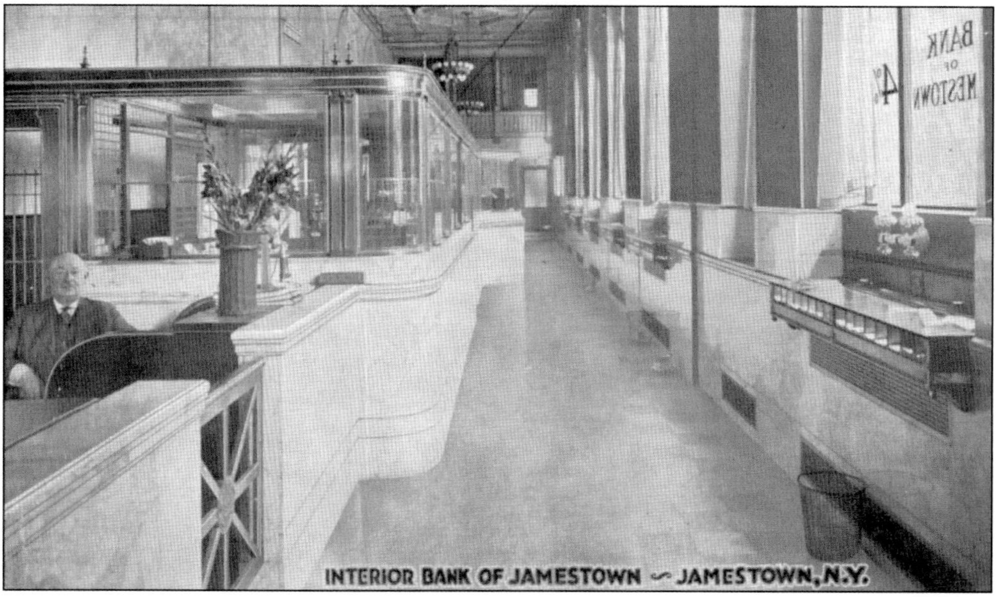

The Bank of Jamestown opened its doors on May 4, 1903. After 16 years at 216 North Main Street, the move to the northeast corner of North Main and East Second Streets was made in 1919. This move gave the bank windows along the south side, as seen in the postcard. In 1932, after merging with another bank, the bank expanded into the building to the north. (Courtesy of FHC.)

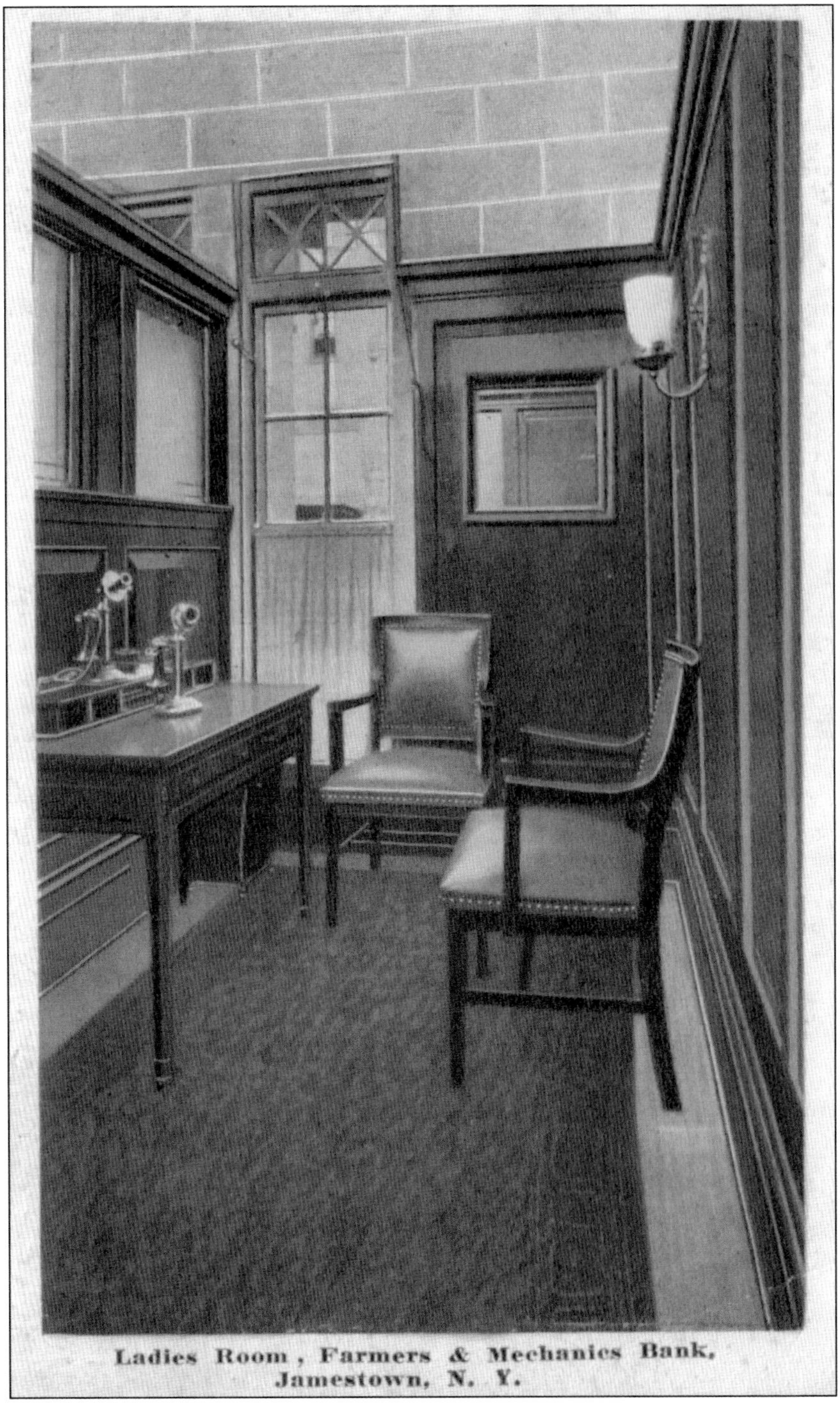

In 1891, the Farmers and Mechanics Bank was started by E.B. Crissey in Jamestown after successful banking in other parts of Chautauqua County. Like many of the other banks in Jamestown, this bank was located on North Main Street, convenient to the business district. The bank had this private area where ladies could transact their banking; it even included two telephones!

Nine

Amenities

Communities begin with basic log homes, necessary businesses, and services, such as stores, the blacksmith, the doctor, and the school. Then, other strongholds arrive when there is a large enough population to support them: the hatter, the lawyer, the carpenter and joiner who make furniture and frame houses, the pail maker, the newspaper editor and printer, and the banker. Businesses develop to fill the needs of the community, whether the community know it needs them or not. Industries develop, exploiting the natural resources and available labor of the area.

As livelihoods thrive, people look for other things to do. The social network, charity work, and recreation begin to occupy the leisure time that people are beginning to enjoy by the early 1900s. Clubs and lodges give members a place to go to meet their friends. Organizations to help the less fortunate spring forth to fill needs. Public transportation is a boon to any community. Cultural and educational institutions add to the fabric of a community. These are all amenities within the city.

Jamestown developed many amenities, from hospitals to lodges to parks and even cemeteries. Photographs of events were seldom turned into postcards, but the static buildings used or built by these organizations were photographed. These photographs became postcards to show others what was available in the city. The members of the organizations were proud of the accomplishments, and postcards were sent to friends to announce these accomplishments.

By no means does this chapter include all the amenities that Jamestown has enjoyed over the years. Hopefully, the organizations and activities captured in these postcards will represent the spirit of Jamestown.

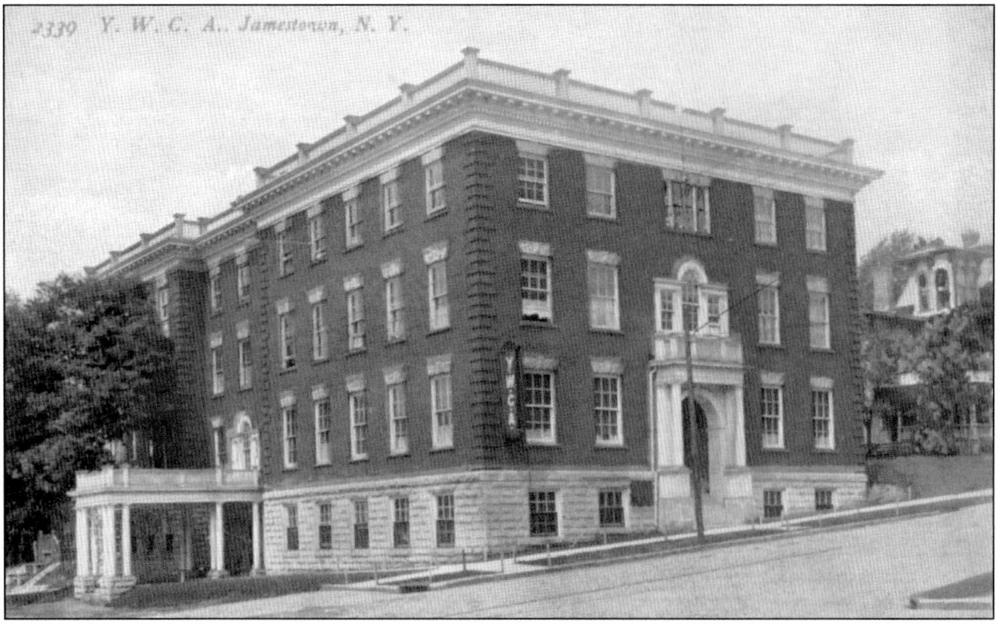

Out of concern for young workingwomen, Jamestown's Young Women's Christian Association (YWCA) was organized in 1888. The YWCA building at the corner of North Main and West Fourth Streets was built in 1908–1909 in the Renaissance Revival style. Offering accommodations and services to women, the YWCA building has adapted to changing times. It has included a restaurant and recently a daycare center.

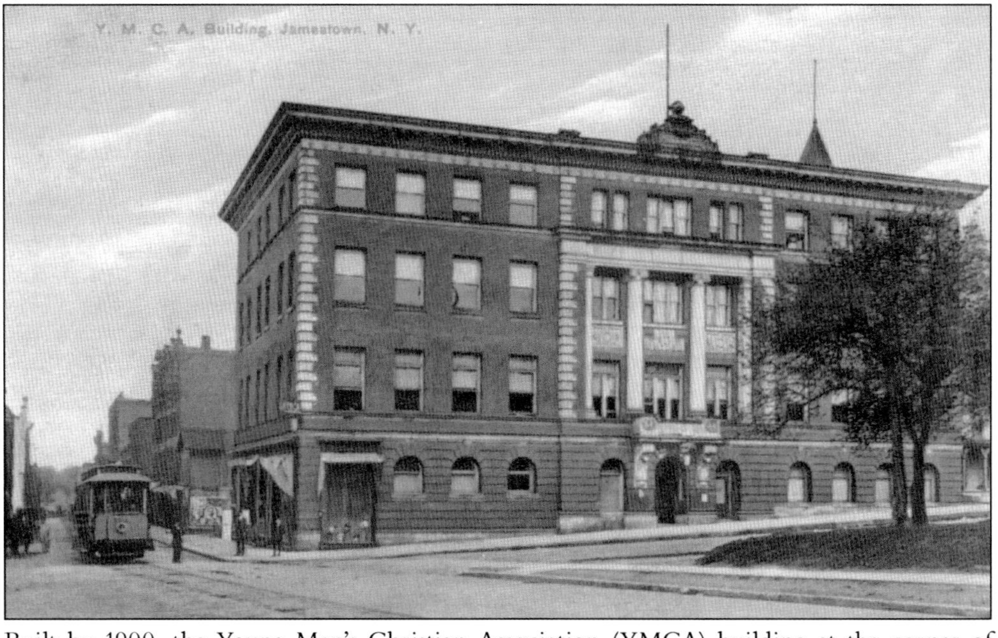

Built by 1900, the Young Men's Christian Association (YMCA) building at the corner of Prendergast Avenue and East Second Street was serving over 700 members by the end of the next decade. Of the 88 rooms, 63 were part of the dormitory serving young workingmen with no local home. Bowling alleys, a gymnasium, and a large plunge were available to members. Retail tenants occupied the ground floor. (Courtesy of FHC.)

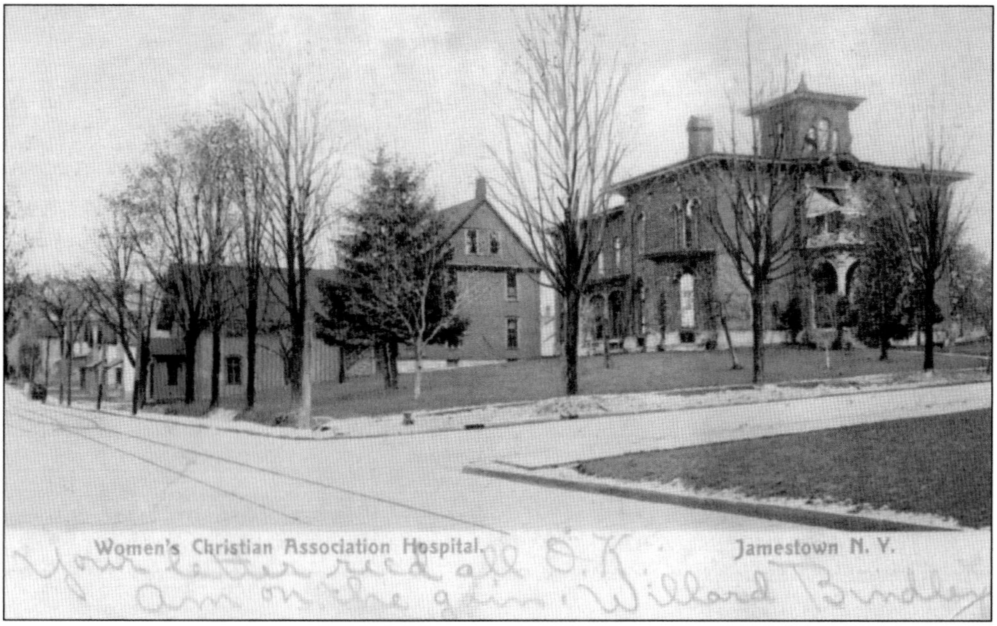

The Fox/Kimball home at the corner of Foote Avenue and Allen Street was purchased by the Woman's Christian Association (WCA) in 1887. This provided a boardinghouse for young workingwomen and one hospital room for Jamestown. Expansion beyond one hospital room was soon undertaken. A nurses' training school opened in 1890. A modern hospital has grown from that one room and continues to serve the Jamestown area.

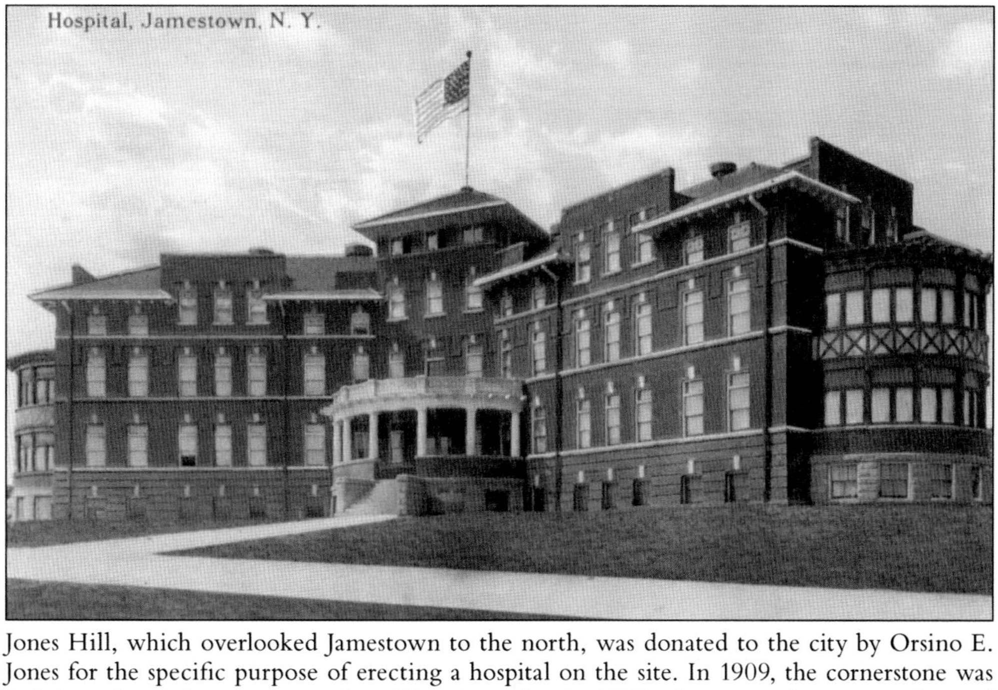

Jones Hill, which overlooked Jamestown to the north, was donated to the city by Orsino E. Jones for the specific purpose of erecting a hospital on the site. In 1909, the cornerstone was laid for a hospital to accommodate 45 patients. In the 1920s, it became Jamestown General Hospital. Additions enlarged the capacity, added equipment, and expanded services. Today, WCA Hospital operates the facilities on Jones Hill.

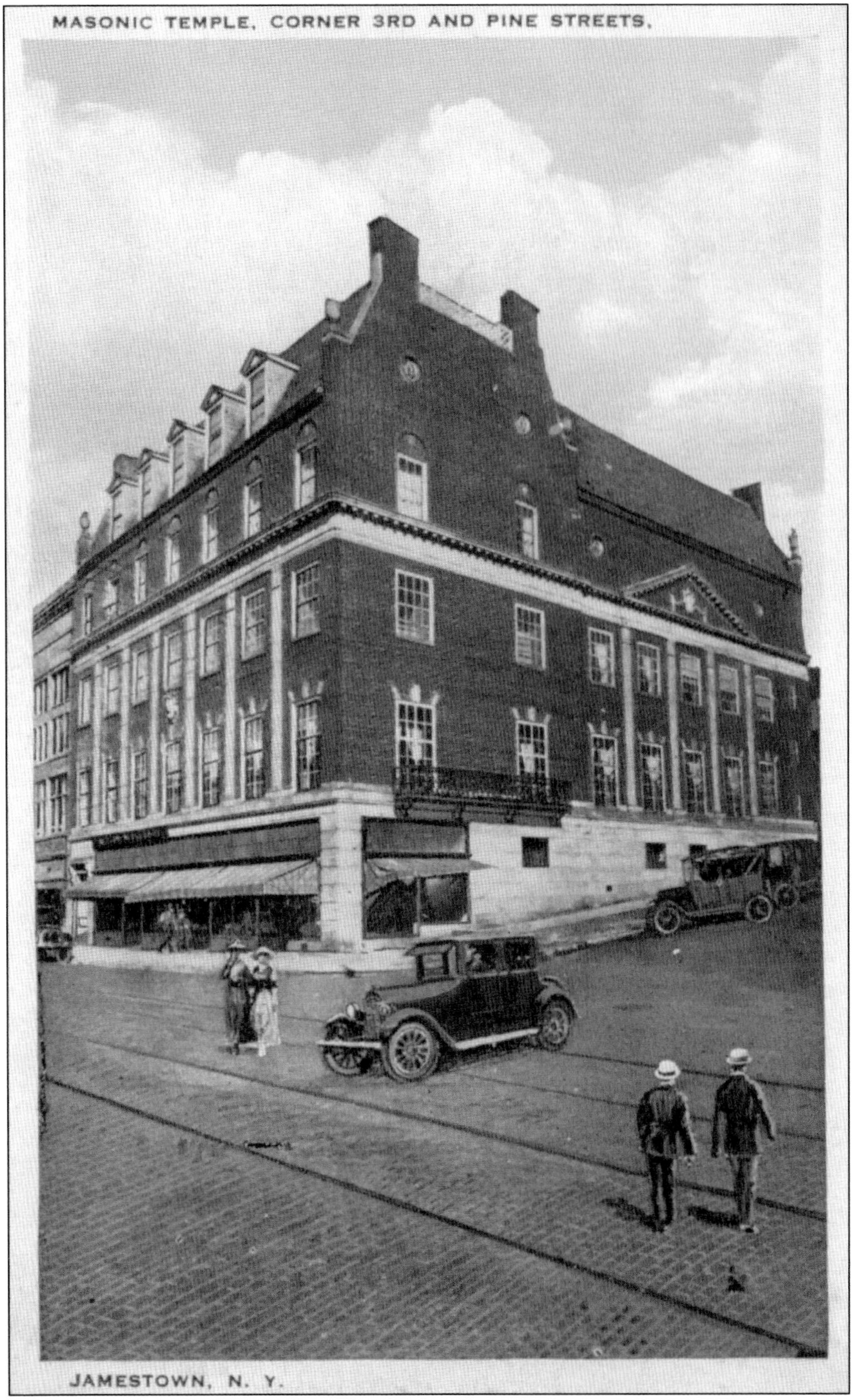

The Masonic temple was not built until 1922. Many different Masonic groups were meeting in many places, and this gave them one place to meet. Retail space was available on the street level. Club rooms were on the second floor; a lodge hall, dining room, and kitchen occupied the third floor; and the large lodge hall with a balcony occupied the fourth and fifth floors.

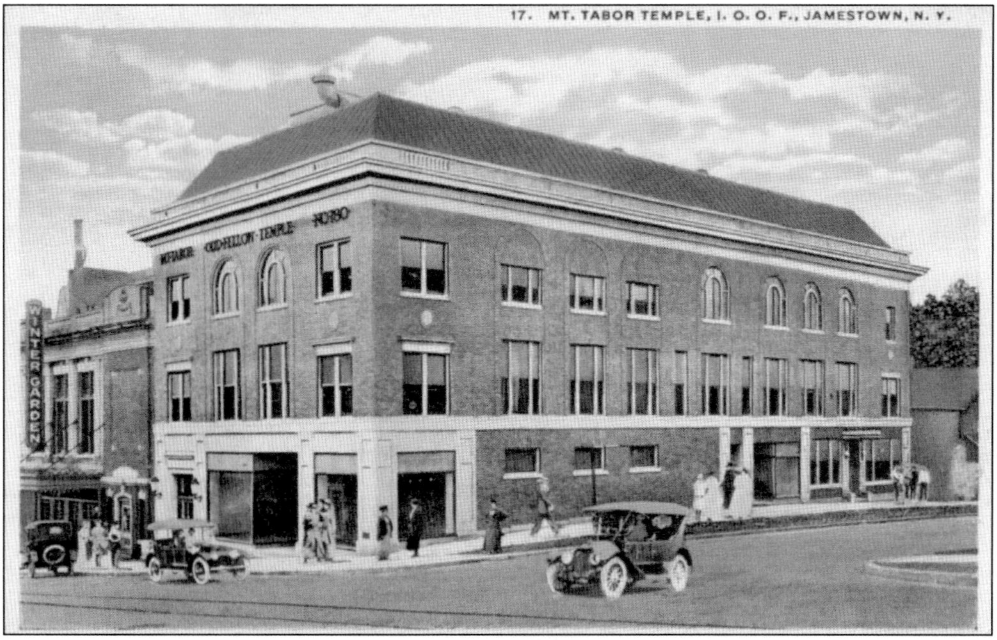

Mount Tabor Lodge, IOOF was instituted in 1897. Its meetings were held in a few locations until 1915, when the Mount Tabor Temple was built at the southwest corner of Washington and West Fourth Streets. Like many buildings in the business district, retail shops were on the street level, with the club rooms and lodge hall on the upper floors.

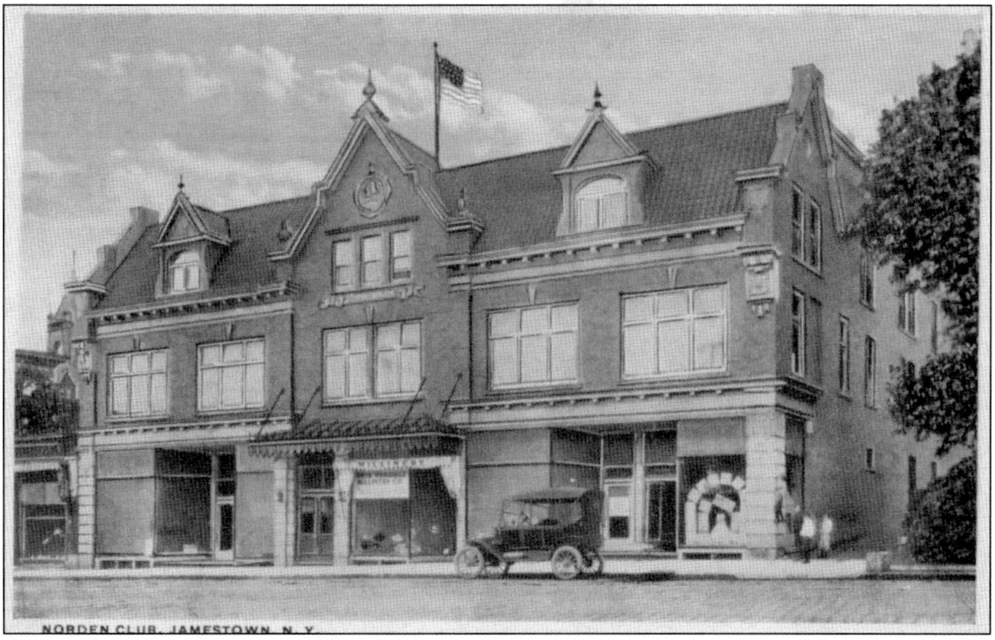

Organized in 1911, the Norden Club is a social organization for men of Scandinavian birth or heritage. The Norden Club's building was dedicated in 1914. Located at the northeast corner of East Second Street and Prendergast Avenue, the building served as a cultural center for the community. Financial difficulties forced its sale in 1937. It was replaced in 1959 by the Federal Building. The Norden Club celebrated its 100th anniversary in 2011.

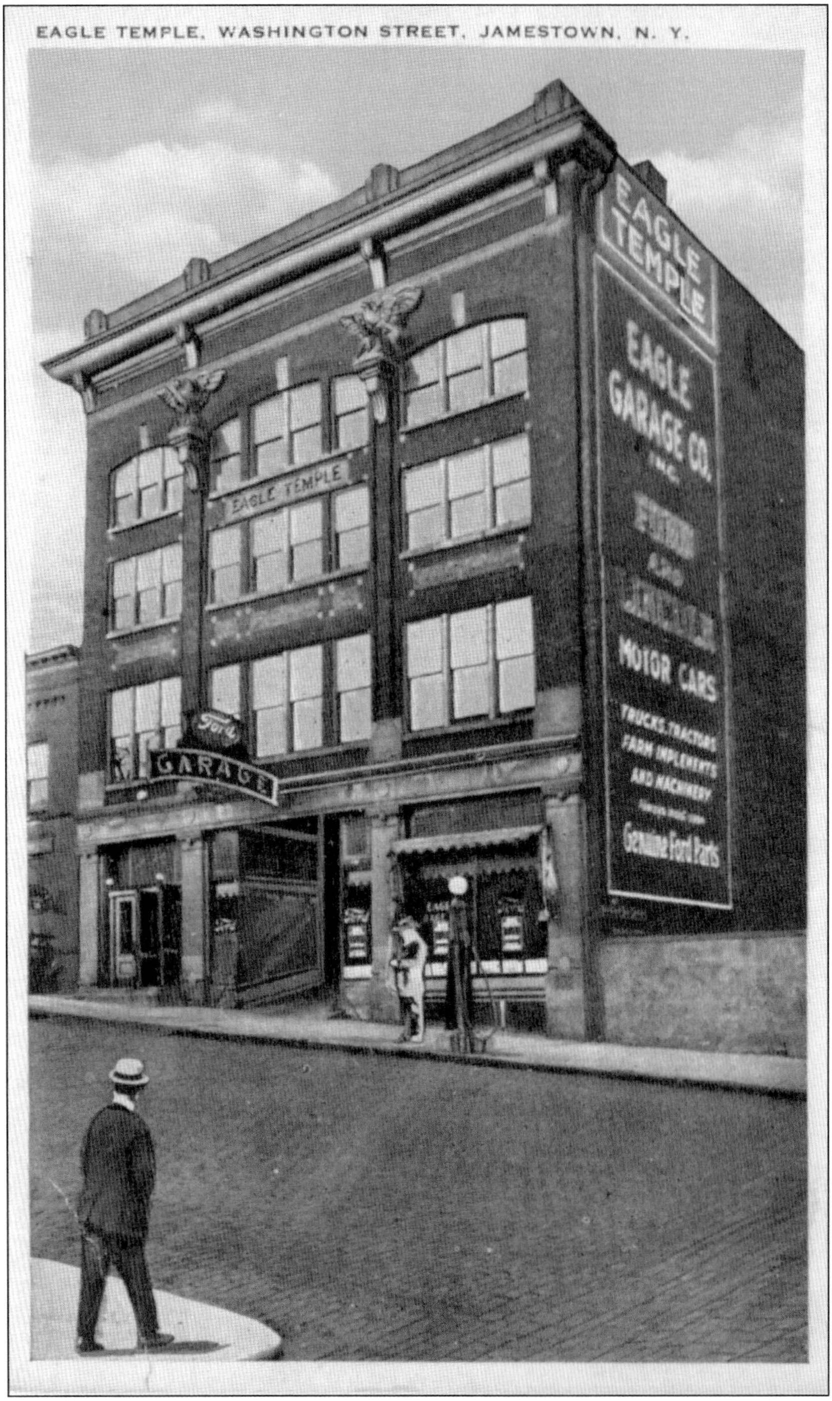

The Fraternal Order of Eagles (FOE), Aerie No. 816, built the Eagle temple on Washington Street between Third and Fourth Streets about 1913. The basement and first floor accommodated the Eagle Garage, catering to the emerging automobile trade. The club rooms and lodge hall occupied the upper floors. In 1941, Ingjald Lodge No. 65, Independent Order of Vikings, purchased the building.

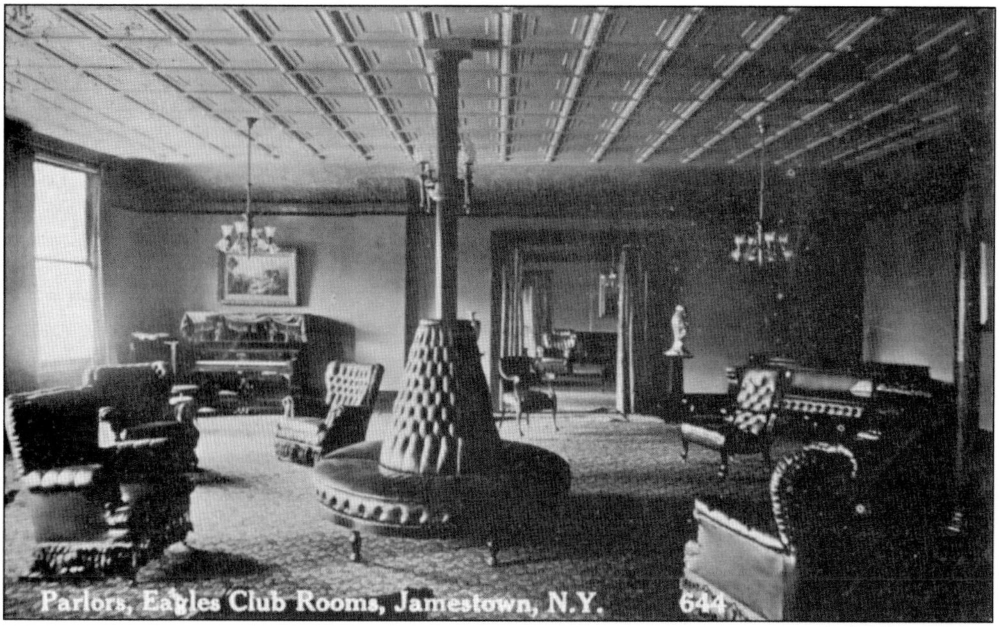

Aerie No. 816, FOE, met in the club rooms in the Arcade Building before it built the Eagle temple. The location of these parlors is unknown, but the furniture may indicate it was in the early years at the Arcade Building.

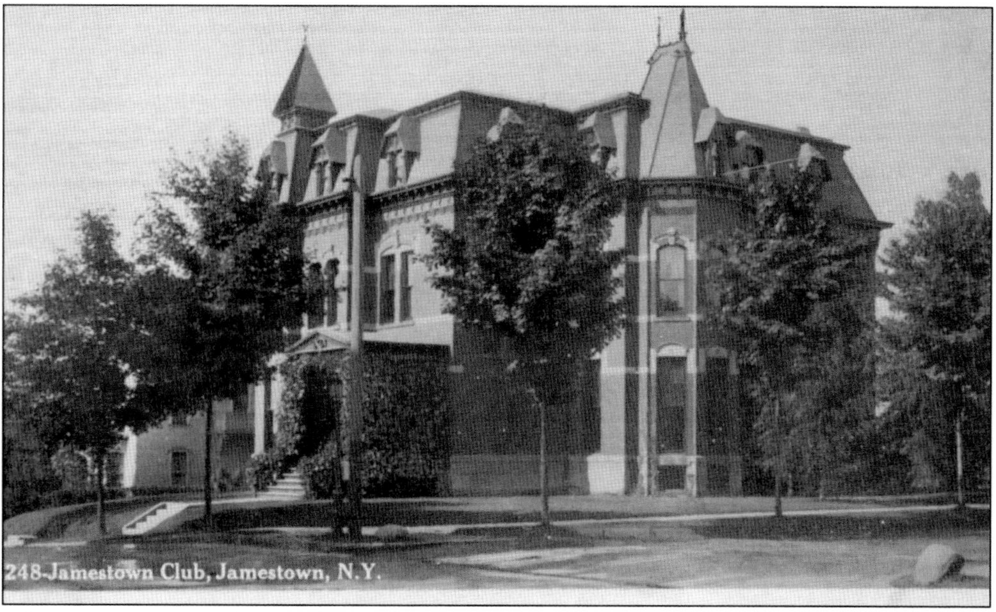

When 13 young men formed the GEC, its meaning was to be kept a secret. A 1940s newspaper article claims it was the Gentlemen's Entertainment Club. It became the Jamestown Club, a local men's social organization, and moved into the William Tew home in 1895. The home at the southwest corner of North Main and Fifth Streets, built in 1881, was remodeled to include bowling alleys and club rooms.

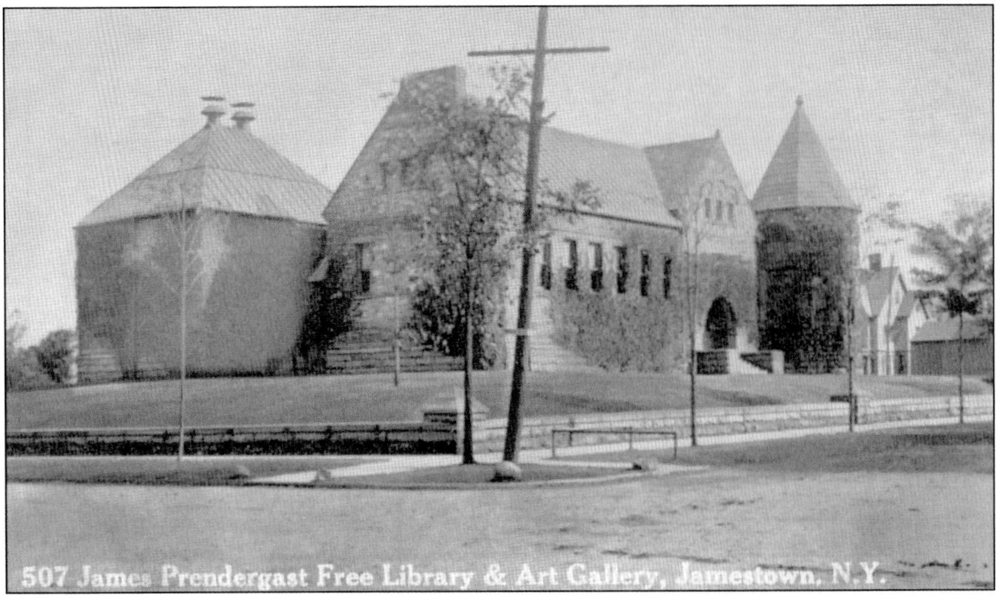

Built in 1891, the James Prendergast Free Library became the library for all Jamestown's residents. Constructed in the Richardsonian Romanesque style, the library was designed by Andrew Jackson Warner of Rochester. It was funded by Alexander and Mary Prendergast in memory of their son James. A hip-roofed art gallery on the northwest side housed the art collection purchased with funds given by Mary Prendergast.

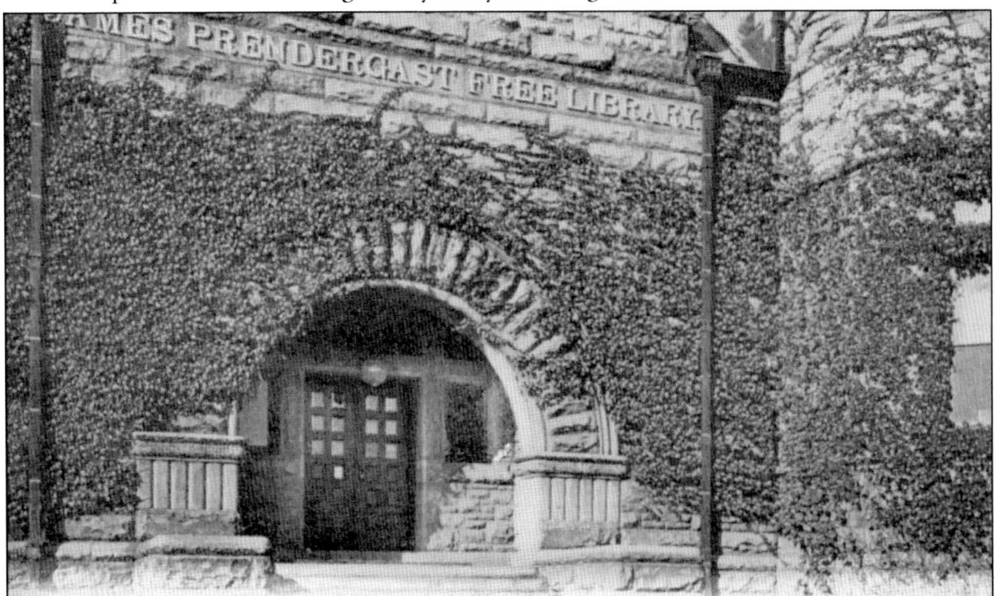

Named for James Prendergast, grandson of Jamestown's founder, the library was a wish he had expressed before his death. The main entrance features a large Syrian arch. Medina sandstone was used as a contrasting colored stone around windows and doors and in horizontal bands, emphasizing architectural features. Occupying an entire city block that had been part of the old cemetery, the library grounds were delineated with a rock-face masonry wall.

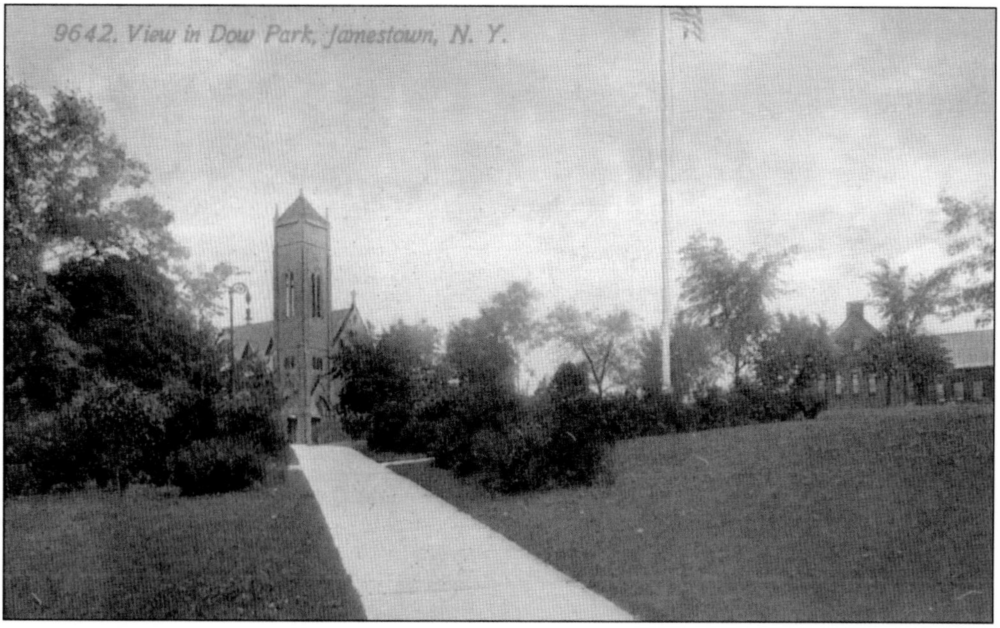

Dow Park, named for Charles M. Dow, is the block bounded by West Sixth, West Seventh, Washington, and Cherry Streets. Here, a sidewalk cuts diagonally across the block. SS. Peter and Paul Roman Catholic Church can be seen at the end of the walk, at the southeast corner of Cherry and West Sixth Streets. At the far right is the James Prendergast Free Library along West Sixth Street.

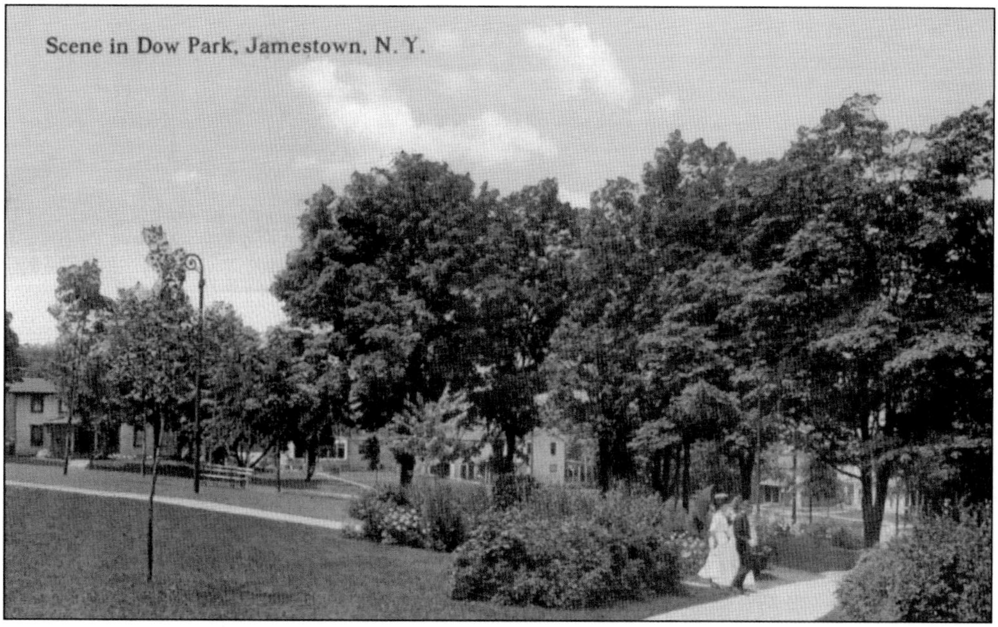

At one time, Dow Park was part of the village's cemetery. Charles M. Dow was interested in conservation and nature and worked on establishing a park system for Jamestown. He took great interest in this park near his home. At his expense, he graded, constructed sidewalks, planted trees and shrubs, and furnished seats and swings. The homes seen border the park along West Seventh and Cherry Streets.

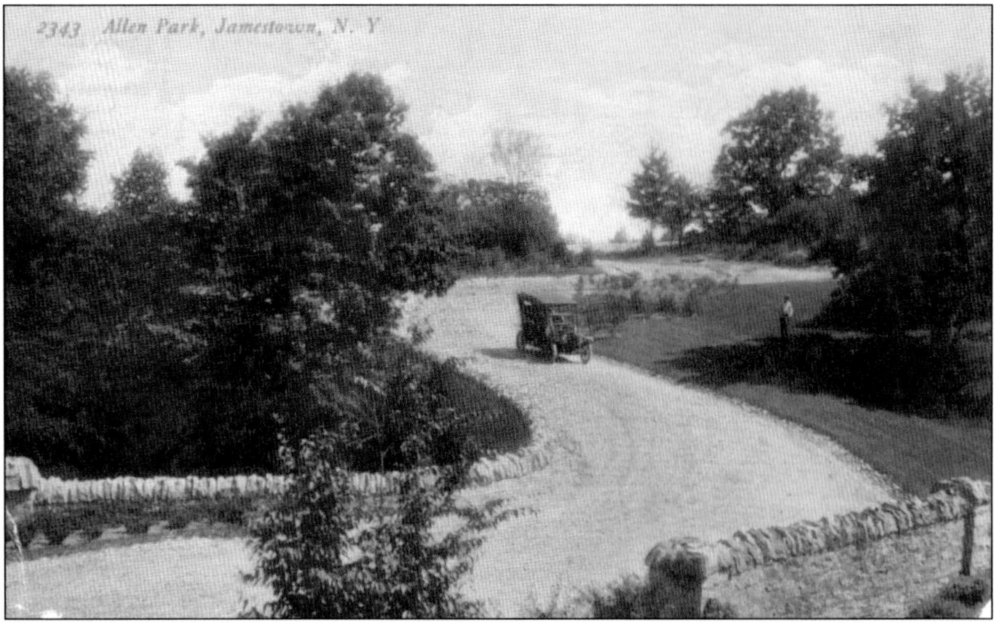

Allen Park was gifted to the city in 1908 by Virginia M. Allen. The 30 acres had been part of the Allen Farm, and the deed called for it to be known as Allen Park, to be used only for park purposes, and to be properly maintained. The park was planned and laid out by Everett D. Johnson. Roads and paths were made and maintained, bringing visitors throughout the park. (Courtesy of FHC.)

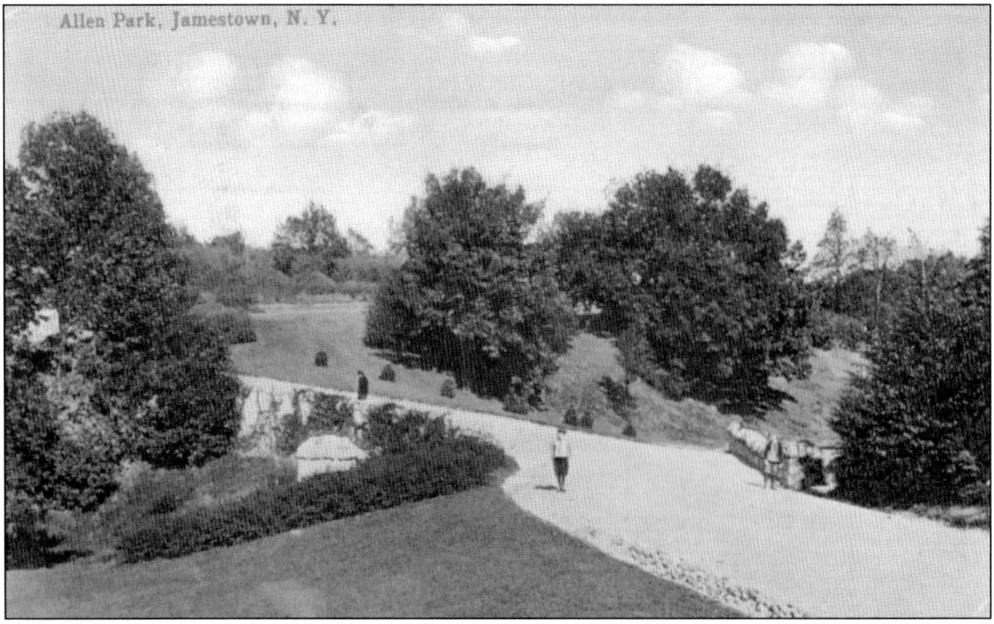

Allen Park was improved through the years. Lawns and views were opened through the dense shrubbery. Park benches were added, and the upper park attracted hundreds of picnickers through the summer. Playgrounds for children and a ball field brought more families to the park all summer, and an ice skating rink extended the enjoyment into the winter. City residents enjoyed the open space, which was Virginia Allen's intent. (Courtesy of FHC.)

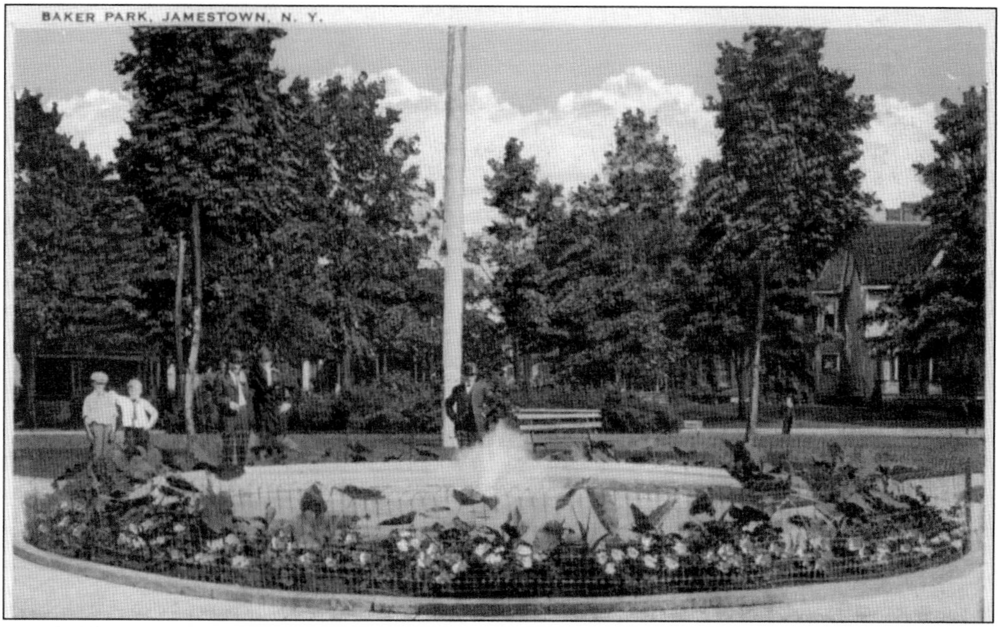

Deeded by Henry Baker to the city with the intent that it remain a park, it bears his name. Baker purchased James Prendergast's unsold Jamestown land in 1840. This park is in the vicinity of—and may include some of—the city's earliest burial ground. The fountain and the flowers are gone today, but the park is an open space near the business district, surrounded by large shade trees. (Courtesy of FHC.)

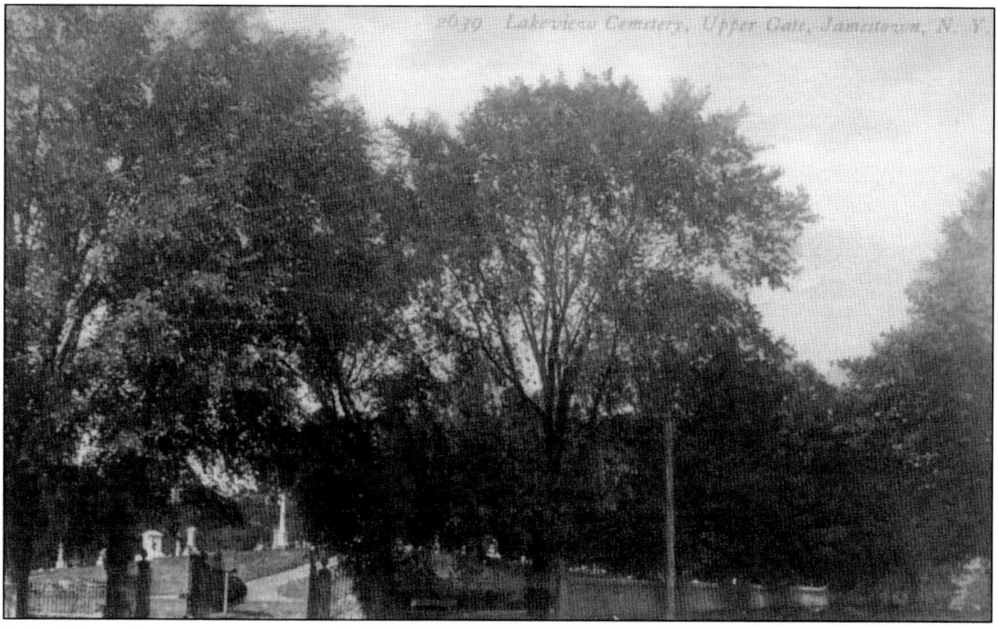

Lake View Cemetery, organized in 1858, was the city's third cemetery and is still used today. Following the popular form of the time, it is a garden cemetery featuring a park-like setting with winding roads, a variety of trees, and landscaped grounds. A stroll or jog through the manicured cemetery continues the tradition of garden cemeteries as places for picnics, walks, and where open public space can be enjoyed.

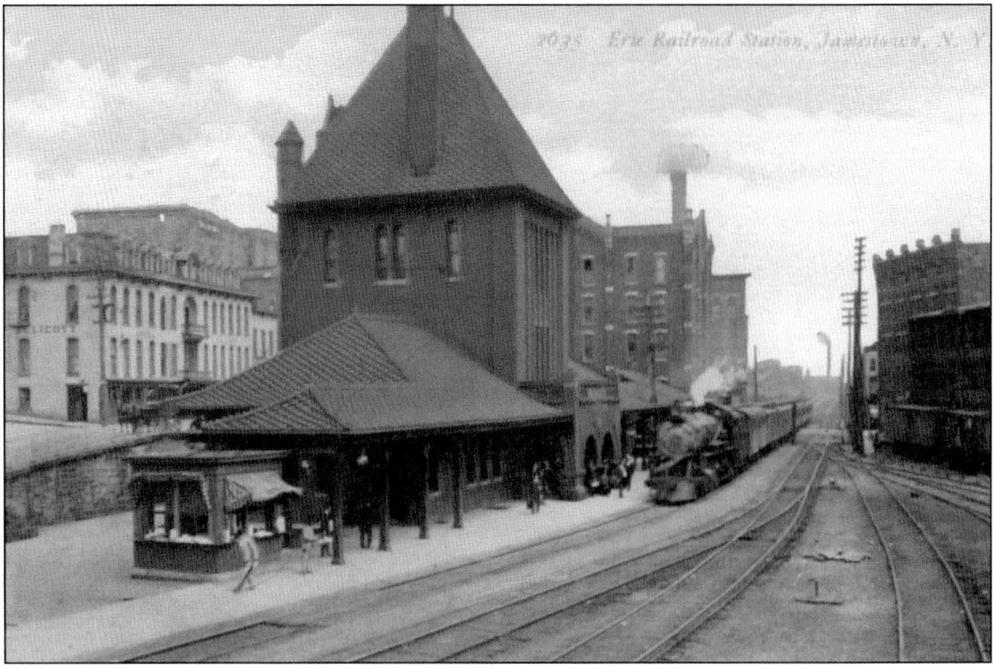

In 1896, this train station was built for $20,000 on First Street at the foot of Cherry Street. Only one block from Main Street and two blocks from Third Street, it was convenient for the traveling public. The building partly obscured by the station is the Hotel Everett, and beyond that is a part of the Arcade Building. To the left is the Hotel Ellicott.

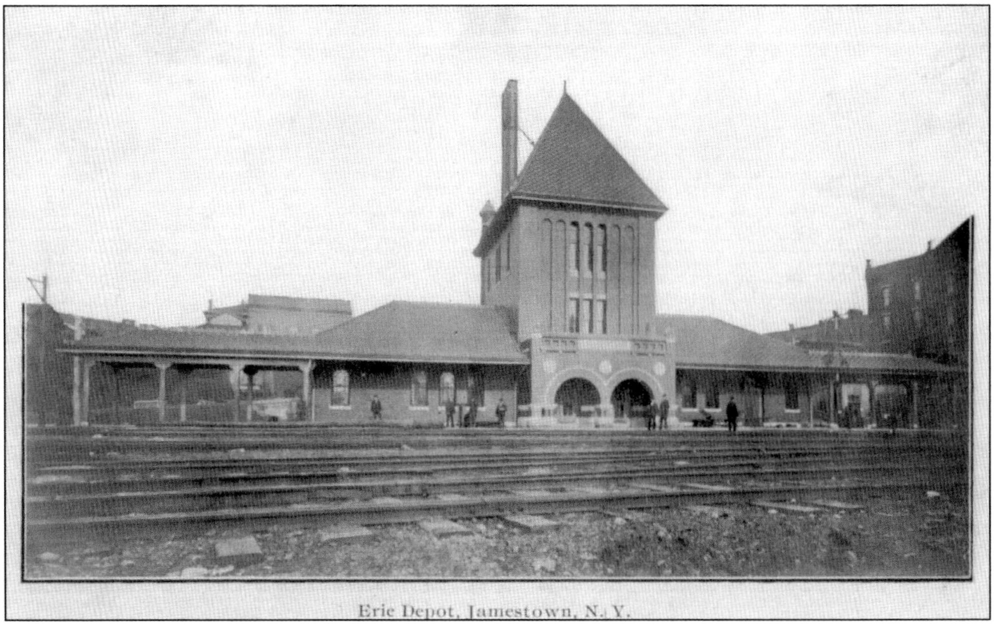

This train station was at track level, as was First Street, which ran in front of the station. After a long controversy, the tracks were elevated to overpasses at Main Street and Foote Avenue. This forced the station to be abandoned in 1926. A temporary station was built farther west until 1932, when a new station was built on West Second Street.

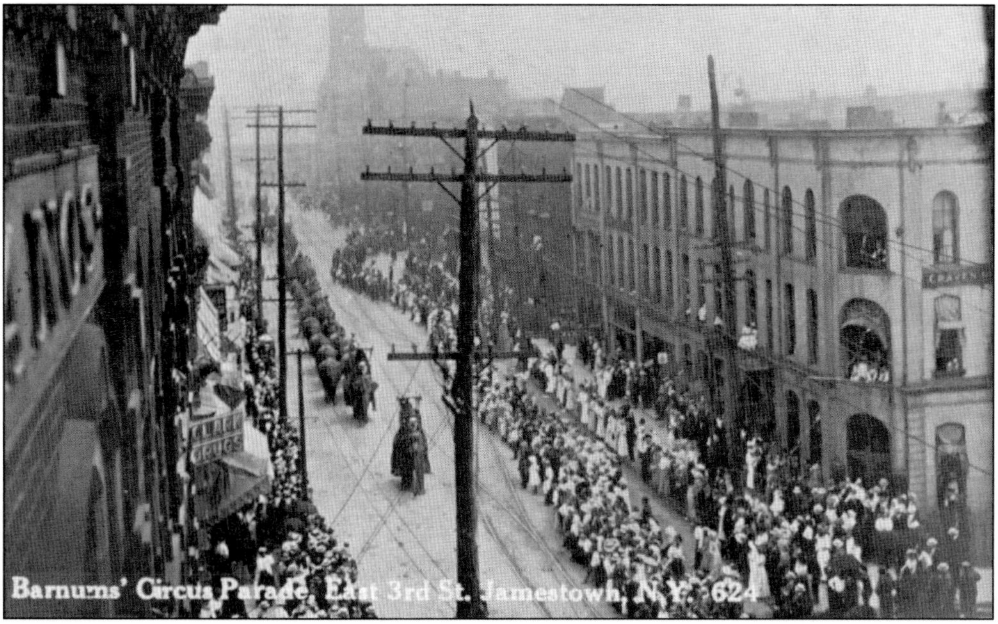

The circus was one of many forms of entertainment that came to Jamestown. Not only were the performances in the big tent an attraction, but the circus parade was a free event. The parade is how the circus animals, people, wagons, and other items from the train got to the place where the circus was set up and back again. This parade is coming west on East Third Street around 1910.

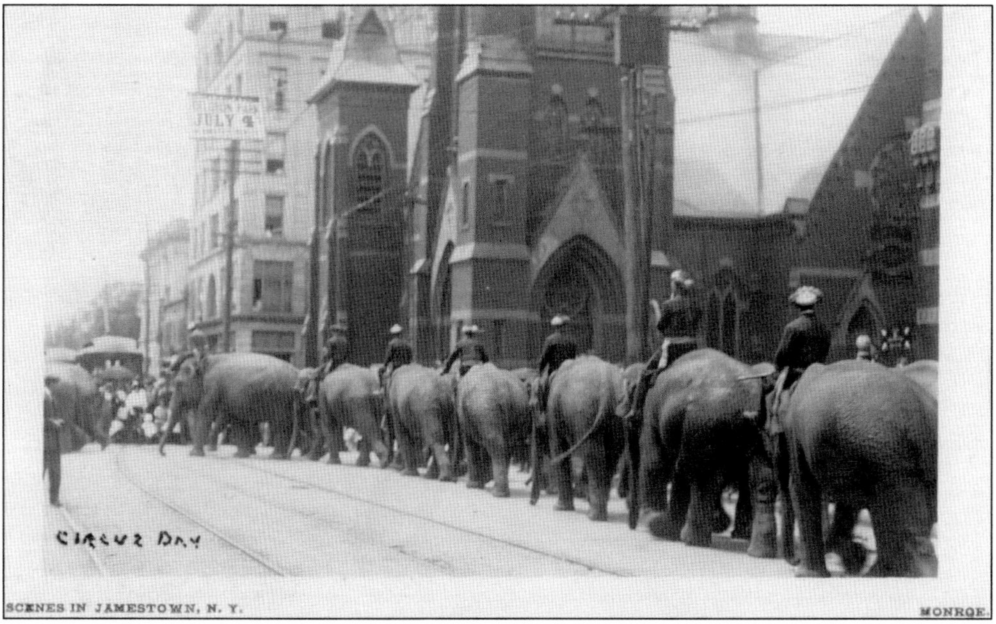

This circus parade is going west on West Third Street, as the First Presbyterian Church and the Chadakoin Building are in the background. It looks as though the elephants are turning left, which puts the parade going down Cherry Street to the train station. The circus at one time set up on the grounds on Sherman Street, where the Sherman Street School was later built. (Courtesy of FHC.)

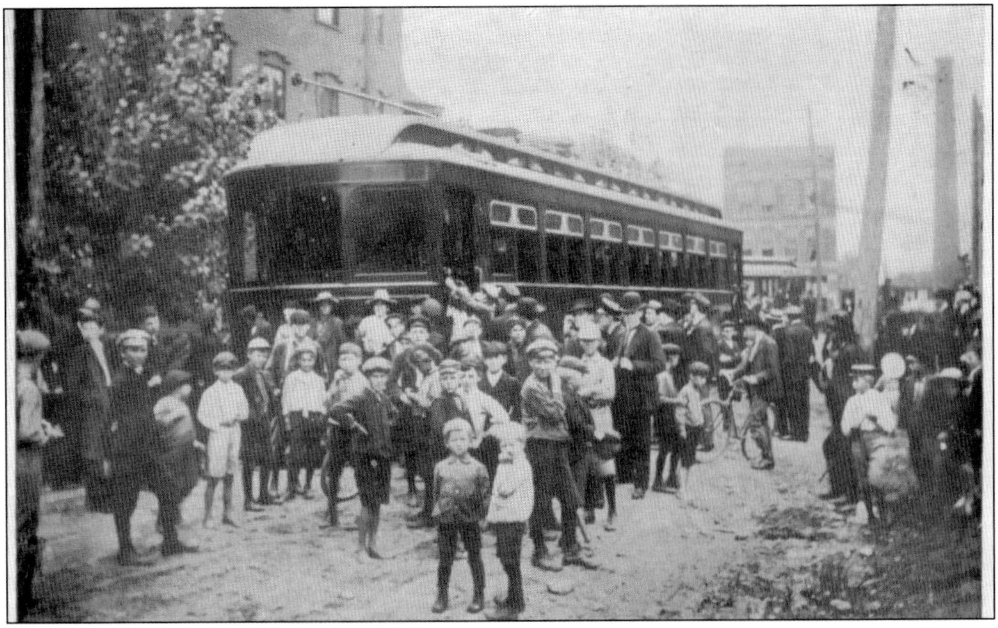

Beginning in 1905 and ending in 1929, an interurban line was established between Warren, Pennsylvania, and Jamestown, New York. A crowd gathered around the first trolley car to arrive at the terminal, located at the Humphrey House in Brooklyn Square. With no track connection to the Jamestown trolley lines, a transfer arrangement was made. The Warren line was the closest trolley to Allen Park and provided service to Jamestown for the Foote Avenue neighborhoods.

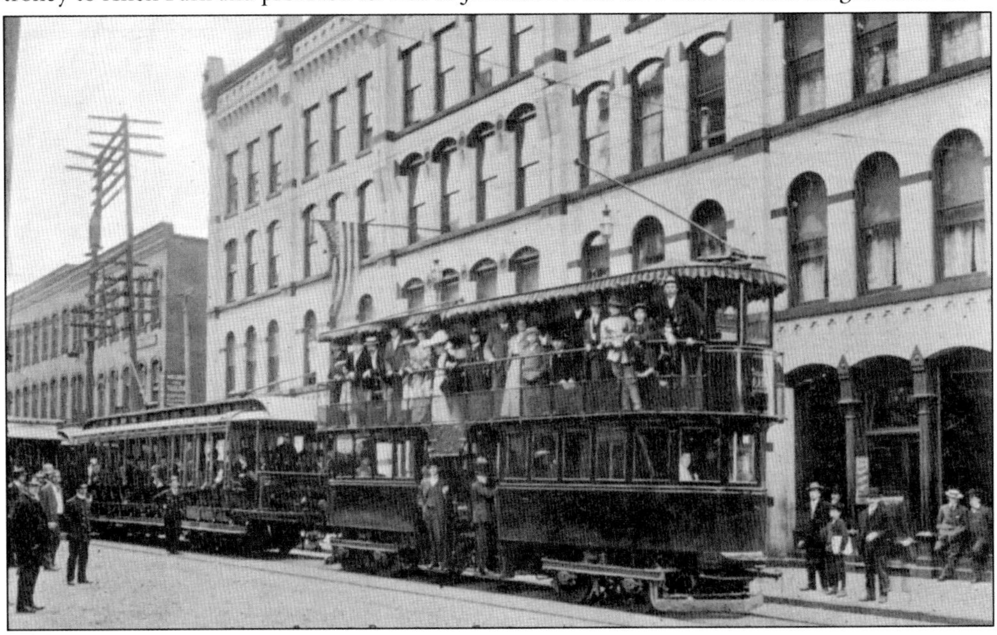

Jamestown's transportation reached a high point when the *Columbia*, a double-decker car, was used on the Celoron Park run for almost 20 years. Here, the Columbia and two smaller open cars are stopped at the terminal at the Sherman House. After the 1910 fire destroyed the Sherman House, the terminal was moved one block west on Third Street. Many passengers let the smaller cars go while waiting to ride the favored *Columbia*.

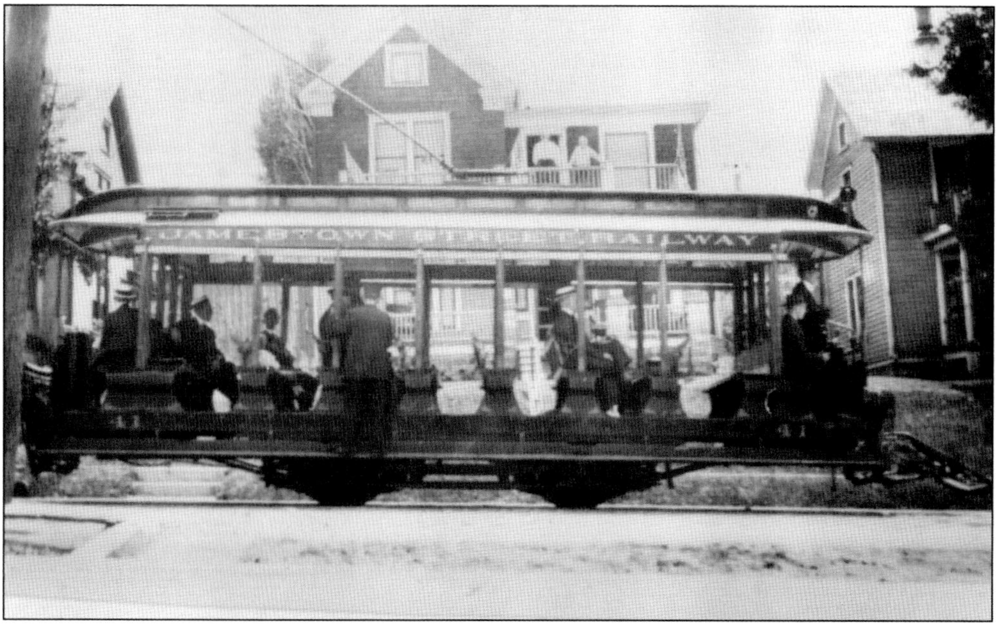

Car No. 41 on the Willard line is stopped in front of a home near Hedges Avenue. When it began in 1913, the Willard Street line was a welcome addition for the residents of Swede Hill. This open car started with the Jamestown Street Railway in 1894. On the Willard line, with a large hill to negotiate, only one car lost its brakes; it jumped the tracks and hit a furniture factory.

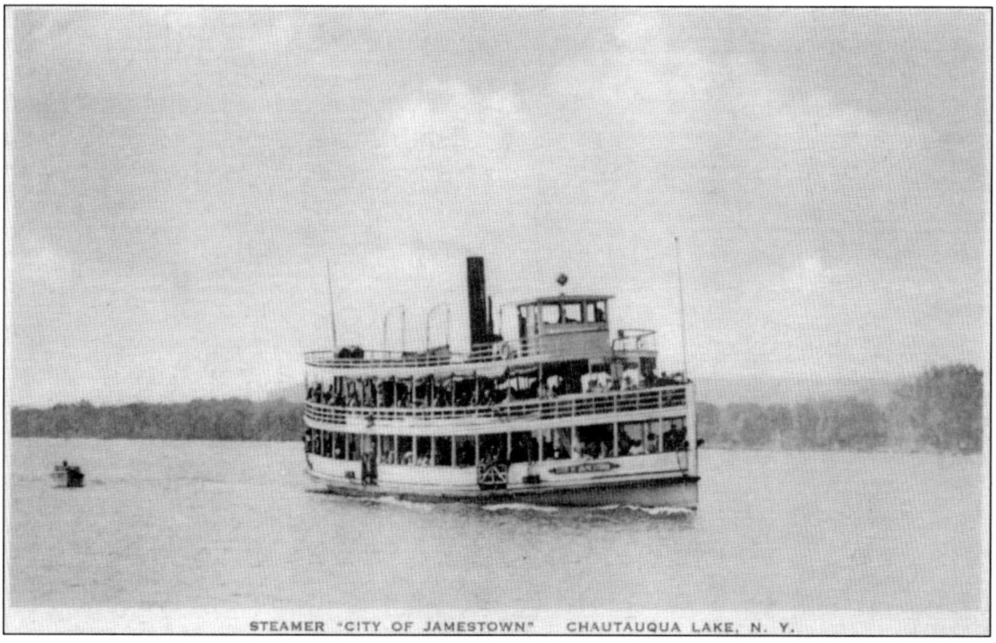

Chautauqua Lake had a least one steamboat operating from 1828 to 1958. This is the last one to navigate the lake and is named *City of Jamestown*. Built in 1891 and spending 38 years as the *City of Cleveland*, she was renamed in 1931. Beginning as transportation, the steamer's last years were for pleasure, with many charters and public boat rides on Chautauqua Lake.